When Religion and Morals Become OCD

When Religion and Morals Become OCD

Understanding and Treating Scrupulosity

Leslie J. Shapiro

BLOOMSBURY ACADEMIC
NEW YORK • LONDON • OXFORD • NEW DELHI • SYDNEY

BLOOMSBURY ACADEMIC
Bloomsbury Publishing Inc
1385 Broadway, New York, NY 10018, USA
50 Bedford Square, London, WC1B 3DP, UK
29 Earlsfort Terrace, Dublin 2, Ireland

BLOOMSBURY, BLOOMSBURY ACADEMIC and the Diana logo are trademarks of Bloomsbury Publishing Plc

First published in the United States of America 2023

Library of Congress Cataloging-in-Publication Data Control Number: 2023017566

ISBN: HB: 978-1-4408-7254-9
ePDF: 978-1-4408-7255-6
eBook: 979-8-216-17257-4

Typeset by Amnet ContentSource

Contents

CHAPTER ONE

Introduction

People with obsessive-compulsive disorder (OCD) suffer from unwanted intrusive thoughts, images, or impulses that provoke anxiety. Rituals (or compulsions), mental or physical, are performed to reduce the anxiety. Along with anxiety, many sufferers also experience strong emotions, especially guilt about obsessions that are considered conscience-related due to the nature of the obsessive thoughts. A range of about 5–33% of people with OCD have religious or moral obsessions (Miller & Hedges, 2008), and this is likely an underestimation of this kind of OCD because it often goes undiagnosed. OCD sufferers with these symptoms may not realize they have a clinical disorder and may believe that they have a problem with their faith or morality. Many clinicians have trouble recognizing as properly assessing these symptoms and clergy are often unaware of the problem being a mental, not faith related, issue.

For example, you are on your daily walk and see a twenty-dollar bill on the ground. You (1) pick up the money and think, "It's my lucky day"; (2) pick it up, thinking, "Well, someone's going to take it, so it might as well be me"; (3) look to see if a person is nearby who might have dropped it to give it back to her; or (4) leave it on the ground because it doesn't belong to you, and taking it is stealing.

For most of us, the decision about whether to take the money would be incidental. Most likely, we would pick it up, feel lucky, maybe have a little extra bounce in our step, and move on. For someone with religious or moral scrupulosity, however, this would be a maddening dilemma because the money could come in handy, but an overwhelming sense of guilt would be punishing for even thinking about it taking it! Imagine facing these unrelenting kinds of decisions dozens of times a day.

Scrupulosity, moral perfectionism, and obsessive guilt are subtypes of obsessive-compulsive disorder (OCD). They refer to OCD symptoms that tend to be overlooked when assessing and treating OCD because the focus is primarily on symptom reduction. It is unclear if this is due to the covert nature of mental compulsions performed to alleviate the anxiety and emotions caused by the obsessions. They may also elicit clinicians' unconscious or affective responses, known as countertransference, to the issues the patient is relating due to the therapist's attitude shaped from their own religious or moral upbringing. Religious or moral lessons learned during the clinician's formative years may have had a lasting effect that is unknowingly communicated in the therapist-patient dynamic. The unconscious responses are typically negative but even positive countertransference can have an influence on the trajectory of treatment.

In the example at the beginning of the chapter, an OCD sufferer might mentally ritualize by thinking, "God, forgive me for even thinking about stealing that money," over and over until a certain "right feeling" is achieved. Another person with OCD may perform a behavioral compulsion by going back to the place where the money was seen on the ground to make sure she didn't take it by mistake. In the meantime, someone may have taken it, and so she checks her pockets to make sure it wasn't her. The mental and physical behaviors never result in a sense of certainty and completion, so she continues to feel anxious and guilty.

Obsessions differ from delusions in that the intrusive thoughts are based on content that is rational. Obsessive thoughts are fears that reflect uncertainties and anxieties that the general population experiences (Rachman & Hodgson, 1980). Nonclinical spontaneous unwanted thoughts may consist of wondering if an accounting of a negative event was accurate, which creates a nagging urge to review it, but the person can let it go. Someone with obsessive morality likens this experience to having lied and has a persistent dread and expectation for punishment if not corrected. "Corrections" often consist of going back to the person to check and see if she really understood the story, mentally reviewing the conversation to achieve certainty, or explaining the situation to someone else as an act of getting reassurance from that person that she was understood. The focus, no longer on the event, is based on the obsessive need to feel "right" (not wrong) and to restore a sense of good moral standing.

Another example is apologizing. People may feel an apology is an appropriate action for having done something wrong to someone else. It is done in the spirit of making amends with the person, accepting responsibility for the act, and restoring the relationship back to mutual respect.

Someone with moral OCD may *feel* like he did something wrong in the absence of evidence that this was true. The "just in case" mentality sets in, and the OCD sufferer may go back to the other person, who has no awareness of any transgression, and apologize again, but this does not eliminate the doubt and "not-right" feeling. So, the person continues to apologize or seek reassurance again, but now the focus becomes not about having offended the other person, but on the self who is busy trying to achieve that "right feeling." Many people who receive compulsive apologies have no idea what the issue was and often become annoyed by the sufferer's persistence. That can start off a whole new round of apologizing for being annoying!

Empirical evidence has shown that conscience-related factors play a role in almost all OCD symptoms and may account for why some people relapse when they go unaddressed in treatment (Shapiro, 2014). As long as people with OCD perform compulsions (the terms *rituals* and *compulsions* are interchangeable), they are fueling their obsessive fear by giving it some "legitimacy" and believing they did something wrong that needs to be "fixed." OCD is classified as an anxiety disorder (American Psychiatric Association [APA], 2013) and has several subtypes. There has been recent interest in establishing scrupulosity and religion as a unique subtype. As such, the Dimensional Obsessive-Compulsive Scale has added this as a fifth subtype that was extracted from the unacceptable thoughts subtype into the dimension of scrupulosity and religion (Abramowitz et al., 2010; Wetterneck et al., 2021).

Even people with the more common OCD symptoms may have unrecognized scrupulosity, moral perfectionism, obsessive guilt, and strong emotions such as anger that can complicate treatment responses. These common obsessions and feared consequences are:

- contamination (getting others sick),
- harming/safety (fear of harming others or the need to protect them from harm),
- intrusive sexual or violent thoughts (inappropriate thoughts about sexual assaulting someone, fear of being attractive to children, fear of physically harming someone or self),
- superstitious ideas (performing lucky/unlucky behaviors, using or avoiding certain numbers/colors),
- the need for symmetry/exactness (the need for things to be perfect in order to maintain existential or personal balance,
- thoroughness (the need to feel complete that communication or tasks are done to completion so as to avoid making mistakes),

Some common obsessions people with OCD scrupulosity and moral perfectionism suffer with are:

- fear of blaspheming/offending God (being punished by God or getting sent to hell)
- fear of having made a deal with the devil (becoming an evil person; thoughts about bargaining with the devil when getting enjoyment)
- fear of becoming possessed by the devil (that OCD is a sign that the devil is taking over the person's soul)
- fear of stealing, lying, cheating (violating personal moral standards as well as committing crimes)
- fear of being selfish (putting one's own needs ahead of others' as an expression of not being caring or compassionate towards others)
- feeling guilty or responsible for having "bad" thoughts (committing sins by having the thoughts, reading meaning into the thoughts that they are meant, taken as signs of being a "bad" person)
- fear of not protecting others from harm (being neglectful of others's safety or well-being if rituals are resisted)

Although hoarding is no longer classified as a subtype of OCD but as its own diagnostic disorder, people who excessively keep or collect things have their own sense of obsessive guilt and moral perfectionism about being wasteful, dishonoring people by throwing away something given to them, feel sad and disrespectful of discarding sentimental items, and have creative ideas about how things can be reused, repurposed, or acquiring items that might be useful to someone else in the future.

Exposure and response prevention (ERP) is the evidence-based gold standard model for treating OCD (Foa & McLean, 2016). Exposure is showing up to situations that trigger the OCD, and response prevention is not thinking or doing anything intentionally to reduce the distress, discomfort, or negative emotions but rather letting them run their course until they pass. The effect of this treatment is the recalibration of the overactive brain chemistry in OCD. For example, someone with an obsessive fear of causing a fire will resist compulsive urges to check the stove and appliances before leaving the house and at bedtime. The person may initially feel an increase of guilt for not checking, but with consistent practice, he will experience relief as the obsessive thoughts start to recede. The ERP will have been effective, but it may have not been sufficient if he continues (not necessarily consciously) to experience a level of guilt about not being careful and conscientious enough (Melli, Carraresi, Poli, Marazziti, & Pinto, 2017).

A word about the seemingly contradictory relationship between religion and science seems *apropos*. We might consider religion and science as two types of divination or prophecy. Though scientists and clergy may not explain human behavior or humanity, the laws of nature, or the origin of the natural world the same way, faith seems to be a concept commonly shared by both—that is, the belief or trust in that which is not yet seen or proven. They may be inspired by existential wonder, curiosity, and imagination about the world, its origin, and the role of humanity in the universe; or they may be driven by fear of the unknown, the need to provide reasons or explanations for what appear to be random events, the need for control, or the need for hope (for some) that there may be more beyond what is concrete or already known. They provide an externalized means of designing control, a way of tapping into a higher consciousness to search for a deeper meaning of our existence. But mostly they appear to be ways of coping with the ultimate fear of death. Some scientific research is based on finding a way to "cheat" death by prolonging the lifespan, while some faith practices address the hope that our lives on earth are rewarded in some form of eternal bliss.

Religion provides a system of faith for believing that there is a relationship with a higher power that oversees and judges our lives in a way that provides meaning and helps us cope with uncertainty and the unknown. It also provides a community where followers can share and practice their sense of spirit in a common, structured manner. Science is a system based on verifying yet-unproven hypotheses about the nature of how things work, and identifying causal relationships or correlations between differing or separate variables, qualities, and attributes (measures, measuring). Researchers conduct their studies in a collaborative and structured format driven by a sense of wonder and curiosity. Their faith in the scientific process motivates their curiosity about finding evidence to prove, or disprove, their hypotheses.

Science and the function of culture also share a factor of the unknown in that they attempt to explain the world of experience by assigning phenomena to definite causes (Dresslar, 1910). In a 2008 study, authors C. H. Miller and D. W. Hedges proposed that existential psychology and scrupulosity are related when people with OCD experience a sense of meaninglessness, fear of a terrifying death, and uncertainty about the afterlife. Beliefs about heaven, hell, purgatory, karma, End of Times, being separated from loved ones in the afterlife, or that our corporeal bodies just decompose are common concerns for people with and without OCD, but they are more distressing for the scrupulous and moral perfectionists due to how obsessive they become about every detail of their lives.

Other researchers have found consistent OCD themes across cultures that may indicate an evolutionary basis of adaptation to ensure human survival (Nicolini, Salin-Pascual, Cabrera, & Lanzagorta, 2017; Polimeni, Reiss, & Sareen, 2005). Evidence from evolutionary anthropology, neuropsychology, and neuroimaging supports the idea that ritualized behavior is an adaptation of an evolved precautionary system conditioned to perceive and react to threats to survival (Boyer & Liénard, 2006, 2008). Another theory is that OCD symptoms are excessive instinctive drives for successful living. Contamination symptoms are behaviors related to maintaining health. Checking behaviors are performed to ensure safety. Excessive ordering and arranging stem from the need for organization and order. Hoarding behaviors mimic nesting. Finally, fear of the unknown and the seemingly randomness of events may relate to the creation of religion and superstitions (Boyer & Liénard, 2006; Dulaney & Fiske, 1994).

This book has many features that will help readers understand the nature of healthy versus obsessive faith, morality, and guilt and how to differentially diagnose and treat them. Chapter 2 depicts practices of extreme religiosity in society that are not related to religious issues in OCD. This is to inform readers about the difference between the social and psychiatric constructs that are implicated in nonclinical and clinical constructs. It also provides historical accounts of religious and notable people who suffered from scrupulosity, which will add to an appreciation for how scrupulosity has been understood or formulated and treated over time. Chapter 3 provides examples of how people prepare and attempt to be in a state of physical, spiritual, moral, and emotional purity before presenting themselves before God. In chapter 4, a deeper examination of "soul cleansing" is provided that depicts the suffering those with scrupulosity endure with the fear of not being worthy of God's grace and forgiveness.

In chapter 5, the moral counterpart to scrupulosity is outlined in the context of the obsessive need to be morally perfect or to perform moral acts perfectly. Existential obsessions are also problematic, as an individual's (or humanity's) reason for existing cannot be proven. On rare occasions, people may experience fleeting moments when they achieve the perfect feeling, but in the next moment, they are back to feeling incomplete and disappointed that they could not sustain their perfect moral standards and must try all over again.

Chapter 6 delves into the minds of people who suffer disturbing obsessions that cause a sense of self-stigma and fear of being stigmatized by others. People may believe they are evil and experience shame and guilt about their thoughts and feel that others should be protected from them. It also explains the differences between cultural rituals and compulsive behaviors, superstitious, and magical thinking. If the onset of OCD was early, religious teachings may affect cognitive and emotional development, especially around sexuality and having "negative" emotions. Sexual obsessions that cause people to believe they are sinning and the obsessive fear of death are topics covered in chapter 7.

Scrupulous and moral perfectionistic eating, orthorexia, is covered in chapter 8. Rigid rules around what is acceptable for eating insidiously limit healthy eating habits and choices. In a similar vein, chapter 9 addresses issues around being "green" enough to save the planet, which can lead to hoarding behaviors. People may save objects to reuse and accumulate items to recycle faster than they can keep up with. They may also pick up others' discarded items or items discarded on roadways to remove litter.

Chapter 10 moves into the theory and science behind OCD and the purposes it serves. Evolutionary biology and neurobiology offer explanations about brain chemistry, its functions, and the effect it has on behavior in OCD. Though these explanations are scientifically based, they are also theoretical, as proving or confirming their validity does not seem possible.

Treatment strategies that are designed to treat scrupulosity and moral perfectionism are outlined in chapter 11. The gold standard of behavioral treatment for OCD is ERP, which is the same treatment approach that is effective in gaining control over the symptoms of these subtypes. Acquiring an understanding of the relevant factors that often make treatment challenging for patients who suffer from the fear of committing sins or moral injustices will provide the help that is sensitive to addressing these particular fears.

Because the context of scrupulosity involves fears around practicing religion and faith correctly enough to avoid displeasing God, chapter 12 covers experience many sufferers have had when they turned to clergy in times of desperation. Depending on the level of psychological training, responses by clergy may be helpful or harmful. As many OCD sufferers are not aware that they have a psychiatric condition, they may approach clergy as the first line for seeking help.

Although ERP is necessary for symptom control, it may not be sufficient for a stable and solid recovery, as everyday life has the same stresses and challenges experienced by people without OCD. As such, treatment strategies that are helpful augmentations for creating a healthy mindset and lifestyle are introduced in chapter 13. Self-compassion is a psychological model that is helpful for changing the pattern of having a negative mindset toward ourselves. The three components are self-kindness and treating ourselves as we would a good friend, participating in the common humanity condition of suffering by connecting with others rather than isolating, and using mindfulness as a strategy to separate over identifying with one's thoughts and emotions. The practice of general mindfulness is reviewed from both the clinical and spiritual perspectives and how it may be used and misused in OCD. Other cognitive and behavioral strategies are also reviewed in this chapter. Finally, the end of the book provides a glossary of common terms and language used in OCD treatment, suggestions for further reading, websites, and organizational resources.

Research on OCD is prolific and informs clinical practice. This book has provided the most current knowledge on the topics it covers, but it is likely that new information will be available from ongoing research, technologies, and psychosocial studies that share the common goal of eradicating the all-too-often devastating effects the disorder has on the lives of all those whom it touches. Medication for OCD is an effective intervention that will not be covered in this book. For information about what medications are prescribed for OCD, please refer to https://www.drugs.com/condition/obsessive-compulsive-disorder.html for a list of primary medications as well as common augmentations that enhance the effects of selective serotonin reuptake inhibitors (SSRIs).

OCD is prevalent in about two to three percent of the Western population (Fontenelle, Mendlowicz, & Versiani, 2006; Ruscio, Stein, Chiu, & Kessler, 2010). Within this prevalence rate, between 5% and 33% of sufferers in the United States reported having religious obsessions and scrupulosity (Abramowitz, Huppert, Cohen, Tolin, & Cahill, 2002; Ruscio et al., 2010; Riley, 2003). In England, 5% of people with OCD had scrupulosity (Dowson, 1977). In the United States, 30% of OCD sufferers had sexual and religious obsessions (Ruscio et al., 2010).

Findings from societies with higher religiosity, compared to secular societies, reported higher rates of religious obsessions. In a Turkish clinical study, religious obsessions were assessed in 42% of a community sample.

In Middle East countries, religious obsessions were highly prevalent. In an Egyptian study, 60% of study participants had contamination and religious obsessions (Okasha, Saad, Khalil, el Dawla, & Yehia, 1994). In Saudi Arabia, the most common obsessions were religious (rate was not identified) (Mahgoub & Abdel-Hafeiz, 1991). In Israel, 41–93% of people with OCD have religious obsessions (Greenberg & Huppert, 2010; Kaiser, Bouvard, & Milliery, 2010). In Bahrain, religious obsessions were found in 40% of a study sample (Shooka, al-Haddad, & Raees, 1998). A study in Iran reported that blasphemous obsessions occurred in 28% of a clinical sample (Dadfar, Bolhari, Dadfar, & Bayanzadeh, 2001).

In the Far East, India's scrupulosity rate was 11% (Akhtar, Wig, Varma, Pershad, & Verma, 1975). In Singapore, the rate was 7% (Chia, 1996). In India, the rate of religious obsessions was 60% (Nazar, ul Haq, & Idress, 2011).

Even atheists suffer from scrupulosity, which speaks to the problem as OCD, not one of God or religion (thescrupulousatheist.com). In unpublished data collected from 355 participants in a residential program who were referred to the symptom-specific scrupulosity group, 5% identified as atheists (Shapiro, Gironda, & Krompinger, 2011).

Changes in cultural and social attitudes toward OCD, and mental illness in general, have led to less stigmatization and a dramatic increase of related resources over the past few decades. There is every reason to believe that the synergy of acceptance by the individual sufferer and others, research that leads to finer-tuned treatments, and the continued establishment of community support structures will result in the recognition of OCD as a human condition people can manage in the same way as any other physical, psychological, emotional, or spiritual challenges.

Much of the clinical and anecdotal content of this book is based on the author's empirical experience spanning over thirty years, most of which has involved treating the most severe cases in a residential-level setting. As such, the concepts and ideas behind the case material may not always appear in the literature, which has been diligently reviewed and included in the text when applicable.

References

Abramowitz, J. S., Deacon, B. J., Olatunji, B. O., Wheaton, M. G., Berman, N. C., Losardo, D., . . . Hale, L. R. (2010, March). Assessment of obsessive-compulsive symptom dimensions: Development and evaluation of the dimensional obsessive-compulsive scale. *Psychological Assessment, 22*(1), 180–198. doi:10.1037/a0018260

Abramowitz, J. S., Huppert, J. D., Cohen, A. B., Tolin, D. F., & Cahill, S. P. (2002). Religious obsessions and compulsions in a non-clinical sample: The Penn Inventory of Scrupulosity (PIOS). *Behaviour Research and Therapy, 40*(7), 825–838. doi:10.1016/s0005-7967(01)00070-5

Abramowitz, J. S., & Jacoby, R. J. (2014). Scrupulosity: A cognitive–behavioral analysis and implications for treatment. *Journal of Obsessive-Compulsive and Related Disorders, 3*(2), 140–149.

Akhtar, S., Wig, N. N., Varma, V. K., Pershad, D., & Verma, S. K. (1975). A phenomenological analysis of symptoms in obsessive compulsive neurosis. *The British Journal of Psychiatry, 127*(4), 342–348. doi:10.1192/bjp.127.4.342

American Psychiatric Association. (2013). *Diagnostic and statistical manual of mental disorders* (5th ed.). American Psychiatric Publishing.

Boyer, P., & Liénard, P. (2006). Why ritualized behavior? Precaution systems and action parsing in developmental, pathological and cultural rituals. *The Behavioral and Brain Sciences, 29*(6), 595–613; discussion 613–550. doi:10.1017/s0140525x06009332

Boyer, P., & Liénard, P. (2008). Ritual behavior in obsessive and normal individuals: Moderating anxiety and reorganizing the flow of action. *Current Directions in Psychological Science, 17*(4), 291–294. doi:10.1111/j.1467-8721.2008.00592.x

Chia, B. (1996). A Singapore study of obsessive compulsive disorder. *Singapore Medical Journal, 37*(4), 402–406. Retrieved from http://www.ncbi.nlm.nih.gov/entrez/query.fcgi?cmd=Retrieve&db=PubMed&dopt=Citation&list_uids=8993143

Dadfar, M., Bolhari, J., Dadfar, K., & Bayanzadeh, S. A. (2001). Prevalence of the obsessive-compulsive disorder symptoms [Original Research]. *Iranian Journal of Psychiatry and Clinical Psychology, 7*(1), 27–33. Retrieved from http://ijpcp.iums.ac.ir/article-1-1963-en.html

Dowson, J. (1977). The phenomenology of severe obsessive-compulsive neurosis. *British Journal of Psychiatry, 131*, 75–78.

Dresslar, F. B. (1910). Suggestions on the psychology of superstition. *American Journal of Psychiatry, 67*(2), 254. doi:10.1176/ajp.67.2.213

Dulaney, S., & Fiske, A. P. (1994). Cultural rituals and obsessive-compulsive disorder: Is there a common psychological mechanism? *Ethos, 22*(3), 243–283.

Foa, E. B., & McLean, C. P. (2016). The efficacy of exposure therapy for anxiety-related disorders and its underlying mechanisms: The case of OCD and PTSD. *Annual Review of Clinical Psychology, 12*, 1–28. doi:10.1146/annurev-clinpsy-021815-093533

Fontenelle, L. F., Mendlowicz, M. V., & Versiani, M. (2006). The descriptive epidemiology of obsessive-compulsive disorder. *Progress in Neuro-Psychopharmacology & Biological Psychiatry, 30*(3), 327–337. doi:10.1016/j.pnpbp.2005.11.001

Greenberg, D., & Huppert, J. D. (2010). Scrupulosity: A unique subtype of obsessive-compulsive disorder. *Current Psychiatry Reports, 12*, 282–289.

Kaiser, B., Bouvard, M., & Milliery, M. (2010). Washing, checking, and rumination: Are the belief domains, obsessions and compulsions specific to OCD subtypes? *Encephale, 36*(1), 54–61. doi:10.1016/j.encep.2008.09.003

Mahgoub, O., & Abdel-Hafeiz, H. (1991). Pattern of obsessive-compulsive disorder in eastern Saudi Arabia. *British Journal of Psychiatry, 158*, 840–842.

Melli, G., Carraresi, C., Poli, A., Marazziti, D., & Pinto, A. (2017). The role of guilt sensitivity in OCD symptom dimensions. *Clinical Psychology & Psychotherapy, 24*(5), 1079–1089.

Nazar, Z., ul Haq, M. M., & Idrees, M. (2011). Frequency of religious themes in obsessive compulsive disorder. *Journal of Postgraduate Medical Institute, 25*, 35–39.

Nicolini, H., Salin-Pascual, R., Cabrera, B., & Lanzagorta, N. (2017). Influence of culture in obsessive-compulsive disorder and its treatment. *Current Psychiatry Reviews, 13*(4), 285–292.

Okasha, A., Saad, A., Khalil, A., el Dawla, A., & Yehia, N. (1994). Phenomenology of obsessive-compulsive disorder: A transcultural study. *Comprehensive Psychiatry, 35*(3), 191–197.

Polimeni, J., Reiss, J. P., & Sareen, J. (2005). Could obsessive–compulsive disorder have originated as a group-selected adaptive trait in traditional societies? *Medical Hypotheses, 65*(4), 655–664. Retrieved from http://linkinghub.elsevier.com/retrieve/pii/S0306987705002732?showall=true

Rachman, S., & Hodgson, R. J. (1980). *Obsessions and compulsions*. Englewood Cliffs, NJ: Prentice Hall.

Riley, C. (2003). *Scrupulosity when being perfect punishes* [sound recording]. Canfield, OH: Alba House Cassettes.

Ruscio, A. M., Stein, D. J., Chiu, W. T., & Kessler, R. C. (2010). The epidemiology of obsessive-compulsive disorder in the National Comorbidity Survey Replication. *Molecular Psychiatry, 15*(1), 53–63. doi:10.1038/mp.2008.94

Shapiro, L. J. (2014). *Understanding OCD: Skills to control the conscience and outsmart obsessive compulsive disorder.* Santa Barbara, CA: Praeger.

Shapiro, L. J., Gironda, C. M., & Krompinger, J. W. (2011). *Scrupulosity response by religion in an intensive residential treatment program* [Poster presentation]. International Obsessive Compulsive Disorder Foundation, San Diego, CA.

Shooka, A., al-Haddad, M., & Raees, A. (1998). OCD in Bahrain: A phenomenological profile. *International Journal of Social Psychiatry, 44*(2), 147–154. doi:10.1177/002076409804400207

Tek, C., & Ulug, B. (2001). Religiosity and religious obsessions in obsessive-compulsive disorder. *Psychiatry Research, 104*(2), 99–108. doi:10.1016/s0165-1781(01)00310-9

Wetterneck, C. T., Rouleau, T. M., Williams, M. T., Vallely, A., La Torre, J. T., & Björgvinsson, T. (2021). A New Scrupulosity Scale for the Dimensional Obsessive-Compulsive Scale (DOCS): Validation With Clinical and Nonclinical Samples. *Behavior Therapy, 52*(6), 1449–1463. doi:10.1016/j.beth.2021.04.001

CHAPTER TWO

Social, Cultural, and Historical Views on Religious Behavior: What Is and Is Not OCD

This chapter reviews the zeitgeist of faith movements and practices since the twentieth century to highlight the differences between religious practices and obsessive-compulsive disorder (OCD)-driven behaviors. The chapter begins with the more recent accounts of attitudes, trends, and contributing factors leading to the rise and fall of religious cults and other faith organizations, followed by historical accounts of scrupulosity. A fuller account of the history of scrupulosity can be found in another book I authored, *Understanding OCD: Skills to Control the Conscience and Outsmart Obsessive Compulsive Disorder* (Shapiro, 2014), which covers saints, historical notables, and celebrities who have publicly disclosed having OCD to help reduce stigma. The remainder of the chapter describes the similar and different topics within the body of literature related to scrupulosity, moralosity, and OCD.

Social Ambivalence toward OCD

"That's just my OCD."

OCD and mental illness in general have been both stigmatized and trivialized in modern society. Saying "That's just my OCD" is a common self-deprecating but prideful response to a "compliment" given for being detailed, picky, perfectionistic, or organized. Such statements diminish the public's understanding of how truly devastating the effects of OCD are on sufferers' lives. Here is a quote from an OCD sufferer on the popularization of OCD:

> Today, I once again saw someone on social media glorifying OCD. In fact, they included in a list of preferred attributes for any potential applicants for a position they were advertising. I constantly hear people say they are "sooooooo OCD!" but for some reason this absolutely triggered me. Yes, triggered me. (Dunbar, 2018)

There is a clear sociocultural ambivalence about whether OCD traits are good or bad. In fact, society has an ambivalent attitude toward and still stigmatizes mental illness in general. According to the National Institute of Mental Illness, the prevalence rate is around 20% and is likely higher as people may not be aware of having an illness or are afraid to seek help. As such, most of us know someone with a mental illness, even if we don't realize it.

When traits or behaviors are diagnosed as a disorder, they are suddenly perceived as bad. On the other hand, when they are an expression of attention to detail and perfection, they are often regarded as endearing or quirky traits. The truth is, most of us have at least a trace of some type of mental health–related issue found in the Diagnostic and Statistical Manual of Psychiatric Disorders (American Psychiatric Association, 2013).

Most people think that OCD is about handwashing or neatness and are not aware of the dark, distressing obsessions that cause sufferers to call their own human decency into question. Even clinicians may not be aware that most OCD symptoms have an underlying moral theme that is ego-dystonic, meaning the content of the obsessions are contrary to the person's true core values and sense of self rather than being ego-syntonic which means the person relates to the thoughts as consistent with their identity. The obsessive trigger ("I might be a pedophile") feels very real and urgent in the moment but has no bearing on the person's identity. In contrast, a pedophile experiences his thoughts and feelings as ego-syntonic (in synch with his desires and wishes) as they are pleasurable and real.

Social systems (legal, religious, and moral) have been put in place to maintain social order and to keep people safe from one another. They also help define the boundaries of what is considered acceptable behavior in accordance with being a good citizen. As with most rules that are set by people, they are subject to interpretation rather than being set as absolutes. There are relative and subjective gray areas where what may be reasonable for one person may be different for another. Someone who is traveling may be okay with skipping going to a religious service while she is away, whereas someone else may consider doing so sinful and will plan her trip around finding places of worship to attend a service.

One function of religion is to help cope with uncertainty (Howell et al., 2019). Some people find comfort in having exact rules and expectations of how to practice a faith belief that is fundamentalist in nature (Hogg, Adelman, & Blagg, 2010). A psychological example of how fundamentalism is defined includes four dimensions: the belief that there is one absolute truth about humanity and God; that religious practice serves to uphold this truth and to fight against evil; that the truth is maintained by adhering to the traditional and resolute practices set out as originally structured; and that those who follow the fundamental practices have a special relationship with God (Altemeyer & Hunsberger, 1992).

A study found a positive association between religious fundamentalism, obsessive-compulsive symptoms, and dysfunctional obsessive beliefs (Inozu, Karanci, & Clark, 2012). Thus, the practices of some strict religions and OCD scrupulosity may appear to be the same but do not share the same function. They become confounded because they are at the extreme endpoint of the religiosity spectrum but with different motivations behind them. Religious practices arise out of tradition, respect for and participation in faith beliefs, love of God, and being in connection with the community. Scrupulosity practices actually serve the opposite purpose. They are born out of fear, are rigidly adhered to as a way to avoid mistakes and to achieve a sense of completion, and result in isolation from the faith community.

We will see how anxiety can manifest in creating communities due to existential uncertainties, coping with social and cultural change, and attracting people who are unsure of their purpose or personal identity. Sometimes people find it easier to be told what to think or do because they don't trust their own sense of themselves.

Late Twentieth-Century Turmoil, Rebellion, and Fundamentalism

Responses to psychological stress can manifest in a variety of ways. The following examples will illustrate nonclinical social, cultural, and political responses to stress and how similar clinical stress response patterns occur in OCD scrupulosity and moral perfectionism. The history and background of some religious movements and trends in society during the twentieth century are reviewed here to highlight what makes them distinct from OCD.

In the 1960s, the country was facing rising national and political unrest/crisis in response to the Vietnam War. One response was the establishment of the secular hippie counterculture movement that was organized around the ideals of love, peace, freedom of expression, and the questioning of authority. There were also burgeoning religious and secular cults that recruited idealistic, lost, and vulnerable souls who sought spiritual direction and community that were different from the traditional "establishment." The sense of free-floating anxiety felt in times of national crisis and upheaval seemed to have ignited the fires of nationalistic, ethnic, and religious fervor that begat secular and religious groups.

Several religious sects and cults emerged that seemed to capitalize on people's fears, uncertainty about the future, and desire to find a place to belong. The Jesus Movement, as one example, consisted of living in communes and called for a return to simple living; asceticism; and a strong belief in miracles, signs, and wonders (Ingersoll, 2012). Others were Heaven's Gate, Scientology, the Peoples Temple, the Unification Church, Hare Krishna, Scientology, the Children of God, and the New Age Movement. Except for the latter, all of these groups demanded the renunciation of material and monetary things, which were to be "donated" to the organization.

There are no academic studies on the prevalence of or a relationship between OCD scrupulosity and moral perfectionism in the participants of these groups. It is unclear if those predisposed or who already had OCD were drawn into the groups as a way of being taught what to do or think by group leaders. Striving to be pure and perfect may be ideals that the groups hold but the effort and expectation by those in the group who have OCD who are unable to reach the ideal standards may be left feeling inadequate, inferior, and hopeless.

Around the same time, evangelical Christianity and religious fundamentalism membership began to sharply rise from the ability to spread the Gospel and its teachings through televangelism (Hadden, 2016). Televangelism was a watershed in reaching millions of Christians by broadcasting services people could attend from the convenience of their homes. One description of evangelicalism is the practice of interpreting select key passages of religious texts to prevent religious identity from falling victim to modernity and secularism (Herriot, 2007). Over time, a style of preaching called "prosperity gospel" emerged that delivered a controversial message to followers with promises of gaining material, financial, physical, and spiritual success through the practice of surrendering one's material possessions to the organization (https://www.christianitytoday.com/ct/topics/p/prosperity-gospel/).

The quote "Give and you shall receive" (Luke 6:38) is a common reference used to urge generosity. In order to enable the televangelists to survive financially, followers were encouraged to purchase books, CDs, DVDs, trinkets, and other media items. The movement lost popularity when famous leaders were caught in sex scandals and displaying opulent lifestyles that included significant material personal wealth, luxury cars, and various transportation vehicles such as private and ministry aircraft. In 1989, the Evangelical Council for Financial Accountability began random on-site checks to verify that cooperating ministries were following their "God-honoring ethical practices" (Tuft & Smith, 2003). The message for the scrupulous was internalized to the extent that not giving "enough" to the church felt greedy and possibly being negatively judged and punished by God. "Give until it hurts" was how some scrupulous sufferers measured the "right" amount of donations, and often, it was money they could ill afford to give away.

During the 1980s, megachurches became another platform for reaching millions of evangelical, charismatic, fundamentalist, and nondenominational believers who could worship under the same roof (Hadaway & Roozen, 1993). One characterization of the ministry leadership is the creation of spiritual entrepreneurship preached by charismatic leaders who may not have had any formal religious training or credentials (Greeley, 1989). Their message was reported to have attracted those who were searching for a more strict and demanding adherence to their Christian faith (Thumma, 2005). This evangelical form of faith might provide a kind of structure that the scrupulous and moral perfectionists might be drawn to as the teachings are presented in a black and white manner. They are likely to take the teachings as literal and feel that falling short of perfection can indicate a lack of or fallen faith, fear being punished by God, and have difficulty dealing with ambiguity about the church teachings and life experience.

The relevance of evangelism to OCD, regardless of tradition, is the black-and-white imperative imposed by the tenets of a religion that its followers attempt to follow to the literal letter of the religious law. Such adherence in the context of religion is a practice of faith. With OCD, it is a fear-based practice to avoid thoughts and behaviors that may be considered sinful and immoral, or to atone for any forgotten or possible mistakes made in the past.

Leadership Traits That Attract Vulnerable People

Common personality traits of the charismatic leaders among the various groups mentioned are often obsessive-compulsive, narcissistic, perfectionistic, and controlling (Kilian, 2018). Marcus J. Kilian explains that the obsessive-compulsive and perfectionistic leader operates with excessive control; has a preoccupation with orderliness, detail, and precision; and uses a micromanaging style to correct guide others' "inadequacies" (Kilian, 2018). A narcissistic leader has a grandiose sense of self, is preoccupied with success and popularity, is self-entitled, exploits others for his benefit, and is threatened by the success of others. This person is typically able to garnish the validation and admiration of his followers but does not necessarily reciprocate. A perfectionistic leader also has an obsessive need for order and control; has inflexible rules, especially regarding morality; selfishly hoards resources or information; and expects others will follow the rigid standards he sets (Kilian, 2018).

Religious leaders with these profiles often may claim to have special powers to the divine that are then proselytized as revelations to the group (Rodia, 2019). Issues such as the end of days, judgment day, the apocalypse, prophecy, and subjective interpretation of scripture are preached with the purpose of instilling fear, but the leader claims to have special abilities to save his following. Charles Kimball stated, "Religious leaders who can package and deliver absolute truths find receptive audiences" (Kimball, 2008, p. 85). These audiences comprise vulnerable people who are looking for answers about how to live faithful, moral lives but have no direction to teach them how. In comparison, mainstream clergy typically serve their parishioners and congregations with a spirit of strong faith, a sense of humility, and, in some cases, a naturally charming personality. They usually lead from a place of love and compassion rather than fear and control.

Overtly narcissistic pastors may demand complete and unquestioning obedience, leading the church to develop cultlike characteristics that influence beliefs and values "along a continuum of various states which include paranoia, obsessive compulsive, dramatic, depressive, schizoid, and narcissistic tendencies" (Hunter, 2013, p. 44). The narrative at the heart of their identity story may be used to strengthen the power of the pastor (Puls, 2020).

What is central to the issues at hand is the way both religious cult members and people with OCD follow and obey strict religious rules that are determined by external influences about how to think and behave righteously. The personalities of leaders may be an attractive trait for the scrupulous or moral perfectionists because of the confidence and conviction the leaders portray. They may feel they are in good hands by others' who preach what to think and feel. Some find relief in finding a structure or system that is exact and prescribed. Deviations from the exact adherence to the rigid rules may result in castigation by clergy or self-imposed punishment in those with OCD to restore obedience and compliance.

There are no findings in the literature identifying the prevalence of scrupulosity within fundamentalist congregations. Like people in cultish groups, one would wonder if some people suffering from OCD gravitated toward fundamentalist denominations because of the extreme forms of belief and behaviors they have in common, as well as fundamentalism's attempt to fulfill the need for certainty.

The accounts above were provided as a way to discern social and cultural religiosity from scrupulosity. This is not to say that, by and large, people who worship through these structures aren't thoughtful, insightful, strongly supported in their faith, or have containing meaningful connections to their religious communities. An institutional structure is not necessary to be faithful but for many it provides a conducive atmosphere for community and connection.

Because OCD manifests from neurobiological imbalances which impact psychosocial functioning, sufferers adopt a literal mindset in pursuit of achieving the perfect standards they feel compelled to maintain as a set, not by God, but by the way OCD interprets the religious rules. "Do as I command you," is a biblical mandate from God that has become corrupted by OCD (Duet. 5:10). In the extreme, literalistic practices by people with OCD eliminate choice and responsibility from making internalized personal decisions, especially when the stakes seem so high.

Appeals from televangelists and other religious denominational leaders for money are triggering for vulnerable people with scrupulosity. They may have interpreted the preacher's charismatic style as speaking directly to them, asking them for donations, or purchasing items in the organization's marketplace as a sign of faith, but instead the funds may be used to provide the means of ensuring financial solvency for the religious institution (Frankl, 1986). The ministries, unwittingly, capitalized on the fear those with scrupulosity had about being greedy by not making contributions, regardless of how the money was spent for the survival of the ministry.

Historical Records and Accounts of Religious, Moral, and Faith Bookkeeping

References to OCD and scrupulosity were discovered on some Babylonian cuneiform Maqlû and Šurpu tablets that referenced concerns about contamination, orderliness of objects, aggression, sex, and religion (Reynolds & Kinnier, 2012). Other early accounts of religious scrupulosity were attributed to Evagrius Ponticus (346–399 AD), a Turkish Christian monk, and Saint John Cassian, aka "John the Ascetic" (360–435 AD). A psychological "case study" assessed Evagrius as likely to have suffered from OCD based on his writings on *logismoi* (literally thoughts) and the DSM-IV diagnostic obsession criteria (American Psychiatric Association, 1994; Hill, 2010). Evagrius's *logismoi* identified eight patterns of thoughts and feelings about temptations (gluttony, lust/fornication, greed/avarice, sorrow, wrath, pride, vainglory/boastfulness, and sloth/listlessness) that would later be shortened by Gregory the Great (c. 540–604) to become the Seven Deadly Sins (minus vainglory) (Hill, 2010; Tilby, 2009). The *logismoi* were interpreted as obsessive because they had an irrational quality:

> Be on your guard for the snares of your adversaries, for it happens, when you are practising [sic] pure and untroubled prayer, that they will suddenly set before you some strange and alien form in order to divert you into the presumption of rashly localizing the Divinity; their purpose is to persuade you that the quantitative object suddenly revealed to you is the Divinity, but the Divinity is without quantity and without form. (Evagrius, as cited in Hill, 2010)

Saint Cassian, a disciple of Evagrius, stated the ultimate goal of monastic life was mystical contemplation (Geger, 2014). To achieve that goal, a monk had to attain *puritas cordis* (purity of heart), which was achieved by the absence of disordered or "harmful" thoughts and the power over the eight desires or vices (Geger, 2014). His strict instruction for the examination of conscience was as follows:

> [W]e should . . . constantly search all the inner chambers of our hearts . . . with the closest investigations lest . . . some beast furtively insinuate itself into the secret recesses of the heart . . . each believer in an effort to rid themselves of their own noxiousness, must scrutinize their untoward desires and thoughts, enumerate them in writing, and divulge them daily to the abbot. (Paden, 1988, pp. 69–72)

Conversely, the Syrian monk John Climacus, whose writings in *The Ladder of Divine Ascent* revealed his own case of scrupulosity, taught clerics to have a more compassionate understanding of people with "unspeakable" blasphemous thoughts (Graiver, 2016). Having spent twenty years with unrelenting blasphemous obsessions, he explained that these thoughts were not acts of free will, were not sins of commission, and that thinking them was not the same as doing them (now defined in psychology as Thought-Action Fusion).

Climacus wrote:

> If you have blasphemous thoughts, do not think that you are to blame. God knows what is in our hearts and he knows that ideas of this kind come not from us but from our enemies [the demons]. (1982, p. 211)

A different depiction of the minds of the scrupulous and moral is that of a double-entry bookkeeping (DEB) system. James Aho's sociological work, *Confession and Bookkeeping: the Religious, Moral, and Rhetorical Roots of Modern Accounting*, discusses the morality and scruples of commerce and outlines the emergence of the DEB system in Italy during the fourteenth century (Aho, 2005). According to Aho, DEB was based on the moral and religious consciousness of Christian merchants in the spirit of indebtedness toward the Creator, church, and community. This system provides a means of honesty and accountability that those with obsessive fears of cheating or stealing can follow.

Profit became a moral issue in the sense that it was contradictory to the prevailing Christian values at the time and was likely regarded as committing the deadly sin of greed. Merchants began keeping meticulous accounts of their commercial transactions to provide evidence of how they earned and spent their income in the name of maintaining a spiritual balance between their trades and their souls. "For everything they earned something of equal value had been returned, and that for everything meted out something else was deserved" (Aho, 2005, p. xiii). The list was an account of behaviors made "meaningful" by the reasons, stories, or accounts given for and about them (Arrington & Francis, 1993) and was brought to clerics in a manner similar to confession, and aspects of the transactions were judged as to whether they had been sinful (Aho, 2005). Some merchants and bankers became morally obsessive about the accuracy of their business dealings and kept scrupulous DEB logs "day by day and hour by hour even the minutiae of transactions . . . never spar[ing] pen and ink" (Lopez & Raymond, 2001, pp. 376–377).

Likewise, in a DEB style, scrupulous records were kept by people who felt compelled to keep track of alleged sinful or moral deeds and to confess them in church on a weekly or even daily basis to placate God and escape hell (Aho, 2005). Aho cites a kind of DEB in Revelation (Rev. 20:11–15) that refers to the Book of Accounts, which kept a legalistic record of every person's debts and credits in life, and the Book of Life, in which the judgments of the behavior of the dead were recorded and determined how the person would exist in the afterlife (Aho, 2005).

Another piece of literature on the topic of DEB examined how, along with Christianity, Judaism, and Islam used the same system of moral accounting as a "faith management" practice during the Reformation (Joannides & Berland, 2010). Such practices were enabled through the development of calculative practices by the clergy and religious people (Joannidès de Lautour & Nicolas, 2010). Islamic and Catholic merchants accounted for their economic transactions "in the name of God" (Carruthers & Espeland, 1991) while in the nineteenth century, Jewish and Protestant vendors kept such books "in the name of God and profit" (Maltby, 1997). Other accounts of moral bookkeeping existed during the Ming Dynasty (1368–1644). Emperor Zhu Yuanzhang, a former Buddhist monk, used this system for conditioning the righteous behavior of his heirs (Maas, 2020).

The relevance of DEB for OCD also has meaning for people with existential obsessions. The belief, and in some sense superstition, is that keeping a moral balance will prevent good from begetting bad. Those with existential obsessions assign themselves legalistic blame for how their privilege has benefited them and harmed others, and they feel a sense of shame for having more than those who struggle to make ends meet. The possibility (despite the improbability) of being responsible for catastrophic outcomes by making wrong choices based on obsessive thoughts paralyzes people from taking action. Regardless of the level of importance, the concept of the "butterfly" effect causes people to feel that any risk is not worth taking. The butterfly effect is the unforeseeable and unintended impact a very small action has on the larger system (Lorenz, 1994). Because there is no way of proving ahead of time what the "butterfly" results may be, people abdicate their responsibility by making no decision at all.

This type of OCD is more characteristic of the type of OCD called the need-to-feel-right or having not-just-right-experiences (NJREs), which is an underlying trait experienced in all OCD subtypes. This is due to the etiology of OCD stemming from the moral center of the brain (and why the content of obsessions is irrelevant) indicating that something is "not right" and the physiological urge to fix what is "wrong." Although people are motivated to restore feeling "right" and "good," the irony is that their obsessive indecisiveness causes negative consequences in almost all aspects of their real lives. Another factor is the moral emotion of deontological guilt, addressed in chapter 4, which motivates people to perform rituals as a means of avoiding feelings of personal guilt, responsibility, and blame for potentially causing a bad outcome of a decisive action.

References

Aho, J. (2005). *Confession and bookkeeping: The religious, moral, and rhetorical roots of modern accounting.* Albany: State University of New York Press.

Altemeyer, B., & Hunsberger, B. (1992). Authoritarianism, religious fundamentalism, quest, and prejudice. *The International Journal for the Psychology of Religion, 2*(2), 113–133. doi:10.1207/s15327582ijpr0202_5

American Psychiatric Association. (1994). *Diagnostic and statistical manual of mental disorders: DSM-IV* (4th ed.). Washington, DC: American Psychiatric Publishing.

American Psychiatric Association. (2013). *Diagnostic and statistical manual of mental disorders* (5th ed.). Washington, DC: American Psychiatric Publishing.

Arrington, E. C., & Francis, J. R. (1993). Giving economic accounts: Accounting as cultural practice. *Accounting, Organizations and Society, 18*, 107–124.

Carruthers, B., & Espeland, W. (1991). "Accounting for rationality": Double-entry bookkeeping the rhetoric of economic rationality. *American Journal of Sociology, 97.* doi:10.1086/229739

Climacus, J. (1982). *Ladder of divine ascent (revised).* Mahwah, NJ: Paulist Press.

Dunbar, J. (2018). *What it's really like to be "sooooo OCD."* Retrieved from https://themighty.com/topic/obsessive-compulsive-disorder-ocd/living-with-ocd-not-a-joke/

Frankl, R. (1986). *Televangelism: The marketing of popular religion.* Carbondale: Southern Illinois University Press.

Geger, B. T. S. J. (2014). Hidden theology in the "Autobiography" of St. Ignatius. *Studies in the Spirituality of Jesuits, 43*(6). Retrieved from https://ejournals.bc.edu/index.php/jesuit/article/view/5771

Graiver, I. (2016). The mind besieged: Demonic obsession in early monastic psychology. *Journal of Cognitive Historiography, 2*(2), 116–131.

Greeley, A. M. (1989). *Religious change in America.* Cambridge, MA: Harvard University Press.

Hadaway, C. K., & Roozen, D. A. (1993). The growth and decline of congregations. In D. A. Roozen & K. Hadaway (Eds.), *Church & denominational growth* (pp. 127–134). Nashville, TN: Abingdon Press.

Hadden, J. K. (2016). The rise and fall of American televangelism. *The Annals of the American Academy of Political and Social Science, 527*(1), 113–130. doi:10.1177/0002716293527001009

Herriot, P. (2007). *Religious fundamentalism and social identity.* Hove, UK: Routledge.

Hill, J. (2010). Did Evagrius Ponticus (AD 346–99) have obsessive–compulsive disorder? *Journal of Medical Biography, 18*(1), 49–56. doi:10.1258/jmb.2009.009056

Hogg, M. A., Adelman, J. R., & Blagg, R. D. (2010). Religion in the face of uncertainty: An uncertainty-identity theory account of religiousness. *Personality and Social Psychology Review, 14*(1), 72–83. doi:10.1177/1088868309349692

Howell, A. N., Carleton, R. N., Horswill, S. C., Parkerson, H. A., Weeks, J. W., & Asmundson, G. J. (2019). Intolerance of uncertainty moderates the relations among religiosity and motives for religion, depression, and social evaluation fears. *Journal of Clinical Psychology, 75*(1), 95–115.

Hunter, M. (2013, January 1). The psychosis of organizations. *Contemporary Readings in Law and Social Justice, 5*, 44–57.

Ingersoll, J. (2012). *Baptist, Methodist, and evangelical faiths in America* (2nd ed.). New York, NY: Chelsea House.

Inozu, M., Karanci, A. N., & Clark, D. A. (2012). Why are religious individuals more obsessional? The role of mental control beliefs and guilt in Muslims and Christians. *Journal of Behavior Therapy and Experimental Psychiatry, 43*(3), 959–966. doi:10.1016/j.jbtep.2012.02.004

Joannides, V., & Berland, N. (2010). Keeping accounts by the book: The revelation(s) of accounting. *Crises et nouvelles problématiques de la Valeur.* Retrieved from https://www.academia.edu/784827/Keeping_accounts_by_the_Book_the_Revelation_s_of_accounting

Kilian, M. K. (2018). *Formational leadership: Developing spiritual and emotional maturity in toxic leaders.* Wipf and Stock. Retrieved from https://www.scribd.com/book/399747125/Formational-Leadership-Developing-Spiritual-and-Emotional-Maturity-in-Toxic-Leaders

Kimball, C. (2008). *When religion becomes evil: Five warning signs.* San Francisco, CA: HarperCollins.

Lorenz, E. (1994). *The essence of chaos.* Seattle: University of Washington Press.

Maas, H. (2020). True grid: Three case studies of moral accounting. *East Asian Science, Technology and Society: An International Journal, 14*, 309–330. doi:10.1215/18752160-8538670

Maltby, J. (1997). Accounting and the soul of the middle class: Gustav Freytag's Soll und Haben. *Accounting, Organizations and Society, 22*(1), 69–87. doi:10.1016/0361-3682(95)00050-X

Paden, W. (Ed.). (1988). *Theaters of humility and suspicion.* Amherst: University of Massachusetts Press.

Puls, D. (2020). Narcissistic pastors and the making of narcissistic churches. *Great Commission Research Journal, 12*(1), 67–92.

Lopez, R. S., & Raymond, I. W. (2001). *Medieval trade in the Mediterranean world: Illustrative documents.* Records of Western Civilization Series. New York, NY: Columbia University Press.

Reynolds, E. H., & Kinnier, W. J. V. (2012). Obsessive compulsive disorder and psychopathic behaviour in Babylon. *Journal of Neurology, Neurosurgery, and Psychiatry, 83*, 199–201.

Rodia, T. (2019, August 29). Is it a cult or a new religious movement? *Penn Today Blog.* Retrieved from https://penntoday.upenn.edu/news/it-cult-or-new-religious-movement

Shapiro, L. J. (2014). *Understanding OCD: Skills to control the conscience and outsmart obsessive compulsive disorder.* Santa Barbara, CA: Praeger.

Thumma, S. (2005). *Exploring the megachurch phenomena: Their characteristics and cultural context.* Hartford Institute for Religious Research. Retrieved from https://scholar.google.com/citations?view_op=view_citation&hl=en&user=NQhwyZYAAAAJ&citation_for_view=NQhwyZYAAAAJ:2osOgNQ5qMEC

Tilby, A. (2009). *The seven deadly sins: Their origin in the spiritual teaching of Evagrius the Hermit.* London, UK: SPCK Publishing.

Tuft, C., & Smith, B. (2003). TV evangelists call signals from the same playbook. *St. Louis Post-Dispatch.*

CHAPTER THREE

Effects of Scrupulosity and Moral Perfectionism on Normal Stage Development

Traditional Western human developmental models belie a linear path, presumably for the sake of understanding what the developmental process consists of. The models help underscore the fundamental challenges of each stage that, when achieved, launch the person to the next adaptive stage. In reality, people are more complex and may have mixed results going from one stage to the next. However, when the challenges of each stage are unfulfilled, which often occurs in those with scrupulosity or moral perfectionism, the results have potentially lifelong consequences. Salient aspects of the particular dimension will be delineated in this chapter.

It is worth including some dynamic concepts in understanding some of the underlying factors that affect the development of early onset obsessive-compulsive disorder (OCD) sufferers. Even though the etiology of OCD is neurobiological, it is important to understand that there are complex and insidious underlying factors that play a significant role in those who have had OCD since childhood.

The psychodynamic theory of OCD is explained by a connection to the subconscious from childhood experiences that are manifested through OCD thoughts and behaviors (UKEssays, 2018). Even though there is no scientific evidence to validate this theory, it suggests that socially unacceptable thoughts and images become repressed and are expressed through compulsions (UKEssays, 2018). The goal of psychodynamic therapy is to create change by resolving unconscious conflicts that have affected the person's relationships and quality of life into the consciousness through increased insights and self-awareness (Fulmer, 2018).

On the other hand, OCD is an overactive system that is hardwired in the brain and responds to evidence-based treatment. The important point here is that treating OCD with analysis or talk therapy can reinforce obsessing with the patient or causing a distraction away from behavioral tasks that result in symptom reduction and increased functionality (McKay, Abramowitz, & Storch, 2019).

The stages presented here will be from puberty to young adulthood. Keep in mind that other contributing developmental factors that complicate OCD episodes during these phases are hormone changes and existential awareness.

For two-thirds of people with OCD, the onset has been shown to begin during the pubescent years of seven to twelve years old (Dell'Osso et al., 2016). For youth predisposed to or who already have OCD, the developmental challenges of each of these dimensions can affect the trajectory of their maturation (see Table 3.1). Understanding that development is dynamic, the proposed outline for age and stage development will rely on the more traditional linear models developed by theorists such as Freud (psychosexual), Erikson (psychosocial), Piaget (cognitive), Kohlberg (moral), Fowler (faith/religion), and Young (values).

Puberty

During puberty, also identified as the latency stage, sexual and aggressive urges that were dormant begin to emerge. These and other difficult emotions, such as anger, disgust, shame, and morality, are managed through unconscious adaptive or maladaptive defense mechanisms to cope with them (Freud, 1975; Sarnoff, 1980). At this stage sublimation and identification are developed as adaptive mechanisms, whereas repression and reaction formation are maladaptive.

Sublimation channels these impulses to actions that are socially approved and contribute to the greater good (Cohen & Kim, 2020). Someone may become involved in community work to channel his anxiety, aggression, or other difficult emotions into productive avocations.

The defense mechanism called identification (also known as introjection) emerges as a way an individual unconsciously adopts aspects or traits of another person that serves as a way of emotionally relating to

Table 3.1 Model of Stage Development within and across Six Intrapsychic Dimensions and Possible Consequences for Developmental Stages and Potential Effects of Scrupulosity

Theorist	Dimension	Stage (Age)				
		puberty/latency (9–12)	early-adolescence (13–14)	mid-adolescence (15–16)	late adolescence (17–18)	young adulthood (19–20)
Freud	psychosexual	puberty/latency	genital			
	consequence	development of overcritical superego	immature defenses employed: reaction formation, isolation, displacement			
Erikson	psychosocial	industry v. inferiority	ego identity v. role confusion			intimacy v. isolation
	consequence	lack of self-esteem	premature commitments out of security need			
Piaget	cognitive	concrete to formal operations				
	consequence	tacit knowledge undeveloped; dichotomous thinking				
Kohlberg	moral	Stage 2 Preadolescence preconventional instrumentalist-relativist level	Stage 3 Early Adolescence conventional interpersonal concordance level	Stage 4 Mid-Adolescence conventional societal level: authority, law, duty	Stage 4 1/2 Late Adolescence hedonistic level	Stage 5 Young Adulthood postconventional autonomous, principled level
	consequence	intolerance of difference	certain thoughts (sexual, aggressive) are wrong/evil		reinforcement of guilt by obeying rules, authority	

(continued)

Table 3.1 *(continued)*

Theorist	Dimension	Stage (Age)				
		puberty/latency (9–12)	early-adolescence (13–14)	mid-adolescence (15–16)	late adolescence (17–18)	young adulthood (19–20)
Fowler	faith	Stage 2: mythical-literal	Stage 3: synthetic-conventional		Stage 4: individuative-reflective	
	consequence	overcontrol, perfectionism	polarized response of rigid conformity, inability to develop autonomous judgements	foreclosed identity due to conformity		
Young	values	primary introjection			initial dissonance: rejection, experimentation	differentiation and secondary introjection
	consequence	homogeneity reinforces traditional values and discourages dissent			perceptual and ego defenses against dissonance, self-castigation, risk aversion	

Sources: Erikson, 1963; Fowler, 1981; Freud, Strachey, Freud, Rothgeb, & Richards, 1953; Kohlberg, 1976; Piaget & Inhelder, 1969; Young, 1981.

them while building self-esteem (Békés & Perry, 2017; Laughlin, 1979; Paradiso et al., 2020). Introjection provides a sense of security and simultaneously leads to anxiety about violations of the conscience (Cramer, 2008). This anxiety of conscience can become obsessive for a scrupulous child, who can then have difficulty internalizing or trusting his own sense of identity. Of note, the neurobiological brain development at this time coincides with the emergence of identification (Ballmaier et al., 2008; Cramer, 2018).

Repression transfers difficult emotions, such as anxiety, guilt, anger impulses, and thoughts from the conscious to the unconscious to minimize feelings of guilt and anxiety (Cramer, 2015; Freud, 1975). Repressed emotions may be expressed through passive-aggressive behaviors such as sarcasm, giving the silent treatment, or blaming others for something the person did wrong.

Reaction formation is a paradoxical response to sexual or other impulses (Bailey & Pico, 2022). According to Freud, sexuality in childhood may account for virtuous behaviors (Freud, 1975). The person will respond to conflict with an opposite behavior, such as being nice to someone with whom he is angry or saying yes to doing favors when he really wants to say no.

Sexual feelings that had been suppressed are now emerging from physiological changes and may cause anxiety, confusion, and fear due to religious teachings that consider sexual thoughts and feelings sinful. Not coincidentally, the content of obsessions during this stage may involve unacceptable sexual obsessions accompanied by religious and moral obsessions. In turn, excessive rituals, such as praying, washing/cleaning, mental undoing rituals and attempts to suppress them are performed, but only serve to reinforce the OCD since they cause a rebound effect that only increases them.

Psychosocially, the child is in the state of "industry versus inferiority" (Erikson, 1969), which entails developing a sense of competency and mastery in task completion and productivity. Academic, extracurricular, enrichment, and performing chores are activities that contribute to having a sense of conscientiousness and accomplishment. Children with OCD may have begun to become perfectionistic and feel a sense of inadequacy. This is especially true if the parents are critical, rigid, and judgmental.

Cognitively, the child begins to think abstractly, not just concretely, about reality (Piaget & Inhelder, 1969). Formal operational thinking begins to open the mind in recognizing and reflecting on contradictions and inconsistencies in information. A shift from literal to more abstract thinking enables the child to be more conceptual and entertain other aspects of how things work (Fowler, 1981). It may be unsettling for scrupulous children when they are exposed to the theory of evolution or the "Big Bang" theory of creation that contradicts the story of Genesis in the Bible.

Morally, the sense of empathy and the ability to put oneself in the place of another are in development during this stage. According to Lawrence Kohlberg, this group is in the preconventional moral stage of "instrumentalist relativist." An increased understanding of societal rules, expectations, and morality fosters respect and empathy (Kohlberg, 1976). According to Kohlberg, "Role-taking, then, is a bridge between logical or cognitive and moral level; it is one's level of social cognition" (Kohlberg, 1976, p. 49). For the scrupulous at this age, obsessive doubt can cause confusion about what the proper moral decision should be for any given dilemma. They may default to not making a decision for fear that it will be wrong or that they will be criticized; furthermore, overempathizing with others contributes to more emotional distress.

According to James Fowler (1981), faith development is at the mythical-literal stage. "Marked by increasing accuracy in taking the perspective of other persons, those in [this] stage compose a world based on reciprocal fairness and an immanent justice based on reciprocity" (Fowler, 1981, p. 149). Fowler warns that "the limitations of literalness and an excessive reliance upon reciprocity as a principle for constructing an ultimate environment can result in . . . overcontrolling, stilted perfectionism . . ." (Fowler, 1981, p. 50). An excessive need for control and perfectionism are characteristic traits of scrupulous adults who find themselves still in this early developmental stage of faith.

The dimension of values at this stage of development is primary introjection (Young, 1981), which is another term for the defense mechanism identification. Under normal circumstances, a child unquestioningly incorporates the values of significant others (parents, teachers, clergy) and those of the culture and society as well as his own. Young warns that a highly homogeneous environment can limit the development of values as the traditional values of that group will be reinforced. If this occurs for a scrupulous child, she risks having a rigid, closed value system that is potentially intolerant of diversity or fearful of those who are ethnically or religiously different as others may have different or foreign values or faith practices.

Early Adolescence

Early adolescence is marked by changes in biology, physical development, increased hormones, heightened cognitive awareness, and social pressures. There is also increased pressure on academic performance as well as competition and judgment, and children begin comparing themselves to their peers in areas such as academics, social acceptability, and appearance (Green, Ferrante, Boaz, Kutash, & Wheeldon-Reece, 2021). Confidence and self-esteem are precarious and vulnerable to increased anxiety and a sense of isolation (Cappella, Schwartz, Hill, Kim, & Seidman, 2017).

The psychosexual transition is to the genital stage of maturity and may continue on to adulthood (Freud, Strachey, Freud, Rothgeb, & Richards, 1953). According to Sigmund Freud, issues in the latency phase result in the integration of the superego and the ego (Freud & Strachey, 1960). However:

> [In] obsessional neurosis these processes are carried further than is normal . . . the super-ego becomes exceptionally severe and unkind, and the ego, in obedience to the super-ego, produces strong reaction-formations in the shape of conscientiousness, piety, and cleanliness. (Freud & Strachey, 1960, pp. 114–115)

According to Freud and Strachey (1960), the early adolescent's budding sexual drives may become defended in the form of reaction formation, isolation, undoing, or displacement (Freud & Strachey, 1960). Further, an early adolescent's scrupulosity may serve as a reaction formation against sexual feelings that become displaced, isolated, or undone through ritualistic behaviors such as compulsive praying, washing, or cleaning (Freud & Strachey, 1960). Joseph Mullen also related scrupulosity and sexual impulses in his early twentieth-century study among 400 girls at a Catholic girls' high school who had experienced episodes of scrupulosity in early adolescence (Mullen, 1931).

In Erikson's psychosocial model, the early adolescent faces the challenge of ego identity versus role confusion, which can cause interpersonal and social pressures that result in scrupulous traits of pleasing others if that becomes the primary or sole social motivator (Erikson, 1963). "The ideological adolescent mind is between a morality learned by the child and the ethics to be developed by the adult. . . . [I]t is the ideological outlook of a society that speaks most clearly to the adolescent who is eager to be affirmed by his peers, and is ready to be confirmed by rituals, creeds, and programs which at the same time define what is evil, uncanny, and inimical" (Erikson, 1963, p. 263).

Erikson warned that to defend against role confusion, adolescents adhere to the norms imposed by their cliques and are intolerant of diversity. If this becomes a lifelong pattern, the limited of experience of relating only to those who are similar may result in xenophobia (fear of strangers).

As private religious educational institutions are homogeneous settings, more investigation is needed into the extent to which parochial, yeshiva, or similar education restricts development and increases scrupulosity. There is no literature on the role of Islamic children who attended a madrasa (religious school).

A ten-year study was conducted of twenty-three Roman Catholic parochially educated children who were referred to for treatment of scrupulosity, fourteen of whom were referred by priests (Weisner & Riffel, 1960). The authors reported that the onset occurred from early to late adolescence, with a higher frequency during early puberty. The study also cited consistent personality among the subjects as being perfectionistic, overly clean, prim and fussy, extremely neat, overly studious, too thorough, shy, oversensitive, serious, nervous, withdrawn, reclusive and lonely, rigid, constricted, and lacking spontaneity. They found that the children's mothers were frequently anxious, denied their children's psychological problems, and, in some cases, even viewed their scrupulosity as a noble or superior trait, thus creating a reinforcing environment for its expression. During the follow-up period, many reported to have had problematic interpersonal and uncomfortable social adjustments (Weisner & Riffel, 1960).

The issue of responsibility is a common obsessive concern for the scrupulous and may show signs of becoming problematic to the early adolescent. One small Jewish study described two cases of scrupulosity that appeared to have been precipitated by the Bar Mitzvah ritual, a Jewish rite of passage that occurs at age thirteen and marks the transition to assuming adult expectations (Greenberg, 1987). If taken too literally, these expectations can cultivate an overly exaggerated sense of responsibility that can affect age-appropriate decision-making and functioning.

Freud's concept of the superego plays a major role in how young OCD sufferers interpret the content of their obsessions as they undergo the normal challenges of self-identity (Freud & Strachey, 1960). The superego has two parts, consisting of the conscience and the ego ideal. The conscience includes information about behaviors that are judged as bad by parents and society and lead to bad consequences, punishments, or feelings of guilt and remorse (Piaget & Inhelder, 1969). Alternatively, "the Freudian notion of a perfect or ideal self- housed in the superego, consisting of the individual's conscious and unconscious images of what he would like to be, patterned after certain people whom . . . he regards as idealthat include the rules and standards for behaviors to which the ego aspires" (Schalkwijk, 2018, p. 89). The all-or-nothing standard of measuring success or failure will likely result in feelings of inadequacy and shame.

Psychodynamic interpretations of the role OCD plays indicate that obsessions and compulsions manifest from the unconscious conflict between an impulsive id (pleasure-seeking) and an inflexible superego (strict and watchful) morality (Besharat & Kamali, 2016). As a result, the ego develops defenses to mediate the conflict between them (Fenichel, 1946). Although OCD symptoms are conscious, they appear to act to control unconscious sexual urges (Esman, 2001). Freud attributed perfectionism to the excessive functioning of superego (Freud, 1924, 1959). Research also shows a positive correlation between perfectionism and scrupulosity or religiousness (Abramowitz, Deacon, Woods, & Tolin, 2004; Inozu, Karanci & Clark, 2012; Sica, Novara, & Sanavio, 2002). Using this reaction formation defense mechanism, the person overcomes unacceptable urges by adopting the opposite impulse or behavior such as hypermorality (Kempke & Luyten, 2007).

A study was conducted that examined whether the superego and ego characteristics predicted scrupulosity and non-religious obsessions and compulsions (Besharat & Kamali, 2016). The authors found that perfectionism and ego control were the best predictors of scrupulosity (Besharat & Kamali, 2016).

In the moral dimension, the early adolescent is in the conventional stage and begins to understand societal rules and the "Golden Rules" of morality. Kohlberg stated that the early adolescent unquestioningly conforms to and upholds social rules and conventions by virtue of the external expectation to do so and the need to please others (Kohlberg, 1976). He further states that the child also begins to expand personal morality by considering the intention of an act rather than merely its consequences, which becomes problematic for those with scrupulosity. Obsessive doubt creates confusion about what a real intention is and causes an exaggerated estimation of an increased likelihood that negative consequences will occur from having obsessions and not performing rituals.

The theme of the early adolescent's faith is "synthetic-conventional" faith, which is motivated by the need to please others (Fowler, 1981). Scrupulous and obsessive concern over what pleases others, or whether others are being pleased enough, may override the ability to test out personal judgment in faith or moral matters, or consider that this is even permissible. Fowler addresses this concern by stating that faith must serve as a means to synthesize the emerging identity and newly acquired points of view as they relate to faith and values (Fowler, 1981). He warns that if concern over the evaluation by others interferes with the development of a self-determined faith, the autonomy of judgment can be jeopardized later on. Scrupulous adults who have been unable to progress through this stage, and, subsequently, trusting one's own judgment are perceived as too risky and to be avoided. As a result, reliance on externally determined rules of morality and faith made by others serves as the sole means of assurance that risk or error in judgment will, and should, be avoided.

Young describes two learning styles that affect cognitive processing of information about values in early adolescence. Convergent thinking entails learning about and conforming to specific facts, principles, rules, and values as presented by teachers, parents, and other authorities. These will continue to be used in their original form when necessary (Young, 1981).

Divergent thinking consists of processing and expressing convergent data in the individual's unique, creative way. Young warns that an overemphasis on convergent thinking may result in a polarized response to rigid conformity. Out of an obsessive need for certainty and safety, the scrupulous may become overly entrenched in convergent thinking and become distressed when inevitable conflicts arise for which divergent thinking is most adaptive. Even benign situations that lie in the "gray" area become perceived as risky and dangerous because of the polarized thinking style adopted by the scrupulous. Yet it is *precisely* the taking of what seems to be a risk and asserting one's own judgment that is the most adaptive, appropriate, reasonable, and functional of recourses.

Middle Adolescence

Middle adolescent morality is oriented toward authority, law, and duty. The general challenge of middle adolescence is whether to risk one's own opinions or conform to the status quo. The individual begins to seek out his or her place within the social or cultural system that defines roles and rules (Kohlberg, 1976). Fear is the primary motivator for obeying fixed rules and authority. Paradoxically, this is also the time when the individual may begin to test the authority and rules, which, until now, were unquestioningly heeded.

During adolescence, there is the risk of acting on immature sexual impulses that may not involve the intimacy of romantic relationships. Teens begin to test authority and rules, react to peer pressure, and act on irrational impulses, whose potential consequences they may not be aware of.

A key question, at this point, is whether rebellion contributes to healthy/adaptive development. The consensus among the theorists is that rebellion is necessary for autonomy. According to Hill, finding a sociomoral identity may include, a "rebellious moratorium" to enable development unfettered by guilt (Hill, 1986). Hill also cautions that conformity and compliance in the church, especially by adolescents, should not always be taken as a sign of maturity (Hill, 1986). She suggests that teenagers who show few signs of rebelling may develop a foreclosed identity status and remain stuck in a conventional level of faith and morality. Further, questioning authority should be considered a healthy process of faith development (Hill, 1986). Undoubtedly, the scrupulous may not have been allowed to rebel, or at least were discouraged from doing so, out of the concern to be "good," do the "right" thing, and remain oriented to pleasing others (Hill, 1986).

Fowler presented the conflicts of the "individuative-reflective" stage of faith development as developing a personal faith identity versus being defined by a group membership (Fowler, 1981). It also involves recognizing "strongly felt but unexamined feelings versus objectivity and the requirement of critical reflection, self-fulfillment or self-actualization as a primary concern versus service to and being for others, and the question of being committed to the relative versus the struggle with the possibility of an absolute" (Fowler, 1981, p. 179).

Regarding value development at this stage, Young stated:

> [I]t is much safer and more predictable to have an absolute rule or regulation to govern every possible human emotion and situation than it is to trust moment-by-moment in the spontaneous leading of the Holy Spirit . . . and [in Romans, 14:14] Paul expresses this fact eloquently when he says, "I know and am convinced . . . that nothing is unclean in itself; but to him who thinks anything to be unclean, to him it is unclean." (Young, 1981, p. 171)

Paul's astute insight belies the chronic dilemma of the scrupulous, who seek absolute certainty in most matters. Acting on subjective judgment is considered equivalent to sinning or acting immorally. It is the nature of obsessions to cause doubt, and for those who obsess, the doubt becomes reality instead of unreasonable worry.

Another prominent theme at this age is the self-determination of values. Initial dissonance, rejection of introjected values, and covert and overt experimentation will be what the late adolescent confronts at this stage of development. According to Young, "the manner in which the individual resolves the dissonance (like the individual's ability to rebel) is vital to the maturing process" (Young, 1981, p. 166). By virtue of the problem of scrupulosity, resolving the dissonance in an autonomous manner is almost an impossible task as it requires asserting one's own values, Young identifies five possible ways of resolving dissonance: (1) perceptual defenses (refusing to see the dissonance); (2) ego defenses (repressing the dissonance); (3) discounting the source of the dissonance (rendering the dissonance invalid); (4) self-castigation (assuming that one's dissatisfaction is a result of one's own inadequacy or failure, and reaffirming one's value system through guilt and renewed efforts at "good" behavior and attitudes); and (5) initial challenge (questioning the validity of one's introjected values) (Young, 1981, p. 168). Young asserts that if any of the first four of these processes are chosen, the individual will remain at the conventional level of faith. Those with scrupulosity seem to resolve the dissonance mostly through self-castigation, by blaming themselves for the negative obsessive thoughts and accompanied affect, and by discounting the source of the dissonance by rejecting information from the laity, in which therapists are included.

People resolving dissonance through initial challenge are likely to experience fear, anger, uncertainty, confusion, moodiness, and conflict with authority figures. However, these are the very stresses that enable the maturing process and that the scrupulous avoid by not confronting the normative challenges presented by this stage. The individual who is allowed to experiment covertly through thoughts and overtly through actions during the transition will stand a better chance of succeeding in developing an autonomous value (as well as moral and faith) system. Kohlberg and Kramer (1969) noted that a period of hedonistic experimentation during late adolescence was experienced by every individual who eventually reached the highest level of moral reasoning.

If the onset of OCD has already occurred, the potential covert and overt operations are now occupied by the symptoms (obsessions and compulsions). As the scrupulous believe the content of thoughts and behaviors should be externally defined, they consider their symptoms to be part and parcel of their identity and hold themselves in contempt. In turn, experimentation is precluded for the scrupulous due to obsessive guilt and anxiety. The performance of compulsions instead of experimenting serves as their moral expression. Ironically, the goals of experimentation parallel those of the behavioral therapy techniques of exposure (confrontation of feared situations) and response prevention (no performance of compulsions). More will be said about this later.

Late Adolescence

People in this stage begin to be more sensitive to and aware of inconsistencies in what they were taught and their own sense of self. Rebellion is common in this stage as a way of individuating and testing the authority of the church (Hill, 1986). Those who are scrupulous may become—and remain—stuck in previous stages of development out of fear of betraying authority figures, religious rules, and even God as well as getting in trouble. Even though they may experience dissonance, they stay with what is familiar and safe.

Another theme of late adolescence is acknowledging and reconciling the absolute versus the relative truth in moral, faith, and values issues. The psychosocial stage of young adulthood is intimacy versus isolation (Erikson, 1963). The progression toward achieving autonomy or intimacy challenges young adults to make independent decisions and commit to actions, even if unpopular, that express their ideology.

Kohlberg and Kramer's notion of a "rebellious moratorium" (1969) and Erikson's call for a "psychological moratorium" (1963) to accommodate the emergence of identity during adolescence speak sensitively to the normal anxieties inherent in moral and psychosocial identity formation (Erikson, 1963; Kohlberg & Kramer, 1969).

Young Adulthood

For many, young adulthood is also characterized by moving away from home. Individuals may pursue college, military service, employment opportunities, or marriage. The level of autonomy involved in such decisions is likely to affect the experience. Even if the endeavor proves unsatisfactory to the autonomous young adult, he or she may not necessarily feel a sense of failure but instead may benefit by learning what can be applied from the experience to subsequent life choices. If individuals embark on an externally determined path, not only might they be unhappy with his/her decisions but they may also have further doubts about their decision-making abilities, risking further erosion of self-esteem. The end result would be a spiraling dependency on others' judgments and opinions for future decisions and further self-doubt.

The individual who has been able to progress to the "postconventional, autonomous, principled" level of moral development comes to accept the underlying principles of society's rules. However, individualistic principles that conflict with these rules are regarded by the postconventional young adult as also being moral (Kohlberg, 1976). Hill (1986) wonders why the transition to postconventionality, so crucial to spiritual and mental maturity, and theoretically a normal developmental process, is so rarely achieved by people. She suggests that this particular juncture represents the basis for the turmoil and rebelliousness of adolescence with regard to religious and philosophical values (Hill, 1986). She explains that Kohlberg has hypothesized stage 4.5, which is considered to be a temporary regression to a hedonistic orientation of morality, to account for the marked transitional characteristics of adolescence (Hill, 1986). Helping the scrupulous to jump the developmental hurdle from conventional to postconventional morality will foster self-reliance, promote self-determination, and establish an internalized and omnipresent authority.

Development along the values dimension in young adulthood consists of "differentiation and secondary introjection," which functions similarly to moral and faith development (Young, 1981). Young adults are more secure about living their lives according to the system of values they have developed to this point. Secondary introjection is the acceptance of these values and the ability to affect them in reality.

Sexuality, socialization, moral dilemmas, and questions of faith and values determination inherent in the maturing process are the very touchstones through which identity is developed. In the preceding examination, it has been theorized that when there is a predisposition to OCD, and familial or religious environments impose rigid rules, scrupulosity can result. Scrupulosity is problematic because it is riddled with obsessive doubt about the issues involved in the dimensions outlined in this paper. When the individual is unable to progress along the developmental lines of the dimensions, future autonomy is jeopardized. The anxiety provoked by the OCD along with the additional problems of being scrupulous make it difficult for individuals to resolve the developmental challenges of their age. When this opportunity is lost, it is difficult to compensate for it later.

Development of autonomy is especially conflictual for the scrupulous because it requires making subjective judgments and decisions. In the religious realm, the ultimate feared consequence of subjective judgments cannot be validated in one's lifetime (e.g., going to heaven or hell, offending God, upsetting the natural order in the universe). The scrupulous feel compelled to ritualize from a "just in case I have sinned" or "better to be safe than sorry" mentality to avoid responsibility for having made a mistake. Resolution of problems, then, is achieved through the least risky and most conforming of solutions. Additionally, the scrupulous mistake anxiety and doubt for sin; hence, they suffer from a chronic, yet false, need for absolution. As this process becomes reinforced from preadolescence into adulthood, it is argued that autonomy is forsaken (Hill, 1986).

Taking the proverbial "leap of faith" must be sanctioned to facilitate development and to reconcile the obsessive need for reassurance from others as to what is right or wrong. Fowler (1981) states that to achieve a higher level of faith, relocating external sources of authority to an internalized system is necessary. In other words, the scrupulous can identify and "borrow" the superego of those they respect as a stopgap measure toward autonomy.

References

Abramowitz, J. S., Deacon, B., Woods, C., & Tolin, D. (2004). Association between Protestant religiosity and obsessive-compulsive symptoms and cognitions. *Depress Anxiety, 20*(2), 70–76. Retrieved from http://www.ncbi.nlm.nih.gov/entrez/query.fcgi?cmd=Retrieve&db=PubMed&dopt=Citation&list_uids=15390213

Bailey, R., & Pico, J. (2022). *Defense mechanisms.* Treasure Island, FL: StatPearls.

Ballmaier, M., Kumar, A., Elderkin-Thompson, V., Narr, K. L., Luders, E., Thompson, P. M., . . . Toga, A. W. (2008). Mapping callosal morphology in early- and late-onset elderly depression: An index of distinct changes in cortical connectivity. *Neuropsychopharmacology, 33*(7), 1528–1536. doi:10.1038/sj.npp.1301538

Békés, V., & Perry, J. C. (2017). Identification (defense mechanism). In V. Zeigler-Hill & T. K. Shackelford (Eds.), *Encyclopedia of personality and individual differences* (pp. 1–4). Cham, Switzerland: Springer International Publishing. doi:10.1007/978-3-319-28099-8_1386-1

Besharat, M. A., & Kamali, Z. (2016). Predicting obsessions and compulsions according to superego and ego characteristics: A comparison between scrupulosity and non-religious obsessive-compulsive symptoms. *Asian Journal of Psychiatry, 19*, 73–78. doi:10.1016/j.ajp.2016.01.003

Cappella, E., Schwartz, K., Hill, J., Kim, H. Y., & Seidman, E. (2017). A national sample of eighth-grade students: The impact of middle grade schools on academic and psychosocial competence. *The Journal of Early Adolescence, 39*(2), 167–200. doi:10.1177/0272431617735653

Cohen, D., & Kim, E. (2020). Sublimation (defense mechanism). In V. Zeigler-Hill & T. K. Shackelford (Eds.), *Encyclopedia of personality and individual differences* (pp. 5275–5278). Cham, Switzerland: Springer International Publishing.

Cramer, P. (2008). Seven pillars of defense mechanism theory. *Social and Personality Compass, 2*(5), 1963–1981. doi:10.1111/J.1751-9004.2008.00135.X

Cramer, P. (2015). Understanding defense mechanisms. *Psychodynamic Psychiatry, 43*(4), 523–552. doi:10.1521/pdps.2015.43.4.523

Cramer, P. (2018). The development of defense mechanisms during the latency period. *Journal of Nervous and Mental Disease, 206*(4), 286–289. doi:10.1097/nmd.0000000000000793

Dell'Osso, B., Benatti, B., Hollander, E., Fineberg, N., Stein, D. J., Lochner, C., . . . Menchon, J. M. (2016). Childhood, adolescent and adult age at onset and related clinical correlates in obsessive-compulsive disorder: A report from the International College of Obsessive-Compulsive Spectrum Disorders (ICOCS). *International Journal of Psychiatry in Clinical Practice, 20*(4), 210–217. doi:10.1080/13651501.2016.1207087

Erikson, E. (1963). *Childhood and society* (2nd ed.). New York, NY: W. W. Norton.

Esman, A. H. (2001). Obsessive-compulsive disorder: Current views. *Psychoanalytic Inquiry, 21*(2), 145–156. doi:10.1080/07351692109348929

Fenichel, O. (1946). *The psychoanalytic theory of neurosis*. New York, NY: Routledge.

Fowler, J. W. (1981). *Stages of faith: The psychology of human development and the quest for meaning*. New York, NY: HarperOne. (New edition, September 15, 1995).

Freud, S. (1924). Obsessive actions and religious practices (A. F. Strachey, Trans.). In *The standard edition of the complete psychological works of Sigmund Freud* (Vol. IX, pp. 117–127). London, UK: Hogarth Press.

Freud, S. (1959). *Inhibitions, symptoms, and anxiety* (A. F. Strachey, Trans.). New York, NY: W. W. Norton.

Freud, S. (1975). *Three essays on the theory of sexuality*. New York, NY: Basic Books.

Freud, S., & Strachey, J. (1960). *The ego and the id*. New York, NY: W. W. Norton.

Freud, S., Strachey, J., Freud, A., Rothgeb, C. L., & Richards, A. (1953). *The standard edition of the complete psychological works of Sigmund Freud*. London, UK: Hogarth Press.

Fulmer, R. (2018). The evolution of the psychodynamic approach and system. *International Journal of Psychological Studies, 10*, 1. doi:10.5539/ijps.v10n3p1

Green, A. L., Ferrante, S., Boaz, T. L., Kutash, K., & Wheeldon-Reece, B. (2021). Social and emotional learning during early adolescence: Effectiveness of a classroom-based SEL program for middle school students. *Psychology in the Schools, 58*(6), 1056–1069.

Greenberg, D. (1987). The behavioral treatment of religious compulsions. *Journal of Psychology and Judaism, 11*(1), 41–47.

Hill, C. I. (1986). A developmental perspective on adolescent "rebellion" in the church. *Journal of Psychology & Theology, 14*(4), 306–318. doi:10.1177/009164718601400407

Inozu, M., Karanci, A. N., & Clark, D. A. (2012). Why are religious individuals more obsessional? The role of mental control beliefs and guilt in Muslims and Christians. *Journal of Behavior Therapy and Experimental Psychiatry, 43*(3), 959–966. doi:10.1016/j.jbtep.2012.02.004

Kempke, S., & Luyten, P. (2007). Psychodynamic and cognitive–behavioral approaches of obsessive–compulsive disorder: Is it time to work through our ambivalence? *Bulletin of the Menninger Clinic, 71*(4), 291–311. doi:10.1521/bumc.2007.71.4.291

Kohlberg, L. (1976). *Moral stages and moralization* (T. Lickona, Ed.). New York, NY: Holt, Rinehart and Winston.

Kohlberg, L., & Kramer, R. (1969). Continuities and discontinuities in childhood and adult moral development. *Human development, 12*(2), 93–120. doi:10.1159/000270857

Laughlin, H. P. (1979). *The ego and its defenses*. New York, NY: J. Aronson.

McKay, D., Abramowitz, J., & Storch, E. (2019, Spring). *Ineffective and potentially harmful psychological interventions for obsessive-compulsive disorder.* Retrieved from https://iocdf.org/expert-opinions/ineffective-and-potentially-harmful-psychological-interventions-for-obsessive-compulsive-disorder/

Mullen, J. J. (1931). Psychological factors in the pastoral treatment of scruples. *Archives of NeuroPsychology, 26*(3), 684. doi:10.1001/archneurpsyc.1931.02230090217022

Paradiso, S., Brown, W. S., Porcerelli, J. H., Tranel, D., Adolphs, R., & Paul, L. K. (2020). Integration between cerebral hemispheres contributes to defense mechanisms. *Frontiers in Psychology, 11*, 1534. doi:10.3389/fpsyg.2020.01534

Piaget, J., & Inhelder, B. (1969). *The psychology of the child*. New York, NY: Basic Books.

Sarnoff, C. A. (1980). Latency-age children. In G. P. Sholevar, R. M. Benson, & B. J. Blinder (Eds.), *Emotional disorders in children and adolescents: Medical and psychological approaches to treatment* (pp. 283–302). Dordrecht, The Netherlands: Springer.

Schalkwijk, F. (2018). A new conceptualization of the conscience. *Frontiers in Psychology, 9*, 1863. doi:10.3389/fpsyg.2018.01863

Sica, C., Novara, C., & Sanavio, E. (2002, July). Religiousness and obsessive-compulsive cognitions and symptoms in an Italian population. *Behaviour Research and Therapy, 40*(7), 813–823. Retrieved from http://www.ncbi.nlm.nih.gov/entrez/query.fcgi?cmd=Retrieve&db=PubMed&dopt=Citation&list_uids=12074375

UKEssays. (2018). *Psychology theories of obsessive compulsive disorder (OCD).* Retrieved from https://www.ukessays.com/essays/psychology/psychology-theories-obsessive-compulsive-disorder-8814.php?vref=1

Weisner, W., & Riffel, P. (1960). Scrupulosity: Religion and obsessive compulsive behavior in children. *American Journal of Psychiatry, 117*, 314–318. doi:10.1176/ajp.117.4.314

Young, R. G. (1981). Values differentiation as stage transition: An expansion of Kohlbergian moral stages. *Journal of Psychology and Theology, 9*(2), 164–174. doi:10.1177/009164718100900206

CHAPTER FOUR

Cleanliness Is Next to Godliness: Getting Physically, Spiritually, Morally, and Emotionally Pure

"I wash my hands of this." We may say this when we want to absolve ourselves of a problem and walk away. The origin of this expression dates back to the Gospel of Matthew (27:2) written around 26–37 AD. The gospel portrays Pontius Pilate washing his hands when he declares, "I am innocent of the blood of this just Person. You see to it," referring to his decree that Jesus be crucified.

Water can safely be called the most common physical and symbolic element for cleansing the body and soul. This chapter covers typical physical, religious, and moral cleansing traditions that turn into convoluted compulsive practices, which lose sight of the essential meaning and spirit of the acts. Examples of how these ritual cleansing practices become problematic for Christian, Muslim, Jewish, and Hindu patients are provided in the section that follows.

Symbolically, washing of the hands can also represent an unconscious act of cleansing oneself from physical and moral contamination or guilt. Lady MacBeth, for example, is suffering from guilt after convincing her husband to kill the king of Scotland. While sleepwalking, she utters, "A little water clears us of this deed" (Shakespeare, 2014, Act II, Scene II), and then in Act V, she cries out while washing her hands for fifteen minutes:

> Out, damned spot! out, I say!—One: two: why,
> then, 'tis time to do't.—Hell is murky!—Fie, my
> lord, fie! a soldier, and afeard? What need we
> fear who knows it, when none can call our power to
> account?—Yet who would have thought the old man
> to have had so much blood in him. (Shakespeare, 2014, Act V, Scene I)

She never does wash the spot or the guilt away.

Scrupulous Cleansing

Religious washing rituals are performed to transform someone from a secular/worldly state to one of purity in order to be presentable to God. Obsessive-compulsive disorder (OCD) washing rituals, however, are attempts to transform someone who seeks purity not for the sake of God but rather to achieve a subjective sense of perfection and completion. Not surprisingly, scrupulosity takes "cleanliness is next to Godliness" to figurative and literal levels of the extreme (Lewis, 1998). The phrase originated from a sermon by John Wesley in 1872 on being properly dressed:

> But, before we enter on the subject, let it be observed, that slovenliness is no part of religion; that neither this, nor any text of Scripture, condemns neatness of apparel. Certainly this is a duty, not a sin. Cleanliness is, indeed, next to godliness. (http://wesley.nnu.edu/john-wesley/the-sermons-of-john-wesley-1872-edition/sermon-88-on-dress/)

Subsequently, according to Joanna Bourke, a professor of History, Classics, and Archaeology at Birkbeck College in London who wrote *Divine Madness, the dilemma of religious scruples in twentieth-century America and Britain* was that "cleanliness became quite literally equated with Godliness, forcing scrupulous people to spend large parts of the day washing" (Bourke, 2009).

Christianity

In Christianity, holy water is used for several religious purposes. Holy water is used in baptisms and to bless individuals, churches, homes, and objects; as a means of removing moral uncleanness; and as protection against evil (https://www.britannica.com/topic/holy-water). It is said to have the power to banish demons, wash the soul from the stain of venial sins, and restore moral good standing (*Tracts on Principles of Divine Worship: No. 3. The Sprinkling of Holy Water*, New York: Men's Guild, St. Ignatius's Church).

But how is it made holy? Holy water consists of salt that is blessed by a priest and then added to the water after the following blessing:

> I exorcise thee, O creature water, in the name of God the Father Almighty, and in the name of Jesus Christ His Son, and our Lord; and in the power of the Holy Ghost; that Thou mayest become water exorcised for the chasing away of all the power of the enemy; that thou mayest have strength to uproot and cast out the enemy himself and his apostate angels, by the power of the same our Lord Jesus Christ, who shall come to judge the living and the dead, and the world by fire. Amen. (Lang, 2016, p. 19)

In Christianity, holy water is used in the sacrament of baptism (or christening) to cleanse the soul of Adam and Eve's original sin. Baptism opens the person to the presence of God, who enters the soul, and acts as a transitional ritual that officially or formally brings the person into the faith (Mick, 2007). Catholics, Orthodox, Lutherans, Methodists, Presbyterians, and Congregational Reformers continue to baptize infants (Renard, 2012).

The priest states, "I baptize you in the Name of the Father, and of the Son, and of the Holy Spirit," while pouring water over the head of the person receiving the sacrament or dipping the person in water. For Catholics, baptism is the sacrament of salvation that allows for the practice of all other sacraments (https://www.saintpatrickchurch.org/sacraments-2).

Holy water is found in a font for Catholic parishioners to dip the tips of their fingers into while genuflecting upon entering and leaving the Church. People make a sign of the cross and recite, "By this holy water and by your Precious Blood, wash away all my sins, O Lord" (https://www.catholic.org/prayers/prayer.php?p=20).

During what was to be a celebratory event for her baby, Ellen was in distress when she became unsure if the priest had performed the ceremony accurately. Did he get all the words right? Could she ask him to repeat the blessings just to make sure her son would be allowed in heaven? When her friends and family went to congratulate her, she removed herself and went into the bathroom to collect herself. She knew asking the priest reassuring questions would create more doubt, so she tried to let it go. She never did settle the doubt and had to rely on her faith that the ceremony was proper and that God would accept her son in the afterlife.

What If the Holy Water Is Dirty?

Interestingly, holy water fonts have been identified as a potential source of bacterial and viral infection (Jurado, Ortiz-Martinez, Gonzalez -delValle, Hermosin, & Saiz-Jimenez, 2002). There have been accounts of contaminated holy water in Italy, the United States, England, Spain, and Ireland. In Italy, staphylococci, streptococci, coli bacilli, Loeffler's bacillus, and other bacteria were found in samples of holy water taken from a church in the nineteenth century (Egbert & Dietetic and Hygienic Gazette, 1898). In England, after a burn patient acquired a bacterial infection after exposure to holy water, samples were taken from thirteen other churches and were found to have bacteria that could cause infection in humans (Rees & Allen, 1996). In 2012, taking a hands-off approach, a church in Italy installed an automatic holy water dispenser due to concerns about the flu (Montagne, 2009). During the swine flu epidemic of 2009, Bishop John Steinbock of Fresno, California, recommended that "holy water should not be in the fonts" due to fear of spreading infections (*California Catholic Daily*, 2009). The holy water fonts from the churches of Seville, Spain, had coliforms, Enterobacteriaceae, and other pathogenic bacteria (Jurado et al., 2002). In Ireland, fonts were removed from churches where drug addicts were found to be washing or rinsing their syringes (Payne, 2001). Needless to say, this caused problems for church-attending people with contamination obsessions—do I follow the traditional behaviors of reverence or risk becoming sick from not being sure the water is pure?

When Stan entered his church, he usually dipped his fingers in the font of holy water and makes the sign of the cross to bless and renew himself. However, after he heard about infectious outbreaks in Europe caused by contaminated holy water, he became unsure if the water in the font was safe. The first time he was triggered by this obsession, he froze, unable to decide whether to take the risk. People waiting behind him began showing their impatience, causing Stan to become more anxious. Not knowing what to do, he left the church and went back home. Having been a faithful Catholic, he was distraught about having missed receiving the sacraments and felt he had betrayed God. Not understanding what was going on, he compulsively prayed for forgiveness until exhaustion overcame his conscience, and he fell asleep.

Islam

In Iranian culture, washing behavior serves to restore "spiritual purity" (Ghassemzadeh, 2018). In the twelfth century, the theologian Abu al-Wafaa al-Aqeel considered a person *manjun* (legally insane) if, after immersing himself in water, he doubted whether he may have missed wetting a part of his body (Keshavarzi, Khan, & Syed, 2020). Presently, this condition has been termed *alwaswâs al-qahri* (Overwhelming Whisperings), which translates clinically to OCD (Rassool, 2019). Further, someone with *iradah* (willful intent) to perform *ikrah* (psychological compulsions) may be considered *junun al-juzi* (partially insane) (Keshavarzi et al., 2020). Junun al-juzi is used to denote a specific area of compromised functioning despite the presence of normative cognitive faculties that are fully intact in other areas of life (Al-Issa, 2000). Depending on the severity of OCD, patients may receive religious accommodations to alleviate the obsessive burden the disorder places on their faith practice, such as sanctions for excessive washing, wasting water, the ability to forego the washing rituals for prayer, or for prayer altogether (Keshavarzi et al., 2020; Muhaizah, 2013).

Taharah (purity) is an important condition in the practice of the five daily prayers in Islam. There are two types of cleansing rituals conducted in order to be in a state of purity worthy of Allah: *wuḍū*ʾ and *ghusl* (Rassool, 2019). wuḍūʾ is performed for minor impurities consisting of washing the face, hands, forehead to crown of the head, and feet (Johari, Hassan, Anwar, & Kamaruzaman, 2013; Rassool, 2019). Muslims with OCD fear that they may become contaminated or have irrational fears that their wuḍū did not adequately purify them for a reverent prayer (Keshavarzi et al., 2020). Obsessive doubt about whether the washing rituals were complete and performed in the right order can cause the person to repeat the process until she is sure she has done a thorough job.

Actions that are considered to invalidate wuḍūʾ include urination, defecation, flatulence, deep sleep, light bleeding, and sexual intercourse (Rassool, 2019). Obsessive doubt that one may have committed any of these acts often leads to compulsive repetitions of both washing and performing the same prayer several times until the person "feels" right. These can recur to the point of missing the actual specified time of the prayer or performing the prayer repetitively. Kesahavarzi and colleagues have stated the importance of understanding that the compulsions are repeated until the level of subjective anxiety subsides, not after having corrected a minor objective flaw in the fulfillment of the ritual obligation (Keshavarzi et al., 2020).

Ghusl is a more thorough cleansing ritual for "major impurity" conditions such as after sexual intercourse, any discharge of semen, the completion of menses, and post-childbirth bleeding, and it is recommended every Friday before the congregational prayer at the mosque (Rassool,

2019). Even though ghusl is not the way each of the five daily prayers is performed, imagine how painstaking even the more simpler prayers are to complete just to get to the prayer!

The following is an abridged version of how Ghusl is conducted (*followed by obsessive thoughts in italics*):

1. Make the following intention in heart without uttering any word with tongue: "I am going to take a bath for acquiring purity" (*Perfectly; but I may have said something out loud—repeat that step*).
2. First wash both hands up to wrist three times (*I'm not sure if I washed them enough, so repeat three more times*).
3. Rinse mouth thoroughly (*Did I get every surface? I'll do it again*).
4. Sniff water through nose (*Not sure if it was thorough. I'll repeat it*).
5. Wash excretory organs, whether impurity is present there or not (*But how do I know they are pure? I will keep washing until I'm sure there is nothing there*).
6. Now, if there is an impurity on any part of the body, remove it (*But maybe something is still there. Keep washing!*).
7. Perform wuḍū as done for ṣalāĥ but do not wash feet (*But maybe some soap got on my feet, so I need to start over*).
8. In case of performing ghusl on some stool, wash feet as well (*I'd better check my feet and keep washing just in case I stepped in something*).
9. Now moisten the body with wet hand, especially in the winter season (during this, soap may be applied) (*Was it wet enough? I'll repeat to make sure*).
10. Now pour water three times over right shoulder, three times on left shoulder, on head, and then three times on the whole body (*I'm not sure if I was paying attention. It might have been four times. I'll start over*).
11. Now shift apart from the place of ghusl and wash feet if not washed during wuḍū (*OK, I'll wash my feet in case I skipped it*).-
12. Do not face toward Qiblaĥ during ghusl (*Let me check to make sure I'm in the right spot*).
13. During bath, rub all the body with hands (*I'll keep rubbing until it feels like I've done it enough*).
14. Take bath at such a place where nobody can see you (*I made sure I'm in a private area, but how do I know? Someone could have seen me without my knowledge*).
15. If such place is not available, a man should cover his *Sitr* (private area) from his navel to his knees with a thick cloth. If thick cloth is not available, two or more thin cloths can be wrapped on *Sitr* as thin cloth will stick with the body and color of thighs (*Am I covered enough? Let me adjust it to make sure*).

16. A woman has to take more precautions (*I'll keep checking and repeating to make sure I've done things perfectly proper*).
17. Neither talk during ghusl nor recite any invocation (*I am keeping my lips sealed until I am finished*).
18. After bath, body may be wiped with a towel, etc. (*Have I dried off enough? I'll keep going and check my skin until I'm sure*).
19. Wear clothes immediately after the completion of ghusl (*Oh no, what if I wasn't fast enough and I exposed myself inappropriately? What if my clothes are dirty?*).

(Amīr-e-Ahl-e-Sunnat, 2011)

Sirah runs through a mental checklist for each step of wuḍū' and ghusl as a way of making sure that she has followed the proper sequence of the ritual. She is caught in a bind of trying to be sure she is clean for prayer but also for how much water she is using and wasting in the process. "Do not waste water even if you were at a running stream" (Qu'ran: Sunan Ibn Majah 42). *When she is finished, she carefully puts her clothes on, making sure they have not become contaminated in a way that would cause her to become impure or contaminate her prayer mat. Sometimes she will go back and rewash, just in case, and then put on a new outfit. Most likely, she will have unexpected triggers while she is performing those tasks and has to decide whether to keep moving forward or go back and ritualize. Her focus has shifted from the spirit and anticipation of praying to being perfectly clean and "getting it right." If this happens during the time of prayer at work, she will stay late to compensate for the lost time.*

Judaism

Water is used throughout the day in Orthodox Judaism. According to *halachah* (custom), hands are washed before and after eating a meal with bread, upon waking in the morning, after using the toilet, and before prayer. Orthodox Judaism, compared to Reform or Conservative, has strict rules around cleanliness. The origin of religious ritual washing in Judaism was referred to in the book of Exodus:

> Then the LORD said to Moses, "Make a bronze basin, with its bronze stand, for washing. Place it between the tent of meeting and the altar, and put water in it. Aaron and his sons are to wash their hands and feet with water from it. Whenever they enter the tent of meeting, they shall wash with water so that they will not die. Also, when they approach the altar to minister by presenting a food offering to the LORD, they shall wash their

> hands and feet so that they will not die. This is to be a lasting ordinance for Aaron and his descendants for the generations to come." (Exodus 30:17–21 NIV)

Judaism has two types of washing: *netilat yadayim* (handwashing with a cup) and *mikveh* (full-body immersion—covered later in the chapter). Handwashing is conducted before the morning prayer, before the other two daily prayers if the hands have touched areas of the body underneath the clothing or the hair, and if bread is served with a meal (Melamed, 2012). If water cannot be obtained, the hands may be cleaned in another manner, such as by wiping them off with a clean cloth (Zalman, Touger, & Kaploun, 2004).

The method of handwashing is to take the cup with the nondominant hand and pour the water twice on the other hand, then switch, and repeat the practice two more times. Prior to washing, the person has to be careful not to touch areas that have openings inside the body such as the mouth, nose, ears, and eyes (*Shulchan Aruch Orach Chaim* 4:3–4; *Mishnah Berurah* 13). Similarly, one must be cautious not to touch food or drink before washing (*Mishnah Berurah* 4:14) (Melamed, 2012).

Mariah washes her hands up to her wrists, and sometimes up to her elbows, with water. Her handwashing has created a red ring between her overwashed hands and wrists and the rest of her arms. Before washing her hands for prayers, she mentally reviews the process to rehearse how she will follow the steps in a perfect manner. Obsessing during the handwashing causes her to doubt whether she has repeatedly pouring the water over her hands twice or thrice. She stays stuck while mentally reviewing what she has done to try to be sure that she is finished and can move forward. Never being able to be sure, she repeats the last step again, even though it might be excessive and not according to the rules. She also repeats the washing ritual before the other daily prayers if she is distracted, which is almost every time due to her children needing her attention.

Hinduism

Washing and purification rituals are common in Hinduism. There are several prayers throughout the day that require the use of water to purify the mind and body. Bathing, especially in cold water, is considered a sacred act.

The *prata-snana* (morning bath, ideally performed at 4:00 a.m.) is considered the most important of Hindu rituals. It is said to remove internal and external contamination to reach a state of purity. Anyone who does not perform the morning bath is considered impure, not fit to perform daily tasks, and a sinner who is to suffer on lower planets (Bharath, 2009).

Psychological and physical benefits of a cold bath are described as giving strength and peace of mind, enhancing personal sensitivity, longevity, increasing knowledge, and enhancing spiritual purity by removing unhappiness and bad thoughts (Bharath, 2009). It is also said to promote appealing personality traits, energy, strengths, purity, hygiene, health, virtue, benevolence, reality, penance, and intelligence (Timilsina, 2015).

The process of prata-snana (morning bath) consists of washing with water while maintaining breath control and placing hands and fingers in the right position and reciting the *Karadarshana* (morning mantra) (Michaels & Harshav, 2004). The bathing ritual entails first cupping water in both hands, facing the sun, and reciting the *Sāvitri* mantra: O Waters, you are the source of all happiness; bestow on us great strength so that we may have the vision of the supreme (Wayman, 1965).

Surya Arghya (offering of water to the sun) is also performed early in the morning facing east as a water offering to the sun for providing peace and energy to the body in the early morning (Badikilaya, 2019). A brass or copper vessel filled with water is raised and then poured in one fluid motion without breaking the stream while looking at the rays of the sun through the water and reciting, "*om Ghrini Suryayte Nahama*," eleven times before the water runs out. Then the person uses the right hand to dab the water from the fingers to the forehead, face, head, mouth, nose, eyes, chest, and shoulders to pray for the deities to expel demons of lust, anger, and greed (Sivananda, 2003). The last step is to close the eyes for a few minutes for silent prayer and to express gratitude for the Sun God's unconditional love (blog.cosmicinsights.net/honor-surya-sun-arghya/; https://rudrasha-ratna.com/articles/why-we-offer-arghya-to-surya).

The ritual *aachaman* is also performed after waking up in the morning. Water is poured into a small ceremonial cup with a small copper or brass spoon placed in it. The water becomes purified by putting the back tip of the right middle finger without the fingernail touching the water with the left hand placed over the right, then reciting a chant. With the left hand, dip the spoon into the water, put some drops of water on hand to rinse it, and then discard the water (this step is performed each time before putting the water into the spoon for the chant). Then put a small amount of water into the spoon and let some drops fall into the right hand, recite the chant, and then hold the right hand up and let the droplets flow into the mouth. Repeat this water process for three more chants. Take a spoon and scoop a few drops of water, say another chant, and let the water flow into the mouth. After the fourth chant, the water is sprinkled over the head and shoulders.

Not surprisingly, excessive washing and purification rituals are common symptoms of Hindus who have OCD (Khanna, Rajendra, & Channabasavanna, 1986). Though there are fifteen types of *Snanam* (religious ritual uses of water), the following five are those most likely to be affected by OCD:

1. Bathing before the pratah-snana (morning prayer ritual).
2. Taking a normal daily bath.
3. Sprinkling holy grass on the head while reciting the mantra to the Sun God and Goddess *Gayathiri*.
4. Being bathed with rainwater kept in specified vessels for auspicious occasions by a designated person while reciting a mantra and special prayer to *Ishta Devatha*.
5. For sickness. (Bharath, 2009)

In the morning, Samesh begins his daily morning routine of washing for purification before prayer. He is slow to move through the steps of the washing ritual to make sure he isn't careless. He checks to make sure he is facing east by looking back and forth at the sky to see that the sun is in front of him. He also wants to embody the proper physical and spiritual mindset to show his reverence to the gods by standing still until he feels he has achieved the right feeling.

While preparing for Surya Arghya, *Samesh fills the water vessel barefoot, standing on the balls of his feet and making sure he is holding the water vessel in the right position. He holds it with arms stretched out from the height of his forehead and makes sure not to step on the spilled ritual water. While pouring the water and looking through it at the sun, he is trying to keep track of how many times he recited the mantra so that the water does not run out before he is done. On bad days, he is so full of doubt that he will repeat the whole process as many times as it takes for him to be certain he has chanted the right words and with perfect timing.*

Menstruation, Attitudes, Ritual Cleaning, and Immersion

> "You shall not approach a woman in her time of unclean separation, to uncover her nakedness."
>
> Leviticus 18:19

Menstruation is considered taboo in many religions. Christian, Islamic, Jewish, and Hindu women are considered unclean and must follow strict religious hygiene rules during and after their menses. These rules are practiced to avoid contaminating others and to restore a state of physical and spiritual purity after the cycle is complete. There is also a social stigma about menstruation to the extent that it is often referred to as "My friend" or "That time of the month" when, if ever, it comes up as a topic needing to be addressed.

The menstrual taboo in Christianity is said to be a major reason women are denied being in positions of power and authority (Phipps, 1980). There are also rules in the Orthodox church against women receiving communion during their menstrual periods, and intercourse is not to be practiced during this phase (Phipps, 1980).

Islamic law treats *ḥaiḍ* (menstruation) as impure, and a menstruating woman may not enter any shrine or mosque, pray, or fast during Ramadan (Engineer, 1992). She is not allowed to touch the Qur'an (Fischer, 1978; Maghen, 1999) or have sexual intercourse for seven full days from when the bleeding starts (Azeem, 1995). A reference about menstruation was made that stated "the 'problem' with menstruating women (reflected in the restrictions placed on certain of their activities) is confined to the ritually threatening properties of their menstrual blood per se" (Maghen, 1999, p. 381). Women must complete *ghusl* (bath) after menstruating, as well as after sexual intercourse, to become "clean" again (Fischer, 1978). The steps to follow for *ghusl* were outlined earlier in the chapter.

Jewish women are in a state of *niddah* (impurity), and *tahor* (purity) is restored at the *mikvah* (ritual bath). Orthodox Jewish men never shake a woman's hands, because they may be menstruating, and Jewish law expressly forbids any physical contact between married Jewish couples during the days of menstruation and for a week thereafter (Eider & Feinstein, 1999; Keshet-Orr, 2003). This includes passing objects to each other, sharing a bed (most couples have two separate beds that are pulled apart during niddah), sitting together on the same cushion of a couch, eating directly from the wife's leftovers, smelling her perfume, gazing on her clothing (whether or not it has been worn), or listening to her sing (Steinberg, 1947. From the "bleeding days" until the end of the seven "clean days" is called the "Niddah (ritually unclean) period" (Guterman, Mehta, & Gibbs, 2007).

The *chafifah* (preparation for the mikvah) begins with the woman removing all foreign elements from her body prior to entering the water (e.g., skin flakes, loose hair, dirt under fingernails) so as not to contaminate it. The quality of the mikvah water itself is to be pure. Two hundred gallons of free-flowing ocean water, natural spring or well water, rainwater from a cistern, melted snow or ice, and rainwater under certain conditions are considered to have the sacred properties for the *mikvah* (Mikvaot 7:1). The woman completely immerses herself in the water all at once. She then recites the blessing for ritual purification and immerses herself two more times (https://www.mikvah.org/article/ocd_mikvah_checklist).

Jewish women who have scrupulosity find it difficult to experience the spiritual aspect of the cleansing process because they are obsessive about removing the foreign particles from their bodies, not only to be in a perfect state of readiness for immersion but also to be certain they are not responsible for contaminating the purity of the water for the rest of the women to come. They spend inordinate amounts of time repeating washing body parts and checking for any remaining particles. The *balanit* (mikvah attendant) may need to step in and firmly help guide the woman to leave the dressing room, go to the water, and get in (Vishne, Misgav, & Bunzel, 2008). On the seventh day after the mikvah ceremony, women will use a *bedikah* (clean cloth) to make sure there is no residual vaginal blood that would preclude resuming sexual relations with her husband.

A rabbi may need to be consulted for helping set structure, limits, or appropriate accommodations for the *mikvah* for scrupulous women, ideally with the balanit (mikvah attendant) present. An appropriate accommodation for practical purposes might be allowing a time limit that is a little longer than usual so the woman can pace herself. Establishing a "contract" that she will move along when prompted by the periodic check-ins from the balanit and to accept the balanit's decision that the preparations has been completed is also helpful.

Hannah worries she will contaminate the ritual bath water if she is not thoroughly rid of impurities. Repeatedly washing body parts and excessive checking double the amount of time it normally takes. She has asked her female relatives and friends about their cleansing process and wishes she could be as fluid and present-minded as they describe their experiences. She seeks reassurance from them about how to know when clean is clean, even though there is no way to be sure. How can anyone tell if the water has been made impure? They typically answer, "Well, you just know!"

She also worries about having the "right" spiritual mindset. Every time she prepares for the mikvah, she remembers the quote from Maimonides: "If a man [sic] immerses himself [sic], but without special intention, it is as though he [sic] has not immersed himself [sic] at all" (Mishneh Torah: Immersion Pools, chapter 11). She constantly asks herself if her mindset is good enough to be worthy of being purified.

Hinduism

Hinduism views the menstruating woman as "impure" (Chawla, 1994), "polluted" (Apffel-Marglin, 1994), or having a "curse" (Sharma, Vaid, &

Manhas, 2006). In a study of women in far-western Nepal during *Chhaupadi* (menstrual cycle), 82% were exiled to a livestock shed, 62% ate meals away from the home, 70% attended to their toileting outdoors, 97% were not allowed to drink or eat milk products, and 70% only took one bath during the entire cycle (Amatya, Ghimire, Callahan, Baral, & Poudel, 2018). Menstruating women cannot do any work, comb their hair, or bathe. They are not allowed to partake in the Naulas, or traditional water springs. They are not allowed to cook and must use separate utensils. They also must not eat fish or meat. Women may not enter the *pooja* room (the prayer room within each home) and may not enter the temple (Chawla, 1992; Phipps, 1980; Sharma et al., 2006). They are not allowed to ride a horse, ox, elephant, or drive a vehicle (Whelan, 1975). Most of all, menstruation is to be a private event. There is a strong taboo against menstruation being made known in a public sphere (Apffel-Marglin, 1994).

For scrupulous Indian women, these restrictions severely affect their ability to trust their judgement about when their menses has ended. In order to resume normal functioning without the fear of contaminating whatever they touch back in the comm unity, they will compulsively check to make sure no blood is visible on the surface of the cloth or paper they use to check their vaginal secretions. As another step to be certain it is safe to return, they may ask other women to inspect the cloth or paper as assurance that they are ready to go back to the community.

Lakshmi holds herself hostage at home during menstruation. Even though there are modern sanitary options that enable women to function during their menstrual cycle, Lakshmi adheres to the traditionally restrictive rules that were set from beliefs that women are impure and taboo while menstruating. Lakshmi feels contaminated during this time and will contaminate or soil whatever she touches. Her mother and other family members encourage her to be more relaxed during the menstrual phase as Hindu religious and cultural attitudes have evolved from women's ability to manage their menstrual flow. Lakshmi says she won't take the risk of contaminating anything she touches, as she would be responsible for defiling the purity of anyone who comes into contact with them. She depends on others to provide for her needs during this time by setting food or items down on the floor so she can pick them up without making physical contact with them.

References

Al-Issa, I. (2000). *Al-Junūn: Mental illness in the Islamic world.* Madison, WI: International Universities Press.

Amatya, P., Ghimire, S., Callahan, K. E., Baral, B. K., & Poudel, K. C. (2018). Practice and lived experience of menstrual exiles (Chhaupadi) among adolescent girls in far-western Nepal. *PLoS ONE, 13*(12), e0208260. doi:10.1371/journal.pone.0208260

Amīr-e-Ahl-e-Sunnat, S.-e.-a. (2011). *Method of ghusl (ritual bath)*. Retrieved from https://en.calameo.com/books/0037095245032555d350f

Apffel-Marglin, F. (1994). The sacred groves. *Manushi, 82*, 22–32.

Azeem, S. A. (1995). Women in Islam versus women in the Judaeo-Christian tradition: The myth & the reality. *Islam—The modern religion*. Retrieved from http://web.fsktm.um.edu.my/~mazliza/essays/annisa.html

Badikilaya, G. (2019). Chhath Puja-A study in religious and cultural tourism. *Atna Journal of Tourism Studies, 14*(2), 71–76.

Bharath, K. (2009). *Bathing (snanam)*. Retrieved from http://bharathkidilse.blogspot.com/2009/10/bathing-snanam.html

Bourke, J. (2009). Divine madness: The dilemma of religious scruples in twentieth-century America and Britain. *Journal of Social History, 42*(3), 581–603.

California Catholic Daily. (2009, May). Holy water should not be in fonts during this epidemic. *California Catholic Daily*. Retrieved from http://www.calcatholic.com/news/newsArticle.aspx?id=4646a566-ae6a-456c-8f28-0d47cb14d3ac

Chawla, J. (1992). *The Rig Vedic Slaying of Vrtra: Menstruation Taboos in Mythology*. Retrieved from https://www.academia.edu/24608298/Mythic_Origins_of_Menstrual_Taboo_in_Rig_Veda

Chawla, J. (1994). Mythic origins of menstrual taboo in Rig Veda. *Economic and Political Weekly, 29*(43). Retrieved from https://www.epw.in/journal/1994/43/special-articles/mythic-origins-menstrual-taboo-rig-veda.html

Egbert, J. H., & Dietetic and Hygienic Gazette. (1898). *Dietetic and Hygienic Gazette* (Vol. 14). New York, NY: The Gazette Publishing Company.

Eider, S. D., & Feinstein, M. (1999). *Sefer hilkhot niddah—Halachos of niddah*. Jerusalem, Israel: Feldheim.

Engineer, A. (1992). *Status of women in Islam*. New York, NY: St. Martin's Press.

Fischer, M. M. (1978). On changing the concept and position of Persian women. In L. Beck & N. Keddie (Eds.), *Women in the Muslim World* (pp. 189–215). Cambridge, MA: Harvard University Press.

Ghassemzadeh, H. (2018). Scrupulosity, sexual ruminations and cleaning in obsessive-compulsive disorder: Novel insights from cognitive perspectives. In D. Geeraerts, D. Divjak, & J. R. Taylor (Eds.), *Cognitive linguistics research* (pp. 293–310). Berlin, Germany: De Gruyter.

Guterman, M., Mehta, P., Gibbs, M. (2007). Menstrual taboos among major religions. *The Internet Journal of World Health and Societal Politics, 5*(2). Retrieved from https://ispub.com/IJWH/5/2/8213

Johari, N., Hassan, O., Anwar, R., & Kamaruzaman, M. (2013). A behaviour study on ablution ritual among Muslim in Malaysia. *Procedia—Social and Behavioral Sciences, 106*, 6–9. doi:10.1016/j.sbspro.2013.12.002

Jurado, V., Ortiz-Martinez, A., Gonzalez-delValle, M., Hermosin, B., & Saiz-Jimenez, C. (2002). Holy water fonts are reservoirs of pathogenic bacteria. *Environ Microbiol,* 4(10), 617–620. doi:10.1046/j.1462-2920.2002.00341.x

Keshavarzi, H., Khan, F., & Syed, B. (2020). Islamically integrated treatment of obsessive-compulsive disorder scrupulosity (Waswasa) in Muslim patients. In N. Tinaz, A. Ayten, M. Zengin, & H. Eksi (Eds.), *Spiritual counseling and care in health and prison services* (pp. 229–251). Instanbul, Turkey: Ensa.

Keshet-Orr, J. (2003). Jewish women and sexuality. *Sexual and Relationship Therapy, 18*(2), 215–224.

Khanna, S., Rajendra, P., & Channabasavanna, S. (1986). Sociodemographic variables in obsessive compulsive neurosis in India. *International Journal of Social Psychiatry, 32*(3), 47–54. doi:10.1177/002076408603200307

Lang, R. J. F. (2016). *Holy water and its significance for catholics from the German of Rev. Henry Theiler.* London, UK: Forgotten Books.

Lewis, C. A. (1998). Cleanliness is next to godliness: Religiosity and obsessiveness. *Journal of Religion and Health, 37*(1), 49–61. Retrieved from www.jstor.org/stable/27511205

Maghen, Z. (1999). Close encounters: Some preliminary observations on the transmission of impurity in early Sunnī jurisprudence. *Islamic Law and Society, 6*(3), 348–392. doi:10.1163/1568519991223784

Melamed, E. (2012). Laws of prayer. In E. Melamed (Ed.), *Peninei Halakhs.* n.p.: Maggid.

Michaels, A., & Harshav, B. (2004). *Hinduism: Past and present.* Princeton, NJ: Princeton University Press.

Mick, L. E. (2007). *Understanding the sacraments.* Collegeville, PA: Liturgical Press.

Montagne, R. (2009, November 12). (2009). *In Italy, an automatic holy-water dispenser* [Radio broadcast]. National Public Radio. Retrieved from https://www.npr.org/transcripts/120340662.

Muhaizah, K. B. A. R. (2013). *The provisions of the psychological patient in Islamic jurisprudence.* Riyadh, Saudi Arabia: Al-Sumaiea Publishing and Distribution House.

Payne, D. (2001). Holy water not always a blessing. *BMJ (Clinical Research Ed.), 322*(7280), 190. Retrieved from https://pubmed.ncbi.nlm.nih.gov/11159605

Phipps, W. E. (1980). The menstrual taboo in the Judeo-Christian tradition. *Journal of Religion and Health, 19*(4), 298–303. Retrieved from www.jstor.org/stable/27505592

Rassool, G. H. (2019). Obsessional compulsive disorder (Waswâs al-Qahri (Overwhelming Whisperings): Case report and spiritual interventions. *Malaysian Journal of Islamic* Studies, 4(1), 115–126.

Rees, J. C., & Allen, K. D. (1996). Holy water—A risk factor for hospital-acquired infection. *Journal of Hospital Infection, 32*(1), 51–55. doi:10.1016/S0195-6701(96)90164-4

Renard, J. (2012). *The handy religion answer book* (2nd ed.). Canton Charter Township, MI: Visible Ink Press.

Shakespeare, W. (2014). *Macbeth* (B. A. Mowat & P. Werstine, Eds.). New York, NY: Simon & Schuster.

Sharma, N., Vaid, S., & Manhas, A. (2006). Age at menarche in two caste groups (Brahmins and Rajputs) from rural areas of Jammu. *The Anthropologist, 8*, 55–57. doi:10.1080/09720073.2006.11890935

Sivananda, S. S. (2003). *All about Hinduism* (7th ed.). Rishikesh, India: Divine Life Trust Society.

Steinberg, M. (1947). *Basic Judaism*. New York, NY: Harcourt, Brace, and Company.

Timilsina, R. R. (2015). Sandhyopaasan: The Hindu ritual as a foundation of Vedic education. *Dhaulagiri Journal of Sociology and Anthropology, 9*, 53–88. doi:10.3126/dsaj.v9i0.14022

Vishne, T., Misgav, S., & Bunzel, M. E. (2008). Psychiatric disorders related to menstrual bleeding among ultra-orthodox population: Case series and literature review. *International Journal of Social Psychiatry, 54*, 219–224. doi:1031177/0020764008083872

Wayman, A. (1965). Climactic times in Indian mythology and religion. *History of Religions, 4*(2), 295–318.

Whelan, E. (1975). Attitidues toward menstruation. *Studies in Family Planning*, 6, 106–108.

Zalman, S., Touger, E., & Kaploun, U. (2004). *Shulchan Aruch: Code of Jewish law*. New York, NY: Merkos.

CHAPTER FIVE

Soul Purification: Confession, Prayer, Repentance, Reassurance Seeking, and Still No Mercy or Forgiveness

> "Comfort, give comfort to my people, says your God. Speak tenderly to Jerusalem, and proclaim to her that her service is at an end, that her guilt is expiated."
>
> Isaiah 40:1–4

Instead of keeping secrets, there is an apparent need for confessing and having someone listen to their guilt for people to feel unburdened and relieved. Many people feel it is wrong to keep secrets about their misdeeds; they feel the need to confess their guilt to someone so they can feel unburdened and relieved. Religious confession is an act of contrition that allows the penitent to perform prescribed acts of penance or atonement. Psychotherapy and close friendships can also provide a nonjudgmental space for moral cleansing by confessing private thoughts and feelings. Essentially, this practice can provide relief and restore a sense of well-being.

Confession

Religious confessions consist of penitents telling a clergy member what transgressions they have committed according to how their particular religion defines sinful behavior. As stated elsewhere, different religions may have different attitudes toward the same obsessive themes. For example, Catholicism considers participating in genetic science as a serious mortal sin, whereas Judaism and Protestantism consider it as something for the greater good (Evans & Hudson, 2007). Some religions display religious icons, whereas in other religions, this is considered idolatry.

Perfectionism characterizes how the scrupulous and moral perfectionists perform soul-cleansing rituals. The standard of perfection and the need to feel "right" overrides the purpose of the confession, which is to acknowledge one's imperfections.

Catholicism

Prior to confession, Catholics examine their conscience by taking an inventory of actions that may have violated any of the Ten Commandments. A review of one's thoughts, words, and actions is conducted to determine whether one adhered to the moral law. The Sacrament of Confession requires penitents to tell their sins to the priest and seek forgiveness. In order to "grow into virtue," it is recommended to do a brief examination of conscience every night before bed. This is a time to recall venial and mortal sins from the day and to ask for God's forgiveness (https://goodconfession.com/examination-of-conscience/).

An examination of conscience is also done during a period of quiet reflection before approaching the priest in confession. The importance of it being thorough is stressed so that you become aware of sins you may have forgotten, and that your conscience can be cleared (https://www.beginningcatholic.com/catholic-examination-of-conscience).

The examination of conscience practice for scrupulous Catholics may become a practice of obsessing. The lack of certainty about whether sins were actually committed can lead to endless and fruitless mental reviewing. The emphasis on thoroughness can lead to endless mental reviewing without ever achieving certainty that the examination was complete. Some faithful Catholics have embellished the severity of a sin, reconfessed sins for which they have received penance, or actually made up sins just in case they were unknowingly committed!

The sins to be sorted through in Catholicism are considered to be either mortal or venial. According to the Catechism of the Catholic Church (#1853), mortal sins are spiritual or carnal. They are of the most serious nature (i.e., murder, rape, cheating on taxes), destroy the soul, and result in being sent to hell unless they are confessed. There are three conditions under which they are committed: the act is considered severe; the person purposefully commits the act knowing it is evil and immoral; and it is done with deliberate consent. Sins are considered venial when they meet only one or two of the conditions of a mortal sin and are minor violations of the moral law (e.g., cutting in line, telling a white lie, or gossiping) (https://www.vatican.va/archive/ENG0015/__P6C.HTM). The Catechism suggests that confessing everyday mistakes (i.e., imperfections) is good practice and is "strongly recommended" (Northridge, 1968).

There are seven deadly sins that reflect excessive and indulgent behaviors by the Catholic Church. These are lust, gluttony, avarice, sloth, anger, envy, and pride, and they can condemn people to hell unless they are confessed and penance is performed (Newhauser & Ridyard, 2012). But what if the sinner isn't sure they actually committed a deadly sin? What if the thoughts weren't those that the church condemns but were really obsessions? Do those count as needing to be confessed? The church tells us that the sins of anger, blasphemy, envy, hatred, malice, murder, neglect of Sunday obligation, sins against faith, sins against hope, and sins against love are also serious (http://www.saintaquinas.com/mortal_sin.html).

An obsessive conscience will cause doubt about whether she lied to the priest by not confessing thoroughly, forgetting any sins she committed since her last confession, and did not do "right" penance. Some people will redo their confessions by church "hopping" in the hope that the confession will be complete and right.

Confession from a Priest about Scrupulous Confessions

The following is an excerpt from a public radio interview between Ira Glass, host of *This American Life*, and Father Santa, director of the *Scrupulous Anonymous* newsletter and author of *Understanding Scrupulosity: Questions, Helps, and Encouragement* (Santa, 2007). The episode is titled "Confession."

Ira Glass

Now, you have an example in your book about you got a letter in a box, and it was 150 pages. Is that what it was? And it was the most unbelievable 150 pages describing this person's struggle with sin, with sexuality, everything that you could possibly imagine. There are 150 pages in the most unbelievable amount of details, all summarized by chapters with questions that would go with it.

And the closing paragraph said, I have two questions for you. One, would you be willing to hear my confession? And the second one is, do you think I'm scrupulous?

Fr. Tom Santa

We'd already been in the confessional for an hour, an hour and a half. And you're extremely vulnerable when you're in the confessional. You never know what the person is that's going to come in, what they're going to talk about. You never know if it's something that's relatively unimportant or it's the deepest, darkest secret. You never know. And it's very draining to give individual energy to each person that comes in, to listen to them with a patient, loving heart. And so after an hour and a half, for instance, and you end up with a scrupulous person that comes in, and all they're doing is engaging in this scrupulous ritual, that has got to be one of the most difficult things I've ever done as a priest, to sit there and be patient and loving. Because all I really want to do is, just slam the door and forget it.
But you can't. You can't. You have to wait and be patient and give them the love that they really, really desire and need.

Ira Glass

These people really test you.

Fr. Tom Santa

Yes. Our own saint Alphonsus Liguori, who was scrupulous, said he exhausted the confessors in Naples, the city he was from. Because whenever they saw Alphonsus enter the city, they would all run because he would exhaust them. And he even admitted that he would do that. (Santa, 2013)

Priests are human, too!

Holy Communion (Transubstantiation or the Eucharist)

"The cup of blessing which we bless, is it not the communion of the blood of Christ? The bread which we break, is it not the communion of the body of Christ?"

Corinthians 10:16

After confession, the penitent will participate in the holiest of sacraments, which is Holy Communion.

Communion serves as converting the embodiment of Christ onto a wafer, which the priest places under the tongue of the parishioner, who is then offered a sip of wine from a chalice that was transformed into the blood of Christ. During these offerings, the priest chants from John (6:53–58):

> Truly, truly, I say to you, unless you eat the flesh of the Son of man and drink his blood, you have no life in you; he who eats my flesh and drinks my blood has eternal life, and I will raise him up at the last day. For my flesh is real food, and my blood is real drink. He who eats my flesh and drinks my blood abides in me, and I in him. As the living Father sent me, and I live because of the Father, so he who eats me will live because of me. This is the bread which came down from heaven, not such as the fathers ate and died; he who eats this bread will live forever (John 6:53–58), Council of Trent, Session xiii (October 11, 1551), *Canones de ss. Eucharistiae sacramento*, can. 1 (DS 1651; TCT 728).

The person receiving responds by saying, "Amen," a Hebrew word meaning, "So be it" (*Catechism of the Catholic Church*, 2856). The person will then return to the pew and engage in silent prayer.

In addition to questioning if they are spiritually worthy enough to take Communion, "eat the bread and drink the cup of the Lord in an unworthy manner" (1 Cor. 11:27), the scrupulous may also fear that they might bite or chew the wafer instead of letting it dissolve under their tongue. As Catholics are taught to fast (except for medicines) for at least one hour before receiving the Eucharist, no matter how well they scrub their teeth clean, or wonder if they have fasted long enough, they may avoid accepting Communion, which is ironic because doing so is denying the sacrament (https://www.usccb.org/prayer-and-worship/the-mass/order-of-mass/liturgy-of-the-eucharist). The following should provide reassurance to the scrupulous:

> Misinterpretation of 1 Corinthians 11:27–32 has caused much unnecessary anguish for Christians, and has caused many to needlessly refuse to partake of this ordinance when they could have and should have done so. Some people wonder if they are good enough to take communion. Often it is those with the most acute sensitivity to sin and the greatest fear of God who decide they are not worthy to take communion, when in fact these people may be the most spiritual members of the congregation . . . the Christian's status before God is "forgiven" no matter whether individual sins committed recently have been specifically confessed or not. He is part of the body of Christ, forever. There is therefore no reason to bar him from

> an ordinance which signifies participation in Christ's body (the church). (https://truthonlybible.com/2016/06/12/what-does-it-mean-to-partake-of-communion-in-an-unworthy-manner/)

The scrupulous may also worry that there may be food remnants in their teeth that would taint the purity of Christ's body by swallowing it. As a result, they often ruminate about being punished as tainting the wafer is considered a mortal sin. As such, the scrupulous will consider themselves unworthy to take Communion as it is uncertain whether they will err and commit a serious act of sin (Cobb, 2014). Some may have an obsessive fear that the Communion chalice might be contaminated by others having taken sips from it, even though disease specialists have not found any evidence that there is an increased risk of contracting an illness (Lobdell, 2005).

After the painstaking process of examining his conscience and completing the confession, Chris wasn't sure he fully confessed all his sins in enough detail to receive the proper penance. He also had doubts that the priest heard his confession clearly. In the past, he would go back and confess all over again to make sure he covered everything. He worried that God would not forgive him if there were any omissions in the confession, even though forgotten sins are forgiven. He is tempted to go back again this time, but his priest told him to refrain from this temptation. He then questioned whether he was worthy of receiving Communion and hesitated to approach the altar due to feeling he was still guilty of an unconfessed mortal sin. He became caught in the scrupulous bind of fear—not knowing whether to skip receiving Communion because of his uncertainty about whether he was in pure enough state of grace to receive it versus believing that not receiving would be tantamount to rejecting Christ and risk being sent to hell.

Protestantism

Protestants confess directly to God rather than through clergy. They recite the Lord's Prayer to seek forgiveness from God. "Forgive us our sins, just as we have forgiven those who have sinned against us" (Matthew 6:9–13). Lutherans differ from other Protestants in how they practice confession and absolution. These rituals are performed communally at the Divine Service, during which the entire congregation pauses for a moment of silent confession and then together recite the *Confiteor* (confessional prayer) to receive God's forgiveness. The pastor is endowed with the power of forgiving as he says the following: "Upon this your confession and in the stead and by the command of my Lord Jesus Christ, I forgive you all your sins in the name of the Father and of the Son and of the Holy Spirit" (https://www.lutheranchoralebook.com/resources/orders-of-service/chief-service/).

Latter-Day Saints/Mormons

According to the Latter-Day Saints edition of the King James Version Bible, "confession is a necessary requirement for complete forgiveness" (John 1:9). Such confessions take place in worthiness interviews prior to baptism into the church, to being set apart for any church callings, or to receiving yearly temple recommends.

The Church of Jesus Christ of Latter-Day Saints (LDS Church) teaches that all people are sinners (Rom. 3:23, Gal. 3:22), and in order that all may be forgiven, repentance is one of the first principles of the gospel. A key element of the five steps of repentance is confession. "By this ye may know if a man repenteth of his sins behold he will confess them and forsake them" (D&C 58:43). First is the conviction of and sorrow for sin, followed by the abandonment of sin, and then the confession of sin, after which restitution for the sin is made; lastly, this is followed by making restitution for sin by doing the will of the Lord (Kimball, 1996).

A proper confession requires the sinner confessing both to God and to those persons wronged by the sin he committed (https://www.churchofjesuschrist.org/study/ensign/1980/11/repentance?lang=eng). It may also be a requirement that confession be made to an authorized priesthood leader, such as a bishop, branch president, stake president, or mission president, and is considered confidential. Although there is no definitive list of sins that require confession to a priesthood leader, "adultery, fornication, other sexual transgressions and deviancies, and sins of a comparable seriousness" are included (https://www.churchofjesuschrist.org/study/new-era/1980/11/confession?lang=eng), as is intentional and repeated use of pornography (https://www.churchofjesuschrist.org/manual/let-virtue-garnish-thy-thoughts/finding-strength-to-abandon-sin?lang=eng&_r=1). Depending on the seriousness of the sin, the priesthood leader may refer the sinner to the authority of a disciplinary council, but ultimately, only God can grant forgiveness. The LDS church believes that confession is one of the steps that is required to secure forgiveness from God (Christofferson, 2011).

Bill was anxious about being honest about his mistakes and misdeeds. As a practice of worship, he would confess to an elder all the things he could remember, even if he had confessed them before. Afterward, he always felt incomplete, that there must have been more he forgot to admit. He would mentally review his actions since his last confession but still had the feeling he missed something. In some instances, he would make up things that he never did, just in case he really did them but couldn't remember.

OCD is ironic in so many ways. Bill actually lied in the pursuit of complete honesty and transparency.

Islam

In Islam, sins are considered acts that defy Allah. Sinful acts are confessed directly to Allah and not to an imam. Repentance through belief and good works restores one's religious standing and is granted forgiveness from Allah. "God will change the evil deeds of such people into good one" (Qur'an, Sura 25 Ayat 70). Those who acted sinfully but repent only to avoid *jahannam* (hell) will not be forgiven. "It is not true repentance when people continue to do evil until death confronts them and then say, 'Now I repent'" (Qur'an, Sura 4 Ayat 18).

Jasmin felt guilty that she may have offended someone or lied during a conversation she had with her mother. "If I am not kind or don't tell the whole truth, I am a bad person and a liar." She wanted to confess her guilt and seek reassurance from her mother by clarifying what she said and asking her mother if she was upset with her. When she did approach her mother, her mother became upset with Jasmin about this pattern of seeking certainty that everything was fine and forgiven.

Judaism

In Judaism, there is no formal confession, but when someone feels the need to unburden herself, she can perform the act of *viduy* (confession), which seeks forgiveness for sins against God and to others. Sins against God are communicated directly to God and not in front of a rabbi or anyone else. The prayers *Ashamnu* and *Al Chet* constitute the Jewish confession and are followed by prayers that ask for forgiveness.

A collective confession by the community is, however, conducted during the service of the highest of holy days, Yom Kippur (Day of Atonement). Together, Jews confess that "*We* have sinned" as a way of taking responsibility for actions that affect the community as a whole.

When a Jewish person has done something that was harmful to another, he should approach the person directly and asks that person for forgiveness; he will then be forgiven by God. If the offended person refuses to forgive, the offender can do his due diligence and ask for forgiveness two more times. According to Jewish law:

> [W]hen you ask someone for forgiveness, he or she is allowed to turn you down. If this happens, you should return a second and third time, with three witnesses, and try apologizing again. If the victim won't forgive you after three tries, then you're considered to have atoned, even if you haven't been granted forgiveness. (Shulchan Aruch, Orach Chayim 606:1)

Moira knew she had hurt her friend's feelings a few months ago. She apologized right away, and after discussing what happened, they agreed it was a misunderstanding and went on to talk about other things. Moira continued to feel guilty and kept replaying the conversation over and over in her head. She texted her friend another apology and her friend reiterated that everything was fine. Not feeling satisfied, Moira repeatedly apologized until her friend expressed how annoying it was, which ironically caused the problem Moira was hoping to avoid.

Hinduism

In Hinduism, *prāyaścitta* (confession) refers to voluntarily accepting one's intentional or unintentional errors and misdeeds, confession, repentance, means of penance, and expiation to undo or reduce the karmic consequences (Lochtefeld, 2002). *Kuttra yinayaru* (confession) is performed as a hymn to a deity and not to a priest. Demonstrations of repentance include admitting one's mistakes, personal sacrifices, fasting, pilgrimage, bathing in sacred waters, adopting an ascetic lifestyle, performing *yajna* (fire sacrifice), praying, yoga, and giving gifts to the poor and the needy (Kāne, 1953).

Sanjeet's form of confession was telling her husband and three children all the things she is grateful for throughout the day, every day, as she worries she is selfish and ungrateful for all gifts that have been bestowed upon her. She makes sure her family has heard her words by asking them to repeat them.

Proper Mindset

Having the proper mindset for prayer is included in most religions to highlight the importance of focus and sincerity rather than going through the motions, and it stands to reason that OCD would insert intrusive or inappropriate thoughts at this most devout time. The scrupulous try to achieve a clear mental state to perform their prayers perfectly to be assured they will be accepted. The very effort made to accomplish this ends up interfering with the ability to do so. If they don't perform up to their perceived expectations, they feel as though they have failed. Overthinking about overperforming only serve to focus too much on the self and not enough on the purpose of clearing the mind to be open to the experience. Once again, perfectionism takes over, and then the goal is to do it "right," "perfectly," and thoroughly.

Christianity

Prior to Communion, a brief self-examination is recommended for having the proper mindset to receive it. A few questions may help a person check her readiness:

- Do I accept that the Word of God was made flesh, dwelt among us, and suffered in human form?
- Do I believe that the shed blood of Jesus was to remove the stain of sin and make an atonement to God?

The saved person with sin in his or her life should not partake of the sacraments of the Lord's Supper. Additionally, the lost or the unsaved should also not participate in the Lord's Supper.

- Do I have an unconfessed sin in my life right now that I need to repent from?
- Am I taking the cup and the bread just because I'm hungry? (https://www.christianity.com/wiki/church/when-should-we-not-take-holy-communion.html).

Prayers to God should be made in a spirit of contrition and humility, especially when a request is being made. A prideful attitude or mindset defeats the purpose of prayer: "And whosoever shall exalt himself shall be abased; and he that shall humble himself shall be exalted" (Matthew 21:12). "Only when we humbly acknowledge that we do not know how to pray as we ought" (Romans 8:26) are we ready to receive freely the gift of prayer (*Catechism of the Catholic Church*, 2019, p. 2559).

Simplicity of words is also encouraged, for Jesus said, "When you are praying, do not heap up empty phrases as the Gentiles do; for they think that they will be heard because of their many words" (Matthew 6:7).

Perseverance is another quality to be practiced for specific prayers. "Ask, and it will be given you; search, and you will find; knock, and the door will be opened for you. For everyone who asks receives, and everyone who searches finds, and for everyone who knocks, the door will be opened" (Matthew 7:7–8).

During Sunday Mass, Chris recites the Our Father prayer but is distracted by seeing someone he beat in a chess game some time ago. He knew he felt prideful and that his participation in the Mass was ruined. He avoided talking to his friend when he was approached by him after the Mass. While waiting to tell his priest about this deadly sin he committed at confession the following week, he asked his friends if they thought he committed a venial sin. He didn't trust their opinions and obsessed about going to confession so he could wipe his sinful soul clean.

Latter-Day Saints/Mormons

The Mormon prophet Moroni warned that if anyone "shall pray and not with real intent of heart . . . it profiteth him nothing, for God receiveth none such" (Moroni 7:9). Prayers must be made with sincerity and "with all the energy of heart" for them to be meaningful (Moroni 7:48). Latter-Day Saints are also advised to be careful not to pray with "vain repetitions" (Matthew 6:7).

Mormons with scrupulosity face the same fears and doubts as those in other religions. For example, Mormons worry about being sincere enough, saying prayers properly, having a focused mindset, and not wanting sacrilegious thoughts to intrude as they raise doubt about whether they feel worthy enough to practice their faith.

Jehovah's Witnesses

Jehovah's Witnesses are instructed to pray with the right attitude, humility, and respect. They adhere to the same Bible verses as Catholics: "Do not say the same things over and over again." Or "do not babble words; do not utter empty repetitions" (Matthew 6:7). Additionally, "It would be wrong, however, to mimic the repetitious prayers of people of the nations [that is, Gentiles, or non-Jews] who are in the habit of mindlessly repeating memorized phrases over and over again" (Matthew 6:7).

Islam

Khushoo is having the proper focus and humility for *salah* (prayer) (https://productivemuslim.com/khushu-in-salah-part-1/). An attitude of selflessness, tranquility, submissiveness, gentleness, humility, yearning, serenity, and absence of ego are conditions conducive to having the proper mindset for prayer and being aware of the power of Allah. It is said that the heart, rather than the mind, determines the quality of *khushoo* and in turn the sincerity of *salah* (Sayeed & Prakash, 2013).

Being distracted at any given moment is often automatic and unintentional. The scrupulous present themselves in prayer with every faithful intention but are mortified by their imperfect attentiveness.

There are two kinds of mind wandering that are prohibited while praying: when the mind wanders, and the heart is distracted from Allah (may He be glorified and exalted) towards something other than Allah (may He be exalted) and when the gaze wanders and one looks around. A teaching on mind wandering during Islamic prayer says that 'Aa'ishah said: "I asked the Messenger of Allah (blessings and peace of Allah be upon him) about looking around whilst praying, and he said: 'That is something that the Shaytaan [satan] steals from a person's prayer'" (al-Bukhari, n.d.). Another principle states "Allah is turning towards His slave so long as he does not look around, so when you pray, do not look around" Narrated by Ahmad (17800); classed as saheeh by al-Albaani in Saheeh al-Jaami' (1724) (from al-Waabil as-Sayyib, Retrieved from https://aboutislam.net/reading-islam/living-islam/try-these-5-tips-to-focus-in-your-prayer/).

Proper prayer practice can become an obsession due to doubts about having physically followed the right set of sequences the correct number of times. The obsession says, "Why stop at two?" causing the penitent to repeat the prostrations in multiples of two just to be sure.

*Jamal is practicing his afternoon prayer in solitude when, as often happens, he has the thought, "This is bull***t." He knows it's an obsession and tries to keep his prayer going, but he loses his khushoo and starts the prayer all over again. Then he thinks, "What if I didn't say my prayers perfectly or with the right words? What if I did something during the steps of salaam that didn't belong?"*

As is the paradox nature of OCD, these intrusive thoughts are interpreted by Jamal as invalidating his true devotion to Allah.

Judaism

Kavanah is considered one of five essential elements of proper prayer. Maimonides said in the *Mishneh Torah*, "Prayer without kavanah is no prayer at all. He who has prayed without kavanah ought to pray once more.

He whose thoughts are wandering or occupied with other things need not pray until he has recovered his mental composure" (Maimonides, 1955). How often do any of us pray with such focus and intention? And, as educators, how do we create a prayerful person, someone who has both the skills to pray traditionally and the ability—and desire—to connect to God?

According to *My Jewish Learning*, the minimum level of kavanah is an awareness that one is speaking to God, free from other thoughts, with an intention to fulfill the obligation to pray. Without this level of kavanah, the action is considered reading, not praying. It is stressed that the person know and understand what he is praying about as well as the meaning of the prayer. Because the same prayers are repeated daily, there may be a risk that they become so automatic as to lose their meaning (https://www.myjewishlearning.com/article/kavvanah-intention/).

The scrupulous Jew will become so preoccupied about this that she will actually do the very thing she is so afraid of and think, "How am I doing? Is my focus sincere and sufficient?" The OCD disconnects the person from fulfilling the religious duties to which she has committed herself.

For the morning prayer, *tefillin* are worn traditionally by men as both a commandment and a *mitzvah* (good action) that binds one to God. Tefillin are a pair of black leather boxes (phylacteries) inside which are handwritten Hebrew parchment scrolls worn by men (and by non-orthodox women). One is placed on the forehead in front of the hairline between the eyes, secured by a strap that is tied in a knot at the back of the head, and then brought to the front with the shiny side of the strap on the outside. The other is secured on the nondominant arm by a strap that is wrapped above the elbow two-finger widths apart. The strap of the arm tefillin is wrapped once around the upper knuckle of the middle finger, then twice on the lower knuckle, with the second wrap extending across three fingers. The arm tefillin should face toward the heart, considered the place of emotions, when the arm is bent (https://www.myjewishlearning.com/article/how-to-put-on-tefillin/).

Arvam's obsessive thoughts are "Did I place it correctly? It doesn't feel right. God will reject my prayer." He repeats taking the tefillin on and off until he feels right, typically for a half hour, checking to make sure the arm box is facing directly to his heart and not crooked. He struggles through the prayer with the same concerns of doing it "right," saying the words perfectly and not leaving any out. His prayer ritual makes him late for the rest of his morning obligations. With all the focus on feeling right, one could say that he did not have the proper kavanah for making a reverent prayer.

Hinduism

Hinduism believes that the person should make sure that his prayer is genuine in order for blessings to be given. The person should address the deity as a child, rather than a beggar, when asking for a share of life's bounties (https://www.beliefnet.com/faiths/hinduism/galleries/your-day-as-a-hindu.aspx).

Hindus pray to many deities that serve different purposes in daily spiritual life. *Iṣṭa-devatā* is the person's preferred and inspiring deity to which he prays. The deity may have been believed to have answered specific prayers made when the person was in despair, or the deity may have appeared in dreams (Knott, 2016). Scrupulous Hindus who become distracted while praying to their Iṣṭa-devatā may fear that they have angered the deity or that their prayers were incomplete. They may say a separate but unnecessary ritualized prayer to appease the deity or repeat the prayer until it feels complete.

Praying in the right environment is recommended for the laity. Christians, Muslims, and Jews are taught to find a place for prayer that is away from distractions. Christians are advised to find a place that is free from distractions and kneel in humility to commune with the Heavenly Father. At times, an extra effort should be made to pray vocally (Doctrine and Covenants 19:28; 20:51).

Proper Environment

Islam

Muslims pray five times a day, and this can take place anywhere. Prayers should be made in a space without distractions such as images, music, sounds, decorations, or anything else that would get in the way of proper focus. At home, the space should be in a secluded area of the house, kept clean, and without clutter. A prayer mat is really the only essential item needed in the prayer room to make it conducive for *khushoo* (http://www.islamhelpline.net/iqa/answer/75/223305/how-can-a-muslim-pray-with-proper-presence-of-mind-and-humble-focus-khushoo-without-being-distracted-by-things-outside-of-the-prayer).

> Whoever is not able to do that, let him bear in mind the greatness of his Lord and humble himself when he is standing, bowing and prostrating, and standing before his Lord with humble focus, *without* letting his mind or gaze wander; let him realise that his Lord is watching him, and let him bear in mind death and its terrors, and let him pray the prayer of one who

is bidding farewell. That will be sufficient to help him focus and not be distracted by anything other than the prayer, and to concentrate in it. (Hawramani, 2018)

Judaism

Shabbat (the Sabbath) takes place from Friday sundown until Saturday sundown. It is the day of rest with specific rules that prohibit any kind of behavior or act that is considered work and is a time devoted to reflecting, praying, and communing.

There is a special candlelighting ritual that is performed by a woman of the household to officially welcome and start Shabbat. It takes place in the room where the Shabbat meal will be eaten. The setting consists of two candles that represent *zakhor* (remember) and *shamor* (keep), which are the first words in Hebrew of the commandment to honor the Sabbath: "Remember the sabbath day and keep it holy" (Exodus 20:8) and "Observe the sabbath day and keep it holy, as the Lord your God has commanded you" (Deuteronomy 5:12). People are free to light as many candles as they wish.

The candlelighting ritual is a bit tricky because striking the match to light the candles is considered work, which is against Sabbath rules. To avoid breaking the Sabbath, the woman first lights the candles and then closes her eyes to "pretend" she didn't see the candles burning and then says the blessing. Another important reason for this backward order is for her to avoid receiving any benefit or pleasure from the candle flames ahead of the recitation of the prayer instead of after (https://outorah.org/p/35448/).

While saying the prayer, the woman waves her hands over the candles toward herself three times. Each wave honors the internal elements of the soul: *nefesh* (the power to live), *ru'ach* (the mind and will), and *neshamah* (the spirit). After the prayer is said, the woman opens her eyes and delights in seeing the candles "for the first time" (https://www.myjewishlearning.com/article/shabbat-candles/).

Sara worried her eyes weren't completely closed when she said the prayer and that she cheated God and the Sabbath. At the Friday night service, she approached the Rabbi and confessed to him what she thought happened. He told her not to worry about it and told her to let it go. She spent the rest of the Sabbath in tears because she could not be sure she properly ushered in the Sabbath in a "kosher" way. Unfortunately, her distress affected the quality of the Sabbath for the rest of the family.

Hinduism

Hindus construct shrines in the cleanest room of their homes. There is a dedicated table or set of shelves on which to place icons, images, or statues of the chosen *murtis* (gods/goddesses) to worship. If the *murti* is stone or metal, place it in a deep bowl recommended) that will catch any sacred water or milk you pour during *murti* bathing rituals. Other items needed are a cup of water, a small spoon, a bowl for kumkum powder (made of turmeric and slaked lime), a bowl for flower petals, and another bowl that covers an offering of fruit or food (https://www.hinduismtoday.com/modules/smartsection/item.php?itemid=1664).

Maintaining ritual purity could be a challenge when non-Hindu visitors to the home, unfamiliar with Hindu rules of pollution, could, unknowingly or inadvertently, compromise its sanctity by walking in wearing shoes or touching the altar or its artifacts with unclean hands (Mazumdar & Mazumdar, 2008). As such, the prayer room is set apart so it is not easily visible or accessible to non-Hindu guests (Mazumdar & Mazumdar, 2009). Hindus see their altar as a private shrine, a sacred space.

The *puja* (worship ceremony) involves all five senses. Items used may include a bell or music for hearing, food offerings for taste, image or statue for sight, incense for smell, and kumkum powder for touch (https://www.bbc.co.uk/bitesize/guides/zvrsv9q/revision/3).

Prayer

Healthy prayers are motivated by creating a loving connection to God, are part of a collective fellowship affinity communal, and have a beginning and an end. OCD "prayers" are motivated by fear, are conducted in isolation, and end when the person achieves the "right" feeling. Traditionally, religions have structured prayers and teach adherents how to pray properly and what words of a prayer are to recite. There is no reference to prayers having to be said perfectly, as their function is to connect with God and to find a calming sense of peace. There is also a beginning and an end. Attention is refocused for the naturally wandering mind, usually without fearing that having done so is a sin.

I have coined the word "prituals" to denote OCD-driven prayer rituals that are performed to quell obsessive fears rather than being done for the purposes of a healthy faith practice. Prituals are done privately, are excessive and literal practices of standard religious prayers, and are typically done until a "right feeling" is achieved. As many people believe their intrusive thoughts are sins that may have an effect in the physical or spiritual world, they feel obligated to neutralize them through prayer in order to restore the "cosmic balance." The person is compelled to say the prayer in a literal manner and will start over if the words are not said precisely out of fear that it won't be acceptable to God.

Compensatory prayer is another way to think about what's behind the role of prituals. This type of prayer is an attempt at atoning for having intrusive thoughts and for seeking redemption for any offense they may have committed, even inadvertently (Berman, Abramowitz, Pardue, & Wheaton, 2010). The scrupulous are constantly questioning the worthiness of their prayer and feel compelled to make up for any that they fear were said insincerely by repeating them throughout the day. Bedtime prayers can run into early morning hours and leave people sleep deprived on top of the guilt and anxiety they feel from the disorder.

It is unclear if prayer works as a placebo, if it is helpful in the same way that meditation works, or that prayer and healing can be unrelated or coincidental events. Studies from a review of the literature on the scientific outcome of prayer have all been inconclusive due to the unquantifiable nature of the variables (identity of God, sincerity, proper mindset, prayer made correctly, etc.) (Andrade & Radhakrishnan, 2009; Cadge, 2012). But just in case prayers actually do work, OCD sufferers feel a moral duty to restore order and the right of the "cosmic balance."

Thought-Action Fusion

> "You have heard that it was said, 'You shall not commit adultery.' But I say to you that everyone who looks at a woman with lustful intent has already committed adultery with her in his heart."
>
> Matt. 5:27–28

Before getting into the specifics about prayer and scrupulosity, it is important to understand the nature of Thought-Action Fusion (TAF) because in the literal world of OCD, and from some religious teachings, thoughts themselves may be considered sinful. Having blasphemous or sacrilegious thoughts, sexual thoughts about religious icons, or images of hell are among many other obsessions people with scrupulosity have. OCD tends to make the sacred profane and latch onto people's sensitivities. Thus, people feel the need to prove they neither mean to have the thoughts nor believe in them; they do this by spiritually prostrating themselves to God through prayer, confession, abstinence, or self-punishment. Being forgiven can never be proven, so the prituals are performed just in case.

TAF is the belief that thoughts are the same as committing the action of the thought and was first identified in people with OCD (Salkovskis, 1985). For example, someone who is angry with a friend may think, "Go to hell," and be convinced that unless he undoes the thought, he will be responsible for sending the person he was angry at to hell. Even though there is no intention or rational belief that he possesses that kind of power, he feels compelled to make amends by thinking, "God have mercy on me and my friend." Or "I'm the one who should be sent to hell." He may make an impossible "pact" with God that he will never curse someone again, even though he does not have control over what thoughts he gets.

There are three types of TAF: likelihood for self (TAF-S), likelihood for others (TAF-L), and moral (TAF-M) (Shafran, Thoradson, & Rachman, 1996). For the purposes of reviewing how TAF is involved in scrupulosity and moral perfectionism, TAF-S will not be included, as there are no relevant findings that pertain to this subject matter.

Research findings show that TAF and OCD have a clinically significant association (Rassin, Merckelbach, Muris, & Schmidt, 2001) and that TAF-M and TAF-LO were correlated with OCD symptoms compared to the measured outcomes of other problems in the study such as sensitivity to body sensations, social anxiety, depression, and worry (Bailey, Wu, Valentiner, & McGrath, 2014). Other research has found that scrupulous or morally "bad" thoughts are not caused by religion, but those predisposed to OCD may develop these subtypes, depending on the teachings of their religion (Siev, Chambless, & Huppert, 2010; Williams, Lau, & Grisham, 2013). Of the nineteen items that make up the TAF Scale, three included religion: "Having a blasphemous thought is almost as sinful to me as a blasphemous action"; "When I think about making an obscene remark or gesture in church, it is almost as sinful as actually doing it"; and "Having obscene thoughts in a church is unacceptable to me" (Shafran et al., 1996).

People with OCD who have harming and sexual obsessions not only feel a sense of over-responsibility for their content but they also experience a high level of guilt and blame themselves for having them (Kim & Lee, 2020; Salkovskis, 1985). It was also found that a sense of over-responsibility and feelings of guilt will potentially result in people with these types of obsessions increasingly avoiding situations they anticipate will trigger obsessive guilt; make it more difficult to resist rituals; and, in turn, increase the belief that the obsessions are meaningful, important, and an obligation to attend to, all of which increases the severity of the episode (Rachman & Shafran, 1999).

Thought-Action Fusion—Likelihood

TAF-L is based on the belief that the content of the obsession is likely to increase the probability that the negative feared consequence will happen, and for which the person will feel responsible. One study found that people with OCD believed not only that their thoughts would cause harm but also that they could *prevent* harm (Amir, Freshman, Ramsey, Neary, & Brigidi, 2001). It is curious that people with OCD only seem to focus on their fear-based TAF but do not give the same legitimacy to love-based TAF—that good thoughts will enact good outcomes. A common double standard is created when people with OCD are asked if other people have the same "psychic" power, and they invariably say no, it is just them. They hold themselves to higher and more perfectionistic moral standards that they do not expect others to need.

With regard to religious behavior, studies found that prayer was minimally used as a thought-neutralizing strategy from a TAF-L standpoint compared to its use for TAF-M (Berman, Stark, Ramsey, Cooperman, & Abramowitz, 2014; Siev & Cohen, 2007). Instead, prayers related to TAF-L were performed to reduce levels of fear and anxiety (Shafran et al., 1996).

Thought-Action Fusion—Moral

TAF-M is characterized by moral and religious perfectionism. Studies on this topic found that Christians and Muslims were higher in TAF in both morality and religiousness than Jews and nonreligious people (Berman et al., 2010; Siev & Cohen, 2007; Siev et al., 2010, 2017). Religious doctrines that have codes of conduct for thinking and acting are said to contribute to the development of TAF-M beliefs, which in turn, ironically, compel people to use religious practices as ways of coping with OCD symptoms (Berman et al., 2014; Salkovskis, Shafran, Rachman, & Freeston, 1999).

Interestingly, research has identified brain activity unique to TAF and in TAF-M specifically. The neurocircuits involved in TAF-M, as well as religious obsessions and feelings of guilt, occur across the ventral caudate nucleus, which is part of the basal ganglia (responsible for motor processes, inhibitory control over action, and learning) and the mid- and antero-basal insular cortex sensory (where emotional awareness/conscious experience of emotions occur) (Gu, Hof, Friston, & Fan, 2013). Evidence of these neurocircuits being more active in people with OCD than controls was supported during functional magnetic resonance imaging studies that presented a difficult moral situation for which the person had to make a decision (Basile et al., 2011; Harrison et al., 2012).

TAF-M has also been identified as a unique predictor and complete mediator between religiosity and the use of prayer (Berman et al., 2014). Berman and colleagues showed that when prayer is used as an OCD coping tool, it is associated with higher scores on religious measures, TAF-M, more frequent praying engagement in prayer, and a greater reduction in anxiety post prayer (Berman et al., 2010).

Another finding from studies was that intrusive religious thoughts in people with TAF-M experienced higher-level emotions such as guilt and responsibility (Williams et al., 2013). Compensatory or ritualized prayers, then, are performed to alleviate the sense of guilt resulting from morally and personally unacceptable thoughts (Shafran et al., 1996) rather than from the fear that something bad will happen now, later, or in the afterlife (Berman et al., 2014).

The findings of a study on Christians who used "compensatory" prayer to "right" the wrong of their obsessions had higher moral TAF that led to more frequent praying. They were also found to be significantly more religious and considered immoral thoughts to be equivalent to immoral actions (Berman et al., 2014). A study of TAF and religiosity in Christians and Jews found that Christians scored higher than Jews on TAF-M. Muslims and Jews participated in a study that examined the relationships between obsessive-compulsive symptoms, scrupulosity, religiosity, and TAF-M (Siev et al., 2017). Findings from a TAF study of Muslims and Jews showed a correlation between religiosity and scrupulosity for both groups; Muslims had a higher level of OCD symptoms and scrupulosity; Muslims had higher scores on TAF-M than Jews; and TAF-M was not found to be related to scrupulosity in Muslims (Siev et al., 2017). The overall findings from these studies indicate that Christians have higher TAF-M than Muslims and Jews (Siev et al., 2017).

A common moral issue that frequently occurs with TAF-M and can affect treatment outcomes is the feeling of selfishness. OCD, by nature, sets up "false" moral dilemmas that affect people's decision-making. People are emotionally torn between praying for a good treatment outcome and obsessively worrying that their intentions are selfish. For example, "Will getting better mean others will suffer?" Another obsessive belief is, "If I am perfect, and if I pray hard enough, I will receive a miracle from God but I'm never good enough, and I never try hard enough." OCD sets up a false moral tradeoff for many that fully participating in treatment and achieving recovery will be at the expense and safety of their moral standards or be responsible for causing their loved ones to suffer.

Functions of Prayer

Prayers can serve many functions. They can facilitate Communion with God, provide a sense of serenity, create a special time for meditation and self-reflection, make spiritual connections with the people in their religious community, be used as a coping strategy, and act as a demonstration of faith (Bänziger, Uden, & Janssen, 2008; Lewis, Breslin, & Dein, 2008).

Catholicism

Scrupulous people are often afraid that they have profaned sacred objects by touching them with contaminated hands. The rosary is considered a sacramental instrument that "speaks of the 'the life, death, and resurrection' of our Lord" (Barrett, 1970, p. 38). The rosary consists of fifty-nine beads strung on a cord in a loop with fifty small beads that are strung in five decades (sets of ten) with a larger bead set in between them. Hail Marys are said on each small bead, and the large beads are for praying the Mystery of the day. There are three small beads, a large bead, and then a crucifix that are attached in a single strand on the end. The order of the prayer starts with the first large bead, and then each subsequent prayer is done on the individual next bead in a clockwise direction. Some people use their fingers instead of the beads to keep track.

The three types of Mysteries are the Joyful Mysteries (about the incarnation of God in Jesus), the Sorrowful Mysteries (about the Passion of Jesus), and the Glorious Mysteries (about Jesus's resurrection). A Mystery is dedicated to each day of the week:

- Sunday—The Glorious
- Monday—The Joyful
- Tuesday—The Sorrowful
- Wednesday—The Glorious
- Thursday—The Joyful
- Friday—The Sorrowful
- Saturday—The Glorious
- Sunday—The Glorious

The rosary takes on a pace of rhythmic repetition, and the suggested amount of time to complete it is twenty minutes. The steps are as follows:

1. Make the sign of the cross
2. Say the Apostles' Creed while holding the crucifix
3. On the first large bead, say an Our Father
4. On the next three small beads, say a Hail Mary on each bead
5. On the next large bead, say a Glory Be
6. Say ten Hail Marys on each bead in the decade
7. Arriving at the next large bead, meditate on the first Mystery
8. Say an Our Father
9. Move clockwise to the next decade (group of ten beads)
10. Say a Hail Mary for each of the next ten smaller beads
11. On the next large bead, say a Glory Be
12. Then meditate on the second recitation of Mystery
13. At the next decade, repeat the cycle saying an Our Father and a Hail Mary for each of the next ten smaller beads
14. Say a Glory Be at the next large bead
15. Repeat the process for the rest of the decades (five in all)
16. When the cycle of the rosary beads is complete, lay the end strand with the three small beads and the crucifix over the finger on the outside of the hand and say the prayer after the rosary
17. Make the Sign of the Cross

(https://howtodiscuss.com/t/how-to-pray-the-rosary/82)

A small research study was conducted on people who regularly prayed the rosary and the perceived effects it had on their issues around health, well-being, spirituality, and religiosity. The use of a tangible prayer cord and the rhythmic repetition of prayers fostered a sense of peace and stability as well as a strong connection to the Divine, and with Mary as a guide and intermediary before God. The participants also described the rosary as being helpful in managing critical life events, and fostering an attitude of acceptance, humbleness, and devotion (Stöckigt et al., 2021).

Steve wakes up in the morning and picks up the rosary beads on his nightstand as the first act of the day. He sits up, and even though he is having sexual images of Mary, he proceeds to pray. He wonders, "Did I mess up the words? Did

I mess up the order? What if I'm punished for praying while I'm having these thoughts in my head?"

Jehovah's Witnesses

Jehovah's Witnesses do not appear to have special rules for prayers but offer guidelines such as talking to Jehovah throughout the day as a way to keep him close. Praying at mealtimes is encouraged as well.

Followers are petitioned to "pray continuously," "persevere in prayer," and "pray constantly" (Matthew 26:41; Romans 12:12; Thessalonians 5:17). These are other suggested Bible passages to help guide Jehovah's Witnesses in prayer:

- Hebrews 11:6—We must have faith.
- Psalm 138:6—We must be humble and respectful.
- James 2:26—Our conduct should be in harmony with our prayers.
- Matthew 6:7, 8—We must be sincere and honest when we pray. We should not repeat the same words in our prayers.
- Isaiah 1:15—We must live according to God's will. (https://www.jw.org/en/library/books/bible-study/how-to-pray-to-god/)

Islam

Muslims pray five times per day. The prayers can be performed individually wherever the person is at the appropriate time, and workplaces should make accommodations accordingly. Muslims also pray communally at the mosque in unison. Women and men pray separately.

OCD can cause *Salah*, the five daily routines of prayer, to be a practice of going through the motions in a mechanistic manner (Rassool, 2019). Once the process of wuḍū has been completed, and the clothing and prayer mat are perfectly clean, the person readies herself for prayer with an internal focus on getting it "right" rather than transcommunion with Allah. Obsessive doubts include fulfilling the proper sequence contained in the eleven steps of Salah, whether other unacceptable thoughts or behaviors were committed during the prayer, and if the words were pronounced correctly for fear that the prayer would be invalidated. The complete prayer can be found here: https://www.instructables.com/How-to-preform-Muslim-prayer/.

When Ali prays at the mosque, he puts his mat down carefully so as not to contaminate others' or his own. He prays in the back because his rituals cause him to be out of step with the communal rhythm of the jama'ah *(community).*

When Ali performs his daily prayers, he doubts whether he pronounced the words of the Qur'an correctly. He is afraid that if he makes a mistake, his prayers will be rejected. He says he is deliberate and focused when saying the syllables of each word, and he checks to make sure he is reading the right passage of the Qur'an and saying the verses perfectly. He has the same obsessive doubts during the Ruku (bowing down and placing hands on knees) and for the Sajdah (prostrating forehead on the prayer mat). It can take him sometimes one to two hours to perform just one Rakat (unit of prayer). Because he is so preoccupied about how he is doing the prayer, he loses sight of the purpose of the prayer, which is meant to humbly communicate his faith to Allah.

Judaism

There are three daily prayers and three types of prayer in Judaism. The prayers are Shacharit (morning), *Mincha* (afternoon), and *Ma'ariv* (evening). The three types are thanking, praising, and requesting. In Jewish orthodoxy, the men and women pray separately.

There are also prayers that require handwashing before being said, including before and after eating meals with bread, waking up in the morning, after bathroom use, after touching semen, and before the three daily prayers noted above. Here are the steps for Jewish handwashing rituals:

1. Make sure your hands are clean. This seems counterproductive, but remember that *netilat yadayim* (handwashing) is not about cleanliness but about ritual.
2. Fill a washing cup with enough water for both of your hands. If you are left-handed, begin with your left hand. If you are right-handed, start with your right hand.
3. Pour the water twice on your dominant hand and then twice on your other hand. Some pour three times, including Chabad Lubavitchers. Make sure the water covers your entire hand up to the wrist with each pour and separate your fingers, so the water touches the whole of your hand.
4. After washing, grab a towel, and as you dry your hands, recite the *bracha* (blessing): *Baruch atah Adonai, Eloheinu Melech Ha'Olam, asher kideshanu b'mitzvotav, vetzivanu al netilat yadayim*. This blessing means, in English, "Blessed are you Lord, our God, King of the universe, who has sanctified us with His commandments and commanded us regarding the washing of the hands." (Gordon-Bennett, 2021)

Some unacceptable behavior in Jewish prayers is mispronouncing words, omitting letters, the interchange of similar-sounding letters in prayer, slurring, swallowing letters, and not enunciating clearly. These are not only *halakhic* requirements—improper pronunciation makes the words meaningless and often an insult to the Creator (Walkenfeld, 1983).

Hinduism

Hindus pray to God each morning when they wake, seeking blessings for the day. The front part of the hands (the fingertips) is ascribed to Goddess Lakshmi, the goddess of wealth; the middle part (the palm proper) to Goddess Saraswati, the goddess of learning; and the root (the part of the hand near the wrist) to Govinda (God). Therefore, every morning, one should have a respectful look at one's hand, which symbolizes honest labor. Hindus also pray before bathing, acknowledging the role of water in their daily lives.

Pūjā is the daily Hindu ceremonial worship of a deity that involves several rituals throughout the day such as bathing, dressing, feeding, and putting it to bed. It can be led by the head household with the family or conducted alone. Traditionally there are sixteen steps:

1. *Dhyaana*: meditate on the deity that is being invoked.
2. *Avahana* (invocation): make a sincere invitation welcoming the deity.
3. *Asana*: offer the deity a seat.
4. *Padya*: wash the deity's feet.
5. *Arghya*: offer water for washing the head and body
6. *Aachamana*: offer water for washing its mouth.
7. *Snana* or *abhisekha*: offer water for symbolic bathing.
8. *Vastra*: wrap clothing around the deity and adorn with ornaments.
9. *Upaveeda* or *Mangalsutra*: put on the sacred thread.
10. *Anulepana* or *gandha*: use perfumes and ointments.
11. *Pushpa*: flowers are offered before the image, or garlands draped around its neck.
12. *Dhupa*: burn incense before the image.
13. *Jyot* or *Aarti*: a burning lamp is waved in front of the image.
14. *Naivedya*: foods such as cooked rice, fruit, clarified butter, sugar, and betel leaf are offered.
15. *Namaskara* or *pranama*: worshipper(s) bow or prostrate before the image to offer homage.
16. *Parikrama* or *Pradakshina*: circumambulate around the deity. (Fuller, 2004, Ch 3, p. 67)

Sometimes, there are additional steps:

1. *Dhyana* ("Meditation"). The deity is invoked in the heart of the devotee.
2. *Acamanıya*. Water is offered.
3. *Aabaran*. The deity is decorated with ornaments.
4. *Chatram*. Offering of umbrella.
5. *Chamaram* Offering of fan or fly-whisk (Chamara).
6. *Visarjana* or *Udvasana*. The deity is moved from the place.

Instead of chanting mantras for calming the mind and soul, minimally demanding repetitive speech may account for the long-established psychological calming effect associated with commonly practiced mantra-related meditative practices (Berkovich-Ohana, Wilf, Kahana, Arieli, & Malach, 2015) may become a ritualized way of trying to suppress thoughts or push them away. Without that necessary awareness, just repeating the sound only brings dullness to the mind. Any repetition of the sound always makes your mind dull.

Sanjay's OCD said that he should chant his mantra seventy-five times so nothing bad happens to his family. It was hard for him to keep track of the number of repetitions while chanting and became so distraught that he gave up. He worried that he broke a pact he made to do this so that his family would be protected. He obsessed that he was irresponsible for not keeping his family safe because he was too lazy to complete the full mantra.

"Oh Goddess Saraswati, my humble prostrations unto Thee, who are the fulfiller of all my wishes. I start my studies with a request that Thou wilt bestow Thy blessings on me."

Intrusive thoughts, doubts about prayers being performed accurately and sincerely, not right feelings, and urges to repeat, mental review, can occur spontaneously during religious practices. Typically, this is seen as a normal occurrence and attention is brought back to the prayer. It is sad that this act that provides comfort, tradition, and community is overtaken by fear, doubts about one's faith, and worry that a vengeful God or mystical power threatens to punish the scrupulous to be eternally damned.

One last thought is this: How are unanswered prayers interpreted by the scrupulous? "Did I not pray hard enough?" "Right enough?" "Did I not have the right mindset?" "Was something wrong or dirty in the prayer setting?" Of course, there is no proof that even if perfection was achieved, with all of those conditions, that the prayers would have been answered. The not (and never) knowing either way is the crux of obsessions.

References

al-Bukhari, S. (n. d.) *Beginning of creation*. Book 59, Hadith 100. Retrieved from https://sunnah.com/search?q=Satan+prayer

Amir, N., Freshman, M., Ramsey, B., Neary, E., & Brigidi, B. (2001). Thought-action fusion in individuals with OCD symptoms. *Behavior Research & Therapy, 39*(7), 765–776.

Andrade, C., & Radhakrishnan, R. (2009). Prayer and healing: A medical and scientific perspective on randomized controlled trials. *Indian Journal of Psychiatry, 51*(4), 247–253. doi:10.4103/0019-5545.58288

Bailey, B. E., Wu, K. D., Valentiner, D. P., & McGrath, P. B. (2014). Thought–action fusion: Structure and specificity to OCD. *Journal of Obsessive-Compulsive and Related Disorders, 3*(1), 39–45. doi:10.1016/j.jocrd.2013.12.003

Bänziger, S., Uden, M. V., & Janssen, J. (2008). Praying and coping: The relation between varieties of praying and religious coping styles. *Mental Health, Religion & Culture, 11*(1), 101–118. doi:10.1080/13674670600748386

Barrett, J. D. (1970). Making the rosary real. *The Furrow, 21*(1), 38. Retrieved from http://www.jstor.org/stable/27678998

Basile, B., Mancini, F., Macaluso, E., Caltagirone, C., Frackowiak, R., & Bozzali, M. (2011). Deontological and altruistic guilt: Evidence for distinct neurobiological substrates. *Human Brain Mapping, 32*(2), 229–239. doi:10.1002/hbm.21009

Berkovich-Ohana, A., Wilf, M., Kahana, R., Arieli, A., & Malach, R. (2015). Repetitive speech elicits widespread deactivation in the human cortex: The "mantra" effect? *Brain Behavior & Immunity, 5*(7), e00346. doi:10.1002/brb3.346

Berman, N. C., Abramowitz, J. S., Pardue, C. M., & Wheaton, M. G. (2010). The relationship between religion and thought-action fusion: Use of an in vivo paradigm. *Behavior Research & Therapy, 48*(7), 670–674. doi:10.1016/j.brat.2010.03.021

Berman, N. C., Stark, A., Ramsey, K., Cooperman, A., & Abramowitz, J. S. (2014). Prayer in response to negative intrusive thoughts: Closer examination of a religious neutralizing strategy. *Journal of Cognitive Psychotherapy, 28*(2), 87–100. doi:10.1891/0889-8391.28.2.87

Cadge, W. (2012). Possibilities and limits of medical science: Debates over double-blind clinical trials of intercessory prayer. *Zygon, 47*(1), 43–64. doi:10.1111/j.1467-9744.2011.01239.x

Catechism of the Catholic Church (2nd ed.). (2019). Vatican City: Libreria Editrice Vaticana.

Christofferson, D. T. (2011). The divine gift of repentance. *Liahona*. Retrieved from https://www.churchofjesuschrist.org/study/liahona/2011/11/saturday-afternoon-session/the-divine-gift-of-repentance?lang=eng

Cobb, K. F. (2014). *Understanding scrupulosity: Psychopathological and Catholic perspectives* (Master of Arts). Iowa, IA: University of Iowa. Retrieved from https://ir.uiowa.edu/cgi/viewcontent.cgi?article=5111&context=etd

Evans, J. H., & Hudson, K. (2007). Religion and reproductive genetics: Beyond views of embryonic life? *Journal for the Scientific Study of Religion, 46*(4), 565–581.

Fuller, C. J. (2004). *The camphor flame: Popular Hinduism and society in India*. Princeton, NJ: Princeton University Press.

Gordon-Bennett, C. (2021). *Jewish handwashing rituals*. Retrieved from https://www.learnreligions.com/jewish-hand-washing-rituals-2076317

Gu, X., Hof, P. R., Friston, K. J., & Fan, J. (2013). Anterior insular cortex and emotional awareness. *Journal of Comparative Neurology, 521*(15), 3371–3388.

Harrison, B. J., Pujol, J., Soriano-Mas, C., Hernández-Ribas, R., López-Solà, M., Ortiz, H., . . . Cardoner, N. (2012). Neural correlates of moral sensitivity in obsessive-compulsive disorder. *Archives of General Psychiatry, 69*(7), 741–749. doi:10.1001/archgenpsychiatry.2011.2165

Hawramani, I. (2018). *The way of the spiritual Muslim: Sayings and aphorisms on Islamic spirituality by Ibn al-Jawzī, Ibn al-Qayyim, al-Ghazālī, Rumi and other great scholars, ascetics and mystics*. Independently published. Amazon Digital Services LLC—KDP Print US. ISBN 10: 1791704964; ISBN 13: 9781791704964

Kāne, P. V. (1953). *History of dharmasastra: Ancient and mediaeval religious and civil law*. Poona, India: Bhandarkar Oriental Research Institute.

Kim, J., & Lee, S. (2020). Thought-action fusion as predictors of obsessive-compulsive symptom dimensions. *Psychiatry Investigation, 17*, 1226–1235. doi:10.30773/pi.2020.0292

Kimball, E. L. (1996). Confession in LDS doctrine and practice. *Brigham Young University Studies, 36*(2), 7–73. Retrieved from http://www.jstor.org/stable/43041988

Knott, K. (2016). *Hinduism: A very short introduction*. New York, NY: Oxford University Press.

Lewis, C. A., Breslin, M. J., & Dein, S. (2008). Prayer and mental health: An introduction to this special issue of mental health, religion & culture. *Mental Health, Religion & Culture, 11*(1), 1–7. doi:10.1080/13674670701701466

Lobdell, W. (2005, January 1). Does communion cup runneth over with germs? *Los Angeles Times*. Retrieved from https://www.latimes.com/archives/la-xpm-2005-jan-01-me-beliefs1-story.html

Lochtefeld, J. G. (2002). *The illustrated encyclopedia of Hinduism*. New York, NY: The Rosen Publishing Group, Inc.

Maimonides, M. (1955). *Mishneh Torah: Hu ha-Yad ha-ḥazaḳah: Mahadurah hadashah metsulemet*. Jerusalem, Israel: Mosad ha-Rav Ḳuḳ.

Mazumdar, S., & Mazumdar, S. (2008). Religious placemaking and community building in diaspora. *Environment and Behavior*, Online First, published. Retrieved from https://escholarship.org/content/qt10n3w3kz/qt10n3w3kz_noSplash_c3aa757e7c02345288453a227cf81531.pdf?t=nhx0p7

Mazumdar, S., & Mazumdar, S. (2009). Religion, immigration, and home making in diaspora: Hindu space in Southern California. *Journal of Environmental Psychology, 29*(2), 256–266. doi:10.1016/j.jenvp.2008.07.004

Newhauser, R. G., & Ridyard, S. J. (Eds.). (2012). *Sin in medieval and early modern culture: The tradition of the seven deadly sins*. Suffolk, UK: York Medieval Press.

Northridge, W. L. (1968). *Psychiatry in pastoral practice* (3rd ed.). London, UK: Epworth Press.

Rachman, S., & Shafran, R. (1999). Cognitive distortions: Thought–action fusion. *Clinical Psychology & Psychotherapy: An International Journal of Theory & Practice, 6*(2), 80–85.

Rassin, E., Merckelbach, H., Muris, P., & Schmidt, H. (2001). The thought-action fusion scale: Further evidence for its reliability and validity. *Behaviour Research and Therapy, 39*(5), 537–544.

Rassool, G. H. (2019). Obsessional Compulsive Disorder (Waswâs al-Qahri (Overwhelming Whisperings): Case Report and Spiritual Interventions. *International Journal of Mental Health & Psychiatry, 5*(1), 1–6.

Salkovskis, P. M. (1985). Obsessional-compulsive problems: A cognitive-behavioural analysis. *Behaviour Research and Therapy, 23*(5), 571–583.

Salkovskis, P. M., Shafran, R., Rachman, S., & Freeston, M. H. (1999). Multiple pathways to inflated responsibility beliefs in obsessional problems: Possible origins and implications for therapy and research. *Behaviour Research and Therapy, 37*(11), 1055–1072. doi:10.1016/S0005-7967(99)00063-7

Santa, T. M. (2007). *Understanding scrupulosity: Questions, helps, and encouragement* (Rev. ed.). Liguori, MO: Liguori/Triumph.

Santa, T. M. (2013). *This American life*. Retrieved from https://www.thisamericanlife.org/507/transcript

Sayeed, S. A., & Prakash, A. (2013). The Islamic prayer (Salah/Namaaz) and yoga togetherness in mental health. *Indian Journal of Psychiatry, 55*(Suppl. 2), S224–S230. doi:10.4103/0019-5545.105537

Shafran, R., Thoradson, D. S., & Rachman, S. (1996). Thought-action fusion in obsessive compulsive disorder. *Journal of Anxiety Disorders, 10*(5), 379–391. doi:10.1016/0887-6185(96)00018-7

Siev, J., Abramovitch, A., Ogen, G., Burstein, A., Halaj, A., & Huppert, J. D. (2017). Religion, moral thought–action fusion, and obsessive–compulsive features in Israeli Muslims and Jews. *Mental Health, Religion & Culture, 20*(7), 696–707.

Siev, J., Chambless, D. L., & Huppert, J. D. (2010). Moral thought–action fusion and OCD symptoms: The moderating role of religious affiliation. *Journal of Anxiety Disorders, 24*(3), 309–312. doi:10.1016/j.janxdis.2010.01.002

Siev, J., & Cohen, A. B. (2007). Is thought–action fusion related to religiosity? Differences between Christians and Jews. *Behaviour Research and Therapy, 45*(4), 829–837. doi:10.1016/j.brat.2006.05.001

Stöckigt, B., Jeserich, F., Walach, H., Elies, M., Brinkhaus, B., & Teut, M. (2021). Experiences and perceived effects of rosary praying: A qualitative study. *Journal of Religion and Health, 60*(6), 3886–3906. doi:10.1007/s10943-021-01299-2

Walkenfeld, C. (1983). On the significance of articulation in prayer. *Journal of Jewish Music and Liturgy,* 6(31), 6–10.

Williams, A. D., Lau, G., & Grisham, J. R. (2013). Thought–action fusion as a mediator of religiosity and obsessive-compulsive symptoms. *Journal of Behavior Therapy and Experimental Psychiatry, 44*(2), 207–212. doi:10.1016/j.jbtep.2012.09.004

CHAPTER SIX

Obsessive Moral Emotions: Demand for Perfection

". . . when a person exercising himself in ignoring the emotion of scrupulosity shows the emotion a bold face, acting in a manner diametrically opposed to its demand for attention, the power of the emotion is broken."

Knight, 1969

We all have a dark side that may flow in and out of consciousness, cause distress, and express itself in dysfunctional ways. Jung framed the unconscious experience of anxiety, anger, shame, and disgust as "shadow emotions" (Jung, 1976). Codes for dealing with these emotions have been structured in several ways. The Ten Commandments has been said to be a code set by God that addresses specific emotions that need to be controlled in order to promote good citizenship. The Golden Rule is a universal precept that expresses the importance of empathy and consideration for treating others as you want to be treated. The seven deadly sins appear to consist of "selfish" traits represented as shadow impulses to be kept in check. These emotions and urges, deemed to be morally unacceptable, are negatively reinforced by the teachings of religion and culture and, sadly, are prime fodder for obsessions. The thought and experience of having the obsessive thoughts are triggering, aside from whatever the triggering event was, and wreak havoc on the consciences of people with obsessive-compulsive disorder (OCD). Disgust is a common response to shadow emotions and is intensified in those with religious and moral OCD, especially when the obsessional content includes sexual violations and moral taboos.

The Ten Commandments are as follows:

1. I am the Lord your God, and you shall have no other gods before me.
2. You shall not take the Name of the Lord in vain.
3. Keep holy the Sabbath day.
4. Honor your father and your mother.
5. You shall not kill.
6. You shall not commit adultery.
7. You shall not steal.
8. You shall not bear false witness.
9. You shall not covet your neighbor's wife.
10. You shall not covet your neighbor's goods.

Sufferers are plagued by fear of being punished by God or being negatively judged and ostracized by others about matters that have no moral significance. The issues addressed on the list are serious and are expected to be followed. If they are broken, the person is guilty of sinning. Not surprisingly, the content of every commandment becomes an obsession for which undoing rituals are performed. Those considered to have healthy faith and morals have the same thoughts across their minds from time to time but do not have the intense reactivity that is provoked in those with OCD. These are all good people with the same thoughts, but the people with OCD are made to suffer.

The Golden Rule says, "Thou shalt not avenge, nor bear any grudge against the children of thy people, but thou shalt love thy neighbour as thyself: I am the LORD" (Leviticus 19:18) and "You shall treat the stranger who sojourns with you as the native among you, and you shall love him as yourself, for you were strangers in the land of Egypt: I am the Lord your God" (Leviticus 19:34). The challenge for the scrupulous and moral perfectionists is to operate on the spirit of the Opposite Golden Rule: "Love thyself as thy neighbor." Although it feels selfish, treating themselves as they treat others brings more love into every interaction and life in general.

Borrowing the term "superego" from psychoanalytic theory, scrupulous and moral perfectionists suffer from excessive guilt by trying, in vain, to obey the religious and moral laws in the most literal way, also known as legalism. The superego is said to be the part of a person's unconscious psyche that is representative of learned social attitudes about right and or wrong, is self-critical and self-punishing, demands repentance or reparation for wrongdoing, and harbors guilt and shame for acts that do not comply with expected behavior (Freud & Strachey, 1960). Freud states:

> [In] obsessional neurosis these processes are carried further than is normal . . . the super-ego becomes exceptionally severe and unkind, and the ego, in obedience to the super-ego, produces strong reaction-formations in the shape of conscientiousness, piety, and cleanliness. (Freud & Strachey, 1960, pp. 114–115)

Franca came home from the grocery store and realized the cashier had given her the wrong amount of change in her favor. Technically this would be stealing. However, most people would probably let it go and consider it not worth the trouble of fixing it. Franca knew that but could not get past the guilt she felt and was stuck about what to do. When she told the customer service person about the mistake, she was told not to worry about it. She persisted a bit to make sure that the person understood that the money belonged to the store but walked away when the person asked to help the next customer in line.

Neurobiology

A functional magnetic resonance imaging (fMRI) study on distorted cognition and morality in OCD patients found an increased level of activity of medial orbitofrontal cortex, the dorsal lateral prefrontal cortex, and middle temporal gyrus in OCD patients (Harrison et al., 2012). Because of cognitive impairments in inhibitory control (the voluntary control over inhibiting cognitive or behavioral responses to unimportant goal-oriented stimuli [Tiego, Testa, Bellgrove, Pantelis, & Whittle, 2018]), OCD misinterprets neutral events as emotional and urgent, and as a result, it triggers deontological guilt by having an erroneous sense of responsibility to ensure the welfare of others (Greene, Morelli, Lowenberg, Nystrom, & Cohen, 2008). An "unsafe" or immoral thought creates doubt about whether it will be acted upon. A married person may have physiological arousal at seeing someone attractive and leaves the situation, not so much as a way to ensure that she will not "cheat" on her husband but more to alleviate guilt associated with being aroused.

Another example of deontologically motivated behavior is when cognitive inflexibility interferes with OCD sufferers' ability to make moral decisions due to their attention being focused on the urge to perform a ritual rather than the sense that not doing the ritual may have negative consequences on others (Hosseinzadeh, Azhdehakosh, & Valibeygi, 2020).

Instead of making utilitarian moral decisions, which are for the greater good, people with rigid moral reasoning make deontological decisions in the absence of morally based events.

Utilitarianism morality advocates for happiness or pleasure that serves the greater good to foster happiness or pleasure and opposes actions that cause unhappiness or harm (Greene et al., 2008). Data from a clinical study indicate that individuals with OCD use more rigid moral reasoning in response to impersonal moral dilemmas compared to healthy individuals, and that this may be associated with reduced cognitive flexibility. Utilitarian moral judgments are driven by controlled cognitive processes, whereas nonutilitarian (characteristically deontological) judgments are driven by automatic emotional responses (Whitton, Henry, & Grisham, 2014).

Disgust

People can feel disgusted with themselves for thoughts and emotions they consider morally and spiritually repulsive. This has been recognized as a clinical factor in OCD (Bhikram, Abi-Jaoude, & Sandor, 2017). Many sufferers report experiencing physical, emotional, and moral disgust in reaction to their obsessions.

Pathogen disgust acts as an evolutionary "behavioral immune system" that sets off a visceral reaction when coming into contact with disease-prone contaminants such as rotten food, biological decay, and malodorous substances (Tybur, Lieberman, & Griskevicius, 2009). Though not a pathogen, physical disfigurement also elicits a disgust response (Stone & Potton, 2019).

The physiology of pathogen disgust and moral disgust have been measured by facial expressions while undergoing electromyography and fMRI. These methods measured facial muscle responses during a game that was stacked to be unfair. The facial responses of the participants while playing an unfair game were the same for pathogen and moral disgust (Chapman, Kim, Susskind, & Anderson, 2009; Sanfey, Rilling, Aronson, Nystrom, & Cohen, 2003), both of which are related to OCD (Tybur, Lieberman, Kurzban, & DeScioli, 2013). Moral disgust was found to be a reaction to bodily violations, sexual taboos such as pedophilia and incest, and moral violations such as deception or betrayal moral (Russell & Giner-Sorolla, 2013).

Sexual disgust appears to play an adaptive evolutionary role by ensuring survival through a selection of mates that are considered compatible for reproduction by creating sensations, such as lust and disgust, specifically for selecting appropriate sexual partners that would likely produce healthy children (Sher, 2009; Tybur et al., 2009; Tybur, Merriman, Hooper, McDonald, & Navarrete, 2010). In OCD, the combination of adaptive sexual disgust and self-disgust from sexual obsessions can affect sufferers' relationships to their sexuality, intimacy, and romantic relationships.

Social disgust also appears to be an evolutionary trait that promotes group cohesion by creating and emphasizing norms that protect the purity, sanctity, and moral standards of the community that may become threatened by intrusions from outsiders (Haidt, 2007, 2012).

Similarly, moral disgust is a reaction to the threat a person poses by committing morally reprehensible acts and is then punished or avoided in order to reduce the risk of harm to the group (Hutcherson & Gross, 2011). Another theory is that moral disgust functions to motivate social, rather than physical, distancing from the person who has committed a serious moral violation and become taboo herself (Curtis & Biran, 2001; Tybur et al., 2009).

A study conducted by Stewart, Adams, and Senior (2020) studied the relationship between disgust and religious scrupulosity in a predominantly Christian sample. The study utilized the Pennsylvania Inventory of Scrupulosity (PIOS), which comprises two subscales that measure fear of sin and fear of God (Sher, 2009), as well as the Three Domains of Disgust Scale, which measures pathogen, sexual, and moral disgust responses. They found a positive relationship between the domains of religious scrupulosity and disgust sensitivity. Sexual and moral disgust was found to predict a fear of sin, whereas pathogen disgust predicted a fear of God. The premise that pathogen disgust acted as a disease-avoidant defense in religious conservatism to defend against outsiders who could undermine the religious doctrine that defined the group's identity was supported. Pathogen disgust may reflect the importance of cleanliness and purity that are emphasized in religious practices and rituals (Stewart et al., 2020).

Religions teach the importance of purity of thought. Clearly, obsessions are at the opposite end of the moral spectrum, and those with high religiosity are likely to experience self-disgust (Abramowitz, Huppert, Cohen, Tolin, & Cahill, 2002). A study found that the relationship between disgust sensitivity and religious obsessions was significant, and interpersonal and contamination fears as well as disgust sensitivity, specifically toward sex and death, best predicted religious obsessions (Olatunji, Tolin, Huppert, & Lohr, 2005).

Myra walked by the play area at the mall and felt a twinge in her body that her OCD interpreted to mean that she was sexually aroused by the children. The twinge could have been a response to feeling joy at seeing the children at play, but it turned into an episode of despair of having offended God for what she thought and felt. After going home and taking a shower, she went to church to confess her sinful feelings to her priest.

Thought-Action Fusion

Six specific cognitive belief domains have been identified in OCD: perfectionism, importance of controlling one's thoughts, overestimation of threat, intolerance for uncertainty, inflated sense of responsibility, and overimportance of thoughts (Obsessive Compulsive Cognitions Working Group, 2011). OCD sufferers in general suffer from feeling overly responsible and perform excessive behaviors for other people's well-being. They also suffer from obsessive guilt when they resist performing ritualistic behaviors, because if something bad happens, it will be their fault. Ironically, if the people who are being "protected" were aware they were being co-opted into the OCD system, they would reject that tole and support the sufferer back to having a healthy relationship with them.

Thought-Action Fusion (TAF), as outlined in Chapter 4, is the belief that thoughts are actions. TAF is included within the domain of overimportance of thoughts. In OCD, TAF-moral (TAF-M) is the belief that obsessive thoughts are interpreted as unacceptable, immoral, and personally meaningful (Rachman & de Silva, 1978). TAF-likelihood (TAF-L) in OCD involves the belief that the content of the obsessive thoughts increases the likelihood that the imagined event will happen, either to oneself or to others (Rachman & Shafran, 1999).

Those predisposed to OCD who may have learned or interpreted religious instructions that morally unacceptable thoughts were considered sins in and of themselves. For example, the tenth commandment in the Bible says that "thou shalt not covet thy neighbor's wife or property" (Exodus 20:17). The Sermon on the Mount claims that "everyone who looks on a woman to lust for her has committed adultery already in his heart" (Matthew 5:27–28). The tenth of thirteen principles of faith according to Maimonides in Orthodox Judaism says, "I believe with perfect faith that the Creator, Blessed be His Name, knows all the deeds of human beings and all their thoughts, as it is written, 'Who fashioned the hears of them all, Who comprehends all their actions' [Psalms 33:15]." People with scrupulosity consider these passages as intended to be taken literally and condemn themselves because their obsessions are committing sinful acts.

Warren became a Jehovah's Witness elder seven years after having converted from Catholicism. He reported having accepted the position against his better judgment due to some subjective disqualifying factors. He told the presiding overseer that he struggled with Matthew 5:28 (as quoted above) because he has committed adultery by having noticed attractive women, which was especially disturbing when he was out with his wife. The elder gave him direction on how to reconcile his thoughts and feelings through religious teachings. Instead, he lied to the elder when he said he moved his family to a Kingdom Hall that was closer to home, when what he was really doing was avoiding the responsibility that was being put forth to him in having a more important role in the community. He was then again offered an elder position in the new congregation and refused it. He stated how ashamed he was of his cowardice and since then repeatedly prays and seeks reassurance from the elders for forgiveness.

TAF and Disgust Sensitivity

People with religious and moral obsessive content often react with the physical feeling of disgust. TAF-M and disgust sensitivity were found to play a mediating role between religiosity and OCD in a Muslim sample (Inozu, Ulukut, Ergun, & Alcolado, 2014). The study also found that higher levels of TAF in highly religious people, who have thoughts or images that threaten their moral integrity, led to strong feelings of guilt and self-disgust and strong urges to perform cleaning behaviors (Inozu et al., 2014).

This and other studies reported that a typical response pattern of people with scrupulosity was to try avoiding blasphemous obsessive thoughts and disgusting feelings by pushing them away, which only increased their frequency (Inozu et al., 2014; Wegner, Schneider, Carter, & White, 1987).

Yosef had intrusive images of his wife in a hospital bed with terminal cancer. Due to the frequency of this image, he persistently asked her how she was feeling and sought reassurance from her that everything was fine. It became less about the concern for his wife's health and more about alleviating the guilt he experienced from the belief that his thoughts could actually cause her to contract a fatal disease.

A study that measured brain function using neuroimaging methods found that disgust had a moderate association with religious obsessions (Olatunji et al., 2005) and disgust sensitivity appeared to be an independent predictor of religious obsessions when contamination concerns and general fearfulness were held constant (Berle & Phillips, 2006). Regarding age of onset and psychosocial development, disgust sensitivity was found to be predictive of moral obsessions and was more resistant to change in a childhood sample (Georgiadis et al., 2020).

Moral Disgust, Mental Contamination, and Cleansing

Compulsive cleaning rituals are performed to restore one's moral standing after a "not right" feeling has set in about whether one violated a personal value (Hollander & Cohen, 1996). A study examined the "Macbeth Effect" on a sample of Muslims who performed a task to recall past mistakes they felt threatened their moral integrity (e.g., guilt) had significantly more cleansing-related thoughts than the control group (Thomas, Grey, & Al-Romaithi, 2018).

Cleaning and washing behaviors also play a role in alleviating deontological guilt in those with OCD (Reuven, Liberman, & Dar, 2013). An experiment that induced deontological guilt found a physiological disgust response for which cleaning behaviors were performed to wash away the feelings (Ottaviani, Collazzoni, D'Olimpio, Moretta, & Mancini, 2019) and that longer times were spent handwashing in conditions that elicited guilt in those with OCD (Cougle, Goetz, Hawkins, & Fitch, 2012). Another report noted that after bathroom use, a patient was motivated to wash his hands, not for contamination purposes but to alleviate the sense of disgust he felt for himself, just as he did after "sinful" sexual behaviors (D'Olimpio et al., 2013).

Mental contamination refers to being triggered by an association of a thought or an experience, rather than from physical contact with something in the environment. Mental contamination often results in a feeling of disgust in OCD sufferers with a sensitivity toward violations of religious, cultural, and moral events that become triggers to be avoided in the future (e.g., certain people, substances, words, physical locations, colors, etc.) (Melli et al., 2017). In an experiment exposing Muslim students to a vignette about nonconsensual kissing, those with high religiosity were found to have stronger feelings of mental contamination, shame, guilt, and humiliation than those with lower levels (Bilekli & Inozu, 2018). The authors also found that the same respondents had stronger urges to wash their hands in order to reduce the feeling of being mentally contaminated (Bilekli & Inozu, 2018).

Deontological versus Altruistic Guilt in OCD

Understanding the distinct role that deontological, versus altruistic, guilt plays in OCD contributes to understanding the roles scrupulosity, moral perfectionism, and obsessive guilt play in the disorder.

Altruism may be a result of guilt, not benevolence. From an evolutionary perspective, altruistic guilt is a prosocial emotion that mediates an individual's wrong behavior and group survival (Basile et al., 2011). Empathy and a guilty conscience are traits that inform an individual of having done, or not done, something that results in a negative outcome to another individual or to his group as articulated as the Golden Rule: Do unto others as you would have them do unto you (Matthew: 7:12). Many religions have their own version of expressing the ability to take another person's perspective as one's own (https://www.goldenruleproject.org/formulations).

Unlike the interpersonal aspects of altruistic guilt that evoke emotions such as sorrow or remorse for not being able to help someone who has been harmed, deontological guilt focuses on preventing or avoiding guilty feelings, and it overrides sufferers' otherwise adaptive response of empathic perspective taking (Mancini & Gangemi, 2015; Mancini, Rogier, & Gangemi, 2021). Deontological guilt is experienced by people when they have a feeling of violating their own moral rules, accompanied by feelings of unworthiness and a need for punishment (Basile et al., 2011). Feelings of deontological guilt have also been correlated with disgust (D'Olimpio et al., 2013). Strong disgust sensitivity was associated with increased deontological judgments for respecting social order and mediated sensitive moral judgment in people with OCD (Robinson, Xu, & Plaks, 2019). OCD patients were found to have an inflated sense of responsibility, be more morally sensitive, make more deontological moral judgments, and experience increased feelings of disgust in response to acts they consider to be immoral than people without OCD (Hosseinzadeh et al., 2020). The neurofunctions of deontological guilt, morality, and OCD are provided in Chapter 3.

The subjective triggering incidents that result in the feeling of having violated one's moral code are caused not from an objective viewpoint but results from having OCD. Some forms of confession, reassurance-seeking questions, acts of compensation, and pursuit of forgiveness are ways some people with OCD seek to alleviate deontological guilt (Giacomantonio, Salvati, & Mancini, 2019). As these are OCD rituals, they never provide the relief or reassurance the person feels he needs in his ongoing journey in trying to cope with his sense of failing to do the right things.

Obsessive doubt about the "right" thing to do for moral perfectionists leads to deferring their own real needs to the assumed needs of others. They mistake the need for self-care for being selfish. Their judgment becomes compromised as they measure their judgment of moral worth on achieving an obsessive "just right" feeling. The bind is: "If I say no to doing a favor for someone, I am selfish and a bad friend." "If I say yes to doing a favor for a friend, even though I don't want to, I am being generous and caring because I put their needs ahead of my own." However, one study showed an increase in selfish responses to a moral scenario that induced deontological guilt, particularly in those with higher disgust sensitivity (Parisi, Mancini, Mancini, Aglioti, & Panasiti, 2021).

One adaptive mechanism that balances feeling indebted to others for their help or generosity is the idea of mutual self-service or reciprocal altruism (RA) (Trivers, 1971). RA is seen as involving altruistic acts that promote future personal gains. It allows people to accept help or favors without feeling selfish because, in the normal course of relationships, it will be naturally reciprocated. Trusting in this interpersonal dynamic requires a level of faith without certainty, which is always a challenge for those in the throes of OCD.

Some people with OCD often focus on doing the right action rather than achieving the best outcome. As stated, they tend to adhere to rules rather than considering the situational context, believing in their feelings of empathy, and trusting their own sense of judgment (Hosseinzadeh et al., 2020). When facing a moral dilemma, OCD sufferers tend to make deontological decisions that are consistent with their subjective rule-based standards and adhere to them rigidly (Mancini & Gangemi, 2015). Those with altruistic guilt will consider the circumstances and context of the situation and make decisions that are for the "greater good."

To this point, an experiment was conducted by subjecting participants to the "trolley problem," a moral dilemma often used to measure which type of guilt is elicited:

> A trolley is headed toward five workmen working on a track. If the trolley proceeds its way, it will run over these five workmen and kill them. But there is also an alternate track for the trolley, on which one workman is working. The only way to save five workmen is hitting a switch, which redirects the trolley toward only workman working on the alternate track leading to his death but rescuing five other workmen. (Foot, 1967)

The aim is not to analyze a right or wrong answer but to highlight that the trend in OCD sufferers with conscience-related symptoms responds higher with deontological guilt than nonclinical subjects (Mancini & Gangemi, 2015; Whitton et al., 2014).

Obsessive doubt causes a person to wonder if there is enough information to make a "right" moral decision. Ultimately, the goal is to be able to tolerate the associated not-just-right-experience (NJRE) feelings and moral emotions that will help the mind be more flexible so that a decision made can be carried out, right or wrong. With practice, the rules around making moral decisions become more flexible so that the person can consider making choices based on altruistic, rather than deontological, guilt.

Charity and Deontological Guilt

Charity presents another obsessive challenge of doing the "right behavior for the wrong reasons." Although tithing and donating to charities are considered altruistic behaviors, people with OCD may be motivated by deontological or obsessive guilt by being overly generous to the point of running into financial stress. Religious guidelines for charity and tithing are:

- Christianity: tithing 10% of salary
- Judaism: *tzedakah* (literally meaning righteousness) *Tzedakah* Jewish law dictates that 10% of net earnings be given to charity.
- Islam: *zaka* (tithing) is one of the five pillars of Islam: 2.5% savings; *sadaqa*, are charitable voluntary acts.
- Indian religions (Hinduism, Buddhism, Jainism): *dāna* (charity) is any action of surrendering the ownership of something identified as one's own and investing the same in a recipient without expecting anything in return. (Glogovac, 2016)

Jamie donated to a religious charity a few years ago. This triggered his name getting on a list that, ever since, has been sending him pleas for donations. Prior to his OCD episode, he was selective and consciously chose the organizations for which he wanted to provide financial support. Now, his deontological guilt urges him to keep giving at least a little to all of the requests in spite of his family's objections. A genuine part of him feels good for helping because he feels fortunate to have so much security in his life, but he knows he lacks judgment about giving to causes he really believes in. His family now tries to intervene when the mail comes and removes the charitable request appeals.

Existential and Deontological Guilt

What could be more uncertain than the meaning of our lives, our purpose, our purpose, where we stand in the cosmic order, and what happens after we die? No studies on this topic and OCD have been identified in the literature, but it is a common obsession in the clinical setting. One case study was conducted on the use of clinical philosophy (Poltrum, 2009), which helped reduce OCD symptoms in a patient with comorbid schizophrenia (Gole, 2015), but it is unclear how helpful this technique would be as a standard intervention.

A common existential question is, "Why do I have so much and others so little?" When people with OCD compare their circumstances to others, some begin to enter into acts of self-deprivation by living in austere conditions, restricting food, avoiding pleasure, and living a life of essential need, not want. Like learning what the function of other OCD behaviors is, we can ask, "Who is it helping?" Self-deprivation doesn't serve its intended purpose of helping people in the Third World (the intended target of the obsession), the poor, or the needy. It stems from deontological guilt by alleviating a sense of personal guilt. Conversely, altruistic guilt would foster a sense of gratitude and performing acts such as volunteering for or donating to a meaningful cause.

Existential OCD involves persistent philosophical thoughts and doubts about the meaning or purpose of life as well as uncertainty about what is real. Thoughts about whether reality, or even the self, exists can lead to endless ruminations and distractions away from attending to the actual real matters that are happening in the moment. As a result, some people seek answers through religion or look for a spiritual path to find meaning and connection to that which is larger than ourselves and may determine their destiny. Faith practice can be motivated by a longing to find acceptance, peace, and serenity about the unknown.

In many instances, personal identity may be based on healthy faith practices developed over time that make meaning of the person's evolving beliefs and from her internal and external experiences. The person often makes spiritual connection by practicing faith communally (i.e., in church, synagogue, mosque, temple). With OCD, however, people may stay stuck in the mythical-literal stage of faith development (Fowler, 1981) and practice their faith in the same exact way as they were taught as children. They are afraid that deviating from the literal letter of the religious law is being disloyal to God and that their souls are in jeopardy.

Osborn refers to Martin Luther's self-reflection that "[b]y fasting, abstinence, and austerity in the matter of work and clothing I nearly killed myself" (Osborn, 2008). He also cited Luther's comments on his early monastery experiences, saying, "When I was a monk, I did nothing but waste my time . . . with all my Masses, with prayers, fasts, vigils, and chastity, I never advanced to the point where I could say that my order and my austere life promoted me heavenward" (Osborn, 2008, p. 63). Clearly, Luther's impact on Christianity was in spite of the OCD, not because of it.

Empathy and Conscience

People with OCD appear to have higher empathy and compassion levels toward the suffering of others (Salazar Kämpf et al., 2021). Feelings of guilt and a sense of over-responsibility that cause increased levels of distress are classic motivators for performing rituals. In order to reduce the distress associated with "proxy" suffering, practicing emotion-regulation skills along with the more traditional interventions has been recommended (Salazar Kämpf et al., 2021). Although not well studied, these skills can potentially help normalize interpersonal relationships because the person with OCD will be on a more emotionally and socially even keel with those with whom they associate (Jansen, Overgaauw, De Bruijn, 2020).

People with OCD also have conscience-related fears and doubts about having lied, cheated, betrayed God or loved ones, or harmed someone spiritually or emotionally; and they tend to overcompensate for the guilt they feel over having possibly committed these "sins." In most cases, people with these doubts try to find ways of checking for mistakes they may have made, check for or seek reassurance from others about their wellness, and perform preemptive prituals to avoid punishment or damnation from God.

Guilt and Pleasure

> "He defers all pleasures because if they are not directly warranted by God he fears he may fail to acknowledge the master provider of all life's gifts and that God may consequently withdraw his benevolent providence."
>
> Vergote, 1978, p. 84

What's so bad about feeling good? When people with scrupulosity or moral perfectionism start to feel good, they automatically jump to feelings of "selfishness." There can also be a superstitious feeling that allowing oneself to feel pleasure will inevitably be offset by something bad happening in order to restore an imaginary stabilizing moral balance. The feeling of enjoyment is experienced as risky due to a superstitious fear that inviting pleasure will be balanced by the punishment of pain.

When asked if they ever have fun, the scrupulous will shrink in mortification because they feel they don't deserve it. They believe pleasure is only for others, even when asked if that would be true if others had the same intrusive thoughts, thus creating a double standard: same thoughts, different rules. Because pleasure is perceived as disrespectful, self-imposed suffering becomes the way to express contrition for alleged past and future indulgent behaviors. They have a superstitious sense that pleasure will upset the "cosmic" balance. Pleasure on the one hand means paying for it on the other. Common obsessive feared consequences are loved ones being harmed, inviting bad luck, being punished by God, or the fear that they are playing with the devil. The binding dilemma is that:

> either one must opt for the purely human plenitude promised by the enjoyment of pleasure or one must love God. . . . Thus, pleasure naturally tends to forget its divine origin and makes man turn in upon himself, recalling what believers often admit: when they are happy, they do not spontaneously think of God. (Vergote, 1978, p. 64)

Obsessive Whispers as a Mistaken Call to the Clergy

Another aspect of religious scrupulosity can manifest as a mistaken call to the clergy. Youth can be a vulnerable time for such events. Though there are no prevalence rates or reports on this phenomenon in the literature, clergy members who have presented themselves in OCD therapy can begin to experience crises of faith and personal identity. Was the commitment to devote one's life to God based on a true calling, or did it result from an undiagnosed OCD episode? In all likelihood, positive reinforcement for such "religious" devotion, admired and respected by family and community, unaware that his soul was suffering from a clinical disorder.

Once ordained, excessive and atypical religious behaviors will eventually emerge. If properly understood, the person may be referred to a psychiatrist. The person can then determine whether he will continue in the role as a religious leader or begin exploring whether it was ever meant to be. Questions and doubts about his religious motivation and uncertainty about his self-identity make treatment more complex. Consultation with someone in the religious community may be a necessary adjunct to help mitigate the emotional turmoil in the throes of coming to terms with the OCD and its impact on life.

The following are a few questions posted on a website for Catholics who are considering a path to the priesthood. They are included so readers have a sense of the decision-making process for those with and without OCD. The list can also be extrapolated for those seeking sisterhood.

Answer "yes" or "no" to the following questions:

1. Does the idea of becoming a priest keep coming back time and time again, even though you thought you had moved on in your life and forgotten about it?
2. Do you feel called to give more, to be more?
3. Does your relationship with God sustain you, enliven you, invigorate you in such a way that you want to share His truth and love with others?
4. Do you long for more than what "the world" teaches us to strive for—money, sensuality, power, self-indulgence, and comfort at any cost?

5. Do you have a sneaking suspicion that you are on the brink of a major life decision?
6. Does the idea of becoming a priest attract you and at the same time frighten you because you feel "unworthy?" (https://www.hbgdiocese.org/clergy/vocations/vocation-discernment/are-you-called-to-be-a-priest/)

There are also four distinct voices of discernment: the Lord's, the person's, the world's, and the devil's. It is said that discernment requires time, patience, and perseverance in the face of struggle. Of the discernments, the voice of the devil and OCD touch on similar themes: the voices that try to lead the person away from turning to Jesus; the voices that doubt the Lord's goodness and tell the person not to trust in Him, saying, "I know more than He does"; and the voices that provoke fears of the temptation to sin (https://dol-in.org/step-6-get-to-know-the-four-voices-of-discernment).

Understanding the complex role moral emotions play—often covertly—in OCD will lead to a more meaningful and stable treatment outcome and recovery. It is hypothesized that when clinicians elicit the moral function that rituals play in the patient's OCD system, bringing these issues into the treatment can contribute toward preventing relapses (Shapiro, 2014).

References

Abramowitz, J. S., Huppert, J. D., Cohen, A. B., Tolin, D. F., & Cahill, S. P. (2002). Religious obsessions and compulsions in a non-clinical sample: The Penn Inventory of Scrupulosity (PIOS). *Behaviour Research and Therapy, 40*(7), 825–838. doi:10.1016/s0005-7967(01)00070-5

Basile, B., Mancini, F., Macaluso, E., Caltagirone, C., Frackowiak, R., & Bozzali, M. (2011). Deontological and altruistic guilt: Evidence for distinct neurobiological substrates. *Human Brain Mapping, 32*(2), 229–239. doi:10.1002/hbm.21009

Berle, D., & Phillips, E. S. (2006). Disgust and obsessive–compulsive disorder: An update. *Psychiatry: Interpersonal and Biological Processes, 69*(3), 228–238.

Bhikram, T., Abi-Jaoude, E., & Sandor, P. (2017). OCD: obsessive-compulsive . . . disgust? The role of disgust in obsessive-compulsive disorder. *Journal of Psychiatry & Neuroscience: JPN, 42*(5), 300–306. doi:10.1503/jpn.160079

Bilekli, I., & Inozu, M. (2018). Mental contamination: The effects of religiosity. *Journal of Behavior Therapy and Experimental Psychiatry, 58*, 43–50. doi:10.1016/j.jbtep.2017.08.001

Chapman, H. A., Kim, D. A., Susskind, J. M., & Anderson, A. K. (2009). In bad taste: Evidence for the oral origins of moral disgust. *Science, 323*(5918), 1222–1226.

Cougle, J., Goetz, A., Hawkins, K., & Fitch, K. (2012). Guilt and compulsive washing: Experimental tests of interrelationships. *Cognitive Therapy and Research, 36*(4), 358–366. doi:10.1007/s10608-011-9359-x

Curtis, V., & Biran, A. (2001). Dirt, disgust, and disease. Is hygiene in our genes? *Perspective in Biology and Medicine, 44*(1), 17–31. doi:10.1353/pbm.2001.0001

D'Olimpio, F., Cosentino, T., Basile, B., Tenore, K., Gragnani, A., & Mancini, F. (2013). Obsessive-compulsive disorder and propensity to guilt feelings and to disgust. *Clinical Neuropsychiatry, 10*, 20–29.

Foot, P. (1967). *The problem of abortion and the doctrine of double effect.* Retrieved from https://www.semanticscholar.org/paper/The-problem-of-abortion-and-the-doctrine-of-double-Foot/450de3aaf2aea1f4c6c24622993f0a4002e00caa

Fowler, J. W. (1981). *Stages of faith: The psychology of human development and the quest for meaning.* New York, NY: HarperOne. (New edition, September 15, 1995).

Freud, S., & Strachey, J. (1960). *The ego and the id.* New York, NY: W. W. Norton.

Georgiadis, C., Schreck, M., Gervasio, M., Kemp, J., Freeman, J., Garcia, A., & Case, B. (2020). Disgust propensity and sensitivity in childhood anxiety and obsessive-compulsive disorder: Two constructs differentially related to obsessional content. *Journal of Anxiety Disorders, 76*, 102294. doi:10.1016/j.janxdis.2020.102294

Giacomantonio, M., Salvati, M., & Mancini, F. (2019). Am I guilty or not? Deontological guilt, uncertainty and checking behavior. *Applied Cognitive Psychology, 33*(6), 1279–1287. doi:10.1002/acp.3600

Glogovac, M. (2016). *Faith and giving: What do various religions have in common?* Retrieved from https://www.huffingtonpost.ca/marina-glogovac/faith-and-giving_b_8861904.html

Gole, M. (2015). Clinical philosophy in the treatment of paranoid schizophrenia and obsessive–compulsive disorder. *Archives of Psychiatry and Psychotherapy, 4*, 53–60.

Greene, J. D., Morelli, S. A., Lowenberg, K., Nystrom, L. E., & Cohen, J. D. (2008). Cognitive load selectively interferes with utilitarian moral judgment. *Cognition, 107*(3), 1144–1154.

Haidt, J. (2007). The new synthesis in moral psychology. *Science, 316*, 1002–1998.

Haidt, J. (2012). *The righteous mind: Why good people are divided by politics.* New York, NY: Pantheon Books.

Harrison, B. J., Pujol, J., Soriano-Mas, C., Hernández-Ribas, R., López-Solà, M., Ortiz, H., . . . Cardoner, N. (2012). Neural correlates of moral sensitivity in obsessive-compulsive disorder. *Archives of General Psychiatry, 69*(7), 741–749. doi:10.1001/archgenpsychiatry.2011.2165

Hollander, E., & L. J. Cohen. (1996). Psychobiology and psychopharmacology of compulsive spectrum disorders. In A. Andrew E. Skodol, Eric Hollander, & John M. Oldham (Eds.), *Impulsivity and compulsivity* (pp. 143–166). Washington, DC: American Psychiatric Press.

Hosseinzadeh, M., Azhdehakosh, E., & Valibeygi, A. (2020). Moral judgments in obsessive-compulsive disorder: A narrative mini-review. *Neuroscience Research Notes, 3*(1), 11–23. doi:10.31117/neuroscirn.v3i1.39

Hutcherson, C., & Gross, J. (2011). The moral emotions: A social-functionalist account of anger, disgust, and contempt. *Journal of Personality and Social Psychology, 100*, 719–737. doi:10.1037/a0022408

Inozu, M., Ulukut, F. O., Ergun, G., & Alcolado, G. M. (2014). The mediating role of disgust sensitivity and thought-action fusion between religiosity and obsessive compulsive symptoms. *International Journal of Psychology, 49*(5), 334–341. doi:10.1002/ijop.12041

Jansen, M., Overgaauw, S., & De Bruijn, E. R. A. (2020). Social cognition and obsessive-compulsive disorder: A review of subdomains of social functioning. *Frontiers in Psychiatry, 11*, Article 118. doi:10.3389/fpsyt.2020.00118

Jung, C. G. (1976). *C. G. Jung Letters: 1951–1961* (G. Adler & J. Aniela, Eds., Vol. 2). Brighton, UK: Routledge.

Knight, J. A. (1969). The many faces of guilt. In *Conscience and guilt* (pp. 91–125). New York, NY: Appleton-Century-Crafts.

Mancini, F., & Gangemi, A. (2015). Deontological guilt and obsessive compulsive disorder. *Journal of Behavior Therapy and Experimental Psychiatry, 49*(Part B), 157–163. doi:10.1016/j.jbtep.2015.05.003

Mancini, F., Rogier, G., & Gangemi, A. (2021). The distinction between altruistic and deontological guilt feelings: Insights from psychopathology. In V. Cardella & A. Mancini (Eds.), *Psychopathology and philosophy of mind* (pp. 75–95). Taylor & Francis. doi:10.4324/9781003009856-6

Melli, G., Bulli, F., Carraresi, C., Tarantino, F., Gelli, S., & Poli, A. (2017). The differential relationship between mental contamination and the core dimensions of contact contamination fear. *Journal of Anxiety Disorders, 45*, 9–16.

Obsessive Compulsive Cognitions Working Group. (2011). Development and initial validation of the obsessive beliefs questionnaire and the interpretation of intrusions inventory. *Behaviour Research and Therapy, 39*(8), 987–1006. doi:10.1016/s0005-7967(00)00085-1

Olatunji, B. O., Tolin, D. F., Huppert, J. D., & Lohr, J. M. (2005). The relation between fearfulness, disgust sensitivity and religious obsessions in a non-clinical sample. *Personality and Individual Differences, 38*(4), 891–902. doi:10.1016/j.paid.2004.06.012

Osborn, I. (2008). *Can Christianity cure obsessive-compulsive disorder? A psychiatrist explores the role of faith in treatment*. Grand Rapids, MI: Brazos Press.

Ottaviani, C., Collazzoni, A., D'Olimpio, F., Moretta, T., & Mancini, F. (2019). I obsessively clean because deontological guilt makes me feel physiologically disgusted! *Journal of Obsessive-Compulsive and Related Disorders, 20*, 21–29.

Parisi, I., Mancini, A., Mancini, F., Aglioti, S. M., & Panasiti, M. S. (2021). Deontological guilt and disgust sensitivity modulate moral behaviour. *Clinical Neuropsychiatry, 18*(4), 196–210. doi:10.36131/cnfioritieditore20210403

Poltrum, M. (2009). Philosophy as cognitive self-medication and noetic resource. *Psychopraxis, 12*, 33–37. doi:10.1007/s00739-009-0155-2

Rachman, S., & de Silva, P. (1978). Abnormal and normal obsessions. *Behaviour Research and Therapy, 16*(4), 233–248. doi:10.1016/0005-7967(78)90022-0

Rachman, S., & Shafran, R. (1999). Cognitive distortions: Thought–action fusion. *Clinical Psychology & Psychotherapy: An International Journal of Theory & Practice, 6*(2), 80–85.

Reuven, O., Liberman, N., & Dar, R. (2013). The effect of physical cleaning on threatened morality in individuals with obsessive-compulsive disorder. *Clinical Psychological Science, 2*, 224–229. doi:10.1177/2167702613485565.

Robinson, J. S., Xu, X., & Plaks, J. E. (2019). Disgust and deontology: Trait sensitivity to contamination promotes a preference for order, hierarchy, and rule-based moral judgment. *Social Psychological and Personality Science, 10*(1), 3–14.

Russell, P. S., & Giner-Sorolla, R. (2013). Bodily moral disgust: What it is, how it is different from anger, and why it is an unreasoned emotion. *Psychological Bulletin, 139*(2), 328–351. doi:10.1037/a0029319

Salazar Kämpf, M., Kanske, P., Kleiman, A., Haberkamp, A., Glombiewski, J., & Exner, C. (2021). Empathy, compassion, and theory of mind in obsessive-compulsive disorder. *Psychology and Psychotherapy: Theory, Research and Practice, 95*(1), 1–17.

Sanfey, A. G., Rilling, J. K., Aronson, J. A., Nystrom, L. E., & Cohen, J. D. (2003). The neural basis of economic decision-making in the ultimatum game. *Science, 300*(5626), 1755–1758.

Shapiro, L. J. (2014). *Understanding OCD: Skills to control the conscience and outsmart obsessive compulsive disorder.* Santa Barbara, CA: Praeger.

Sher, A. (2009). *Amen, amen, amen: Memoir of a girl who couldn't stop praying (among other things)* (1st Scribner hardcover ed.). New York, NY: Scribner.

Stewart, P., Adams, T., & Senior, C. (2020). The effect of trait and state disgust on fear of God and sin. *Frontiers in Psychology, 11*, 51. doi:10.3389/fpsyg.2020.00051

Stone, A., & Potton, A. (2019). Emotional responses to disfigured faces and disgust sensitivity: An eye-tracking study. *Journal of Health Psychology, 24*(9), 1191–1200. doi:10.1177/1359105317692856

Thomas, J., Grey, I., & Al-Romaithi, S. (2018). Macbeth Arabia: Moral threat and cleansing-related construct accessibility in Arab women. *Mental Health, Religion & Culture, 21*(2), 131–138. doi:10.1080/13674676.2017.1381675

Tiego, J., Testa, R., Bellgrove, M. A., Pantelis, C., & Whittle, S. (2018). A hierarchical model of inhibitory control. *Frontiers in Psychology, 9*, 1339. doi:10.3389/fpsyg.2018.01339

Trivers, R. L. (1971). The evolution of reciprocal altruism. *Quarterly Review of Biology, 46*, 35–37.

Tybur, J. M., Lieberman, D., & Griskevicius, V. (2009). Microbes, mating, and morality: individual differences in three functional domains of disgust. *Journal of Personality and Social Psychology, 97*(1), 103.

Tybur, J. M., Lieberman, D., Kurzban, R., & DeScioli, P. (2013). Disgust: Evolved function and structure. *Psychological Review, 120*(1), 65.

Tybur, J. M., Merriman, L. A., Hooper, A. E. C., McDonald, M. M., & Navarrete, C. D. (2010). Extending the behavioral immune system to political psychology: Are political conservatism and disgust sensitivity really related? *Evolutionary Psychology, 8*(4), 599–616. doi:10.1177/147470491000800406

Vergote, A. (1978). *Guilt and desire: Religious attitudes and their pathological derivatives* (M. H. Wood, Trans.). New Haven, CT: Yale University Press.

Wegner, D. M., Schneider, D. J., Carter, S. R., & White, T. L. (1987). Paradoxical effects of thought suppression. *Journal of Personality and Social Psychology, 53*(1), 5.

Whitton, A. E., Henry, J. D., & Grisham, J. R. (2014). Moral rigidity in obsessive-compulsive disorder: Do abnormalities in inhibitory control, cognitive flexibility and disgust play a role? *Journal of Behavior Therapy and Experimental Psychiatry, 45*, 152–159. doi:10.1016/j.jbtep.2013.10.001

CHAPTER SEVEN

Righteous Eating

> "Or do you not know that your body is the temple of the Holy Spirit *who is* in you, whom you have from God, and you are not your own?"
> Corinthians: 6:19

Food, like water, is part of religious culture and has many roles, rules, and customs. Adopting certain food lifestyles is often done for moral reasons (i.e., veganism, pescatarianism, etc.). In these contexts, obsessive-compulsive disorder (OCD) creates a perfectionistic system to ensure complete adherence to the letter of the food rules. Inadvertently, the demands of OCD result in self-sacrifice, self-imposed suffering, and self-deprivation. This chapter focuses on the role religious and moral fasting and dietary practices play in OCD.

Fasting

The practice of fasting has many functions. In medicine, it cleans the system before procedures. Hunger strikes have been staged as acts of political or social protest, during a personal crisis, and are part of an ascetic lifestyle. Almost every religion has a practice of individual or community fasting for physical and spiritual purification, to express atonement or grief, as a form of sacrifice, or to commemorate holy events.

A study was conducted on the use of religious and moral language found in popular culture and advertising for food (Griffin & Berry, 2003). The study commented that food advertising has included words such as "temptation," "decadent," "heaven," and "purity" to suggest an association between food, religious or moral virtues, and sinning. The authors identify the description of chocolate as an indulgence or temptation. A brand of cream cheese is branded with a halo as part of its logo symbolizing holiness (Griffin & Berry, 2003).

Fasting References in the Judeo-Christian Bible

The Bible cites Moses and Jesus as having fasted for forty days on Mount Sinai (Deut. 9:9; Matt. 4:2). Nehemiah said, "When I heard these words I sat down and wept, and mourned for days, fasting and praying before the God of heaven" (Neh. 1:4). Fasting has also been noted as a sacrificial rite in seeking God's favor by Jews (Neh. 9:1).

In the early third century, Tertullian said:

> An emaciated body will more readily pass through the narrow gate of Paradise, a light body will resurrect more rapidly, and in the grave a wasted body will be preserved best. (Cited in Vandereycken & Deth, 1994, p. 15)

Miraculous Maids

The relationship between women and food has been historically complicated. Accounts dating back to AD 300 cite women starving themselves to death as a form of religious ascetism (Pearce, 2004). Although not technically considered scrupulosity, there are depictions dating back to sixteenth-century Europe of fasting women whose behavior was termed as *Anorexia Mirabilis* (AM) (Forcen, 2013). Other terms referred to these women as Holy Anorexics, Miraculous Maids, and Fasting Saints.

Several Catholic saints have been noted to be Miraculous Maids. Most notable is Catherine of Siena (1347–1380), who fasted for most of her life, and the only intake she would allow at the end of her life was a single Eucharist wafer given to her as part of the daily Eucharist (Gardner, 1908). Gardner further accounted Catherine's fasting behavior as defying orders from her religious superiors. Catherine began restricting food as a teenager as a protest of an arranged marriage to her late sister's husband and claimed that her inability to eat food was a punishment from God (Gardner, 1908). During this time, rejecting or restricting food was one of the few ways women could exercise power and control in their lives, and it still serves the same function for girls who suffer from what is now classified as *anorexia nervosa* (Pittock, 2014). The denial of food was in response to the Catholic categorization of gluttony as one of the seven deadly sins that could cause one to be sent to hell. Often, women entering religious orders would starve themselves as punishment for bodily desires or previous sins. This religious belief meant that they sometimes starved themselves to death as part of excessive bodily denial (Pittock, 2014). For some, it was said to be a way of enacting the Passion (the suffering of Jesus) and to serve as acts of contrition (Bell, 1985).

The similarities between scrupulosity, moral perfectionism, and AM are acts of severe self-imposed, self-depriving penance for allegedly sinning; acts demonstrating devotion; and exerting physical and spiritual control over the body. In the context of this type of religious fasting, the anorexic behavior was not driven by weight concerns or body image but rather by a desire for purity and perfection.

There are times when the function of rigid food rules and restricting are clinically misunderstood, and referrals to eating disorder treatment are made, usually for young women, when the actual problem is OCD. Scrupulosity will set rules to control the deadly sin of gluttony as well as a means to deny pleasure as penance for any sinful behavior that may not have been consciously accounted for.

Traditional Religious Fasting Occasions

Christianity

Fasting is a condition of taking the Eucharist (Holy Communion, or Host), the wafer said to be the body of Christ, and one of the sacraments of Catholicism. During Mass, regular bread and wine are consecrated by the priest, through God's power, when he repeats Jesus's words, "This is my body" and "This is the chalice of my blood" (Matt. 26:26). Although there is no directive saying the host should not be chewed, it has become tradition that it should dissolve under the tongue. Holy wine is considered Christ's blood.

Bob worries that residual toothpaste or food stuck between his teeth from the night before will interfere with being in a pure enough state to receive the Eucharist. Even if those substances were there, they are considered digested and are of no consequence. Even so, Bob rinses his mouth several times before leaving for church but is still anxious he may have missed something. He is so afraid of biting into the host that he clenches his teeth and holds his breath while it melts under his tongue.

Other obligatory fasting occasions for Catholics occur on Ash Wednesday (the beginning of Lent) and Good Friday (commemorating the death of Jesus). Fasting is optional for Lent, but eating meat is proscribed.

Islam

The holy month of Ramadan is a mandatory fasting period that commemorates the period when the Qur'an was first revealed to the Prophet Muhammad. "When the month of Ramadan starts, the gates of heaven are opened and the gates of hell are closed and the devils are chained" (al-Bukhari & Uddin, 2020, p. Hadith 9). Each day, Muslims do not eat or drink during the daylight hours from sundown to sundown.

For the entire month of Ramadan, from sunup to sundown, Issa's fast will include not eating, drinking, swallowing, smoking, using profane language, or having sexual intercourse. When she gets up in the morning, she wipes off saliva into a facial tissue if she thinks a speck of something got in her mouth that she could swallow. She spends the day preparing the Iftar (evening meal). She finds it difficult to be sure that she has not accidently ingested something and washes her hands often to get any residual food particles off her hands. She is also worried about making enough food for everyone who will be ravenously hungry. Even though she makes more than enough food, she eats less than her share just to make sure everyone is fed.

Latter-Day Saints

Members are encouraged to fast on the first Sunday of each month, designated as Fast Sunday. During Fast Sunday, members fast for twenty-four hours. The money that would have been spent on the food is donated to the church as a fast offering to help people in need, and people are invited to be more generous (https://newsroom.churchofjesuschrist.org/article/fast-sunday). Church apostle Gordon B. Hinckley stated:

> Think . . . of what would happen if the principles of fast day and the fast offering were observed throughout the world. The hungry would be fed, the naked clothed, the homeless sheltered. . . . A new measure of concern and unselfishness would grow in the hearts of people everywhere. (https://www.churchofjesuschrist.org/study/ensign/1991/05/the-state-of-the-church?lang=eng)

Fasting is also considered a way to grow closer to God, to enhance prayers, and to exercise self-mastery of spirit over body. The decision to fast can be made on a personal level, with family, or with a group to invite special blessings from God (https://www.churchofjesuschrist.org/study/manual/doctrines-of-the-gospel-student-manual/12-prayer-and-fasting?lang=eng).

Judaism

Yom Kippur, the Day of Atonement, is the highest of holy days during which Jews fast from sunset to sunset. No food or water is to be ingested, although medication can be taken as health takes precedence over the fast. The purpose of the fast is to atone for misdeeds and mistakes made that had a negative impact towards others over the year for which atonement may be considered necessary. It is also believed that God's Book of Life, which is a "record" of one's religious and moral standing, will be sealed at the end of the holiday.

Hannah, who we met in Chapter 4, has the same anxieties as Issa's about serving the role of mother, wife, and religious observer while preparing the break-the-fast meal. She feels guilty about not being sure she has the right mindset to honor the spirit and intention of the holiday, as she is so busy with her tasks. Even though she knows health takes precedence over fasting, she delays taking her heart and OCD medication until the fast is broken. She worries about how she will be written into the Book of Life for the next year.

Hinduism

Fasting for religious purification (*upavasam*) is optional for Hindus and is structured by standards such as purpose, time, place, deity, and purity (https://www.hinduwebsite.com/hinduism/essays/fasting-guide-for-hindus.asp). Fasts are conducted based on the *panchanga* (solar and lunar calendar) and do not have to be rigorously followed (Kannan, Mahadevan, Seshadri, Sadacharan, & Velayutham, 2016).

A few types of fasting are *nirahara* (fasting without food), *phalahara* (fasting with fruit and milk), and *alpahara* (eating broken grains) (Kannan et al., 2016). Aspects of fasting for purity consist of physical purity and purity of intention and are chosen according to a diety that is specific for the days in a month, season, year, or week which have particular significance to them (https://www.hinduwebsite.com/hinduism/essays/fasting-guide-for-hindus.asp).

Ekadashi is a fast that takes place on the eleventh day of each ascending and descending moon to honor the god Vishnu (https://www.alimentarium.org/en/fact-sheet/fasting-hinduism). Some Hindus fast on Mondays and Saturdays during the months of July and August to respect Shiva's acts of protecting the world (https://www.astroved.com/astropedia/en/fasting/fasting-on-monday). A particular female fasting ritual (*Karwa Chauth*) is performed on Mondays to better ensure finding a suitable husband (Sharma, 2014).

According to the yogic concept of nutrition, food has been categorized as *Sattvic*, Rajasic, and Tasmaic. A *Saattvic* diet is considered the most pure, while *Rajasic* food is defined as overstimulating, and *Tamasic* as unhealthy (Agte & Chiplonkar, 2007). Hindus with scrupulosity, like other people with orthorexia, halal, or kosher food practices, may severely restrict their food intake and eat only when they are sure the food is not "contaminated" with traces of *Rajasic* or *Tamasic* particles.

Sattvic fasting is considered the purest form of fasting and is done with the purpose of seeking unity with a person's favorite deity by eating eight hours of the day and followed by fasting for 16 hours as often as every night or several times a week (https://thesattvicmethodcompany.com/secrets-of-sattvic-lifestyle-simplified-science-of-fasting/). As is the case with scrupulous behaviors that stem from religious or spiritual practices, *Sattvic* fasting can be taken to an extreme and result in a disconnection between what would be a traditionally healthy ritual versus acting out of perfectionistic and fear driven purposes.

Some fasts may also involve *suchi* (physical cleanliness). Other types of fasts include multiple baths during the day, while for others there is bathing at all until the fasting is complete (https://www.hinduwebsite.com/hinduism/essays/fasting-guide-for-hindus.asp).

Fasting with a mindset of moderation is an important virtue, especially in extreme fasting. One risk of extreme fasting is when it is performed in a spirit of *tamas* (darkness), out of which traits such as pride, vanity, laziness, anger, attachment, depression, dependency, self-doubt, guilt, boredom, irritation, addiction, apathy, confusion, grief, ignorance are manifested (https://www.yogapedia.com/definition/5608/tamas).

The following are some common religious fasting holidays. *Maha Shivaratri* is an all-night, solemn, introspective, and meditative fasting holiday that takes place at temples to honor Shiva and to reflect on forgiveness, honesty, and compassion (Jones & Ryan, 2006). *Navratri* is a nine-day fasting event that takes place in April and October. It is a celebration of the victory of good over evil by the goddess Durga, who vanquished a deceitful demon who pursued his evil ways by shape-shifting (Gupta, Khandelwal, Singla, Gupta, & Kalra, 2017). *Karwa Chauth* is a fast practiced by married women for the sake of the well-being, prosperity, and longevity of their husbands (Pearson, 1996). During this time, some will fast on the day of the week that is reserved for the worship of their chosen god(s), while others will fast during the entire month (https://hinducouncil.com.au/new/fasting-in-my-religion/).

The sacrifice of food, and sometimes water, is a frequent practice for Hindus throughout the *panchanga*. Each holiday has its own set of rituals, values, deities, and guidelines. Scrupulous Hindus, as is the case with practicing any religion, may be so overwhelmed by the need to perfectly follow the strictures that they give up and, ironically, live with the shame and guilt of caring too much to participate in faith practices.

Fasting as Social and Political Statements/Protest

A famous hunger striker is Mahatma Gandhi, an Indian lawyer, politician, social activist, and writer who became the leader of the nationalist movement against the British rule of India. Gandhi fasted for twenty-one days in 1932 to protest the British government's plan to set the electoral system by caste. Cesar Chavez, a Mexican American who founded the National Farmworkers Association, was another political notable who fasted for thirty-six days in 1962 to protest how migrant workers were treated in the United States. Both of these protests were widely covered in the media, which helped gain support for their causes.

Elena is a scrupulous idealist and has taken on the task of only eating enough food to sustain her body as an act of solidarity with her brother. Her brother has no idea she is doing this, but she says she is motivated by guilt for not having stood up for him when their father was abusive. She justifies this behavior by citing philosophical ideas by said by other social justice activists who fast. She includes some of these causes in the spirit of her food sacrifice, such as people being held as political prisoners and food insecurity. She also talks about the sinfulness of gluttony and food being used for emotional soothing.

Differential Diagnosis

OCD and other disorders have common symptoms that need to be assessed by their function. Anorexia and OCD can be misdiagnosed due to the issues surrounding perfectionism and control. The clearest distinctions between them are body image distortion in anorexia and morally motivated food restriction in OCD. However, there are some people who have these as comorbid disorders that require differential treatment.

After Baruch finished high school, he and his family of ten moved around the United States and then to Israel. Each move caused stress to the family but especially for him as change exacerbated his OCD. On arriving at his new home, he would basically shut down because adjusting his rituals to his new environment was too overwhelming.

Baruch felt the need to do things in extremes, perfectly, and in a certain order until he felt "right." He said this made him feel relaxed and less pressured. At one point, he stopped talking for a period of four months. He also went through phases of fasting for days to achieve a state of spiritual purity and perfection. He also had a diagnosed history of anorexia based on his belief that being slender was both aesthetically and morally correct. Having any body mass beyond his stature was considered wasteful and gluttonous. Along with the sense of control he had with setting up perfectionistic rules about eating, his behavior was reinforced by experiencing states of euphoria.

Orthorexia Nervosa

The organic food movement from the 1940s gained momentum during the 1970s as a holistic culture of natural living began to take shape. Since then, cultural trends have promoted more healthy eating consisting of eating fresh food that has not been treated with pesticides, avoidance of consuming processed foods, avoiding foods produced from caged animals, and not consuming animals or other foods treated with growth hormones.

In the 1960s and 1970s, a vegetarian food movement emerged as part of the counterculture in the United States. It focused on concerns about diet, the environment, and a distrust of food producers that led to increasing interest in organic gardening. This was followed by a wider cultural trend called "clean eating" that started in the early 2000s (Allen, Dickinson, & Prichard, 2018). This trend involved avoiding foods that are processed, caged, and fed with growth hormones. People adopting vegetarian diets were on the rise, with vegan diets becoming increasingly mainstream by the 2010s (Raphaely, 2015).

Sarah wants her body to be a pure vessel in spirit and deed. She used to enjoy eating things like cheeseburgers without thinking much about the source or processing of the foods she ate. After driving by a sign that said, "Meat is Murder," she became preoccupied with the Sixth Commandment, "Thou shalt not kill," and started avoiding food with any trace animal or animal products. When grocery shopping, Sarah compulsively checks food labels to make sure there are no meat-related ingredients. Sometimes the checking does not end in certainty, and she puts the item back on the shelf. At the checkout she realizes how few items she has for meals and opts to shop at expensive health food stores. Sarah still craves foods she is depriving herself of and has become anemic.

As with all good intentions, problems can arise when rules around lifestyle choices become strict and rigid. Although not an official DSM-V diagnosis, orthorexia nervosa (ON) has been recognized as an obsession with righteous eating (Bratman, 2017) and extreme dietary purity (Cena et al., 2019). People develop a ritualized pattern of eating and a rigid avoidance of foods believed to be unhealthy or impure (Koven & Abry, 2015). It is not considered an eating disorder, as perfectionism and rigidity are related to morality and not body image (Zickgraf, Ellis, & Essayli, 2019). It is considered to be more OCD-like because the motivation is one of strictness and perfection about food purity, extreme fasting, and restrictive rules and behaviors around eating (Tremelling, Sandon, Vega, & McAdams, 2017). People report deriving moral satisfaction from transcending food craving urges and "lazy eating behavior."

Other aspects of ON are avoidance of foods containing fats, preservatives, food additives, animal products, or other ingredients considered to be unhealthy. Excessive amounts of time (e.g., three or more hours per day) reading about, shopping for, or preparing specific types of foods that consist of proper quality and ingredients, even if their cost is beyond an affordable budget, may also be aspects of ON. Feelings of guilt and self-criticism occur when the person "cheats," and the person may have an intolerance of others' food beliefs and practices (Moroze, Dunn, Holland, Yager, & Weintraub, 2015).

When a person with OCD follows the rules of ON, as well as vegetarianism or veganism, he is not necessarily driven by the same ethical reasons made by those without OCD. It is less of a conscious choice made for the right reasons and more of a deontological compulsion to feel morally "correct" and to avoid guilt. The person is likely responding to a moral or scrupulous imperative that says, "If I can, I should," which is similar to the motivation of performing religious rituals for the sake of avoiding divine punishment even though the person does not normally participate in religious behavior (i.e., strict adherence to the Jewish rules around restricting exertive behaviors during the Sabbath or fasting during certain holidays).

Jon feels compelled to eat "righteously." When shopping, he checks labels for calories, vitamins, salt, fat content, and preservatives. Even though he is five feet ten inches tall and weighed 154 pounds, Jon began limiting his daily food intake to 1,500 calories when his moral perfectionism started making new rules around what was acceptable. According to health charts, the recommended intake for his size would be 2,000–3,000 calories per day (https://health.gov/our-work/food-nutrition/2015-2020-dietary-guidelines/guidelines/appendix). He now weighs 124 pounds with an underweight body mass index of 18. He feels a sense of pride by avoiding sweets and desserts as they are indulgent and unnecessary. He punishes himself for the sin of gluttony if he eats more than his "fair share" by fasting the next day. He is at risk of becoming medically and cognitively compromised due to the effects of malnutrition.

Religious Dietary Practices

Latter-Day Saints

Since the Great Depression, Mormons have embraced a strong ethic of economic self-reliance and have been encouraged to keep at least a three-month supply of food in storage in case of emergencies. People have dutifully secured this food supply in case the need arises. They also follow the health and dietary tenets prescribed in *The Word of Wisdom*, a code of health that Mormons believe God revealed to Joseph Smith in 1833. It contains a list of healthy foods people are encouraged to eat, with an emphasis on plant-based whole foods. Vices, such as alcohol, tobacco, tea, coffee, and illegal drugs, are prohibited.

As is recommended, Barbara's house has a safe room in the basement of her house. She compulsively checks the room before going grocery shopping to make sure there is an adequate amount of food to eat in an emergency, even though no food has been eaten from there; in fact, she has made a household rule that no one is allowed to enter the room to ensure that everything is intact. If she sees items on sale, she will buy them and store them in the room, which has become quite crowded.

Islam and Judaism

Following religious dietary guidelines is an expectation for the practicing faithful. The problem is, it becomes a clinical problem when the obsessive parsing out of minute details of the rules and compulsive rule-following becomes unsustainable and the meaning of the rules become meaningless.

Islam and Judaism have similar dietary laws, *halal* and *kashrut*, respectively, around meat being properly slaughtered for consumption and avoidance of eating pork, as handed down in the Qur'an and the Torah. Foods that are *haram* and *treif* (unlawful) are by-products of pork; carnivorous animals; birds of prey; foods containing ingredients such as gelatin, enzymes, emulsifiers, and flavors that are questionable because the origin of the ingredients is unknown; and any foods contaminated with any of the above products (https://www.halalcertified.in/halal-guidelines/). In Islam, the consumption of alcohol is also prohibited.

For Muslims, there are grocery stores that conveniently ensure food is in compliance with halal. If someone does not live in an area where these stores are available, these symbols are provided on food labels:

There are also kosher grocery stores for Jews to safely shop in for their food products. To identify kosher and *pareve* (neutral) foods in secular supermarkets, Jews look for these symbols:

Rules are also established for managing the kitchen, storing food, and meal preparation in order to maintain halal and kosher households. Both Muslims and Jews store their halal and kosher foods separately from haram and *treif* items (https://hygienicworld.com/wp-content/uploads/2016/06/Halal-GUIDELINES-FOR-THE-PREPARATION.pdf; https://www.jewishvirtuallibrary.org/how-to-keep-a-kosher-kitchen). It is not surprising for there to be a concern that someone with OCD would perform compulsive visual checking rituals to ensure that the food items are separated enough to adhere to the religious requirements. Some people may also check cabinets and refrigerators after someone else has used them.

Rima is strict about following the rules of halal in her household. She is anxious when she invites people over for dinner. If they are Muslim, she worries about whether the food she is making is within the religious guidelines. If she is entertaining non-Muslims, she becomes extremely triggered if they bring something to give as a contribution to the meal. She may be polite and not seek

reassurance from them about the ingredients. Sometimes she is not so polite and "forgets" to serve it, at which point her husband or her guest will retrieve it and eat it as part of the meal.

Because of how social Rima is, she is often invited to non-Muslim events such as weddings and birthday parties. She values these relationships but has begun to turn down invitations since her OCD has flared up. The food and beverages served at these events are not within her religious guidelines, and she is extremely uncomfortable in places where alcohol is served and around people who are drunk. She makes excuses for why she can't attend but is afraid her social circle will start becoming increasingly smaller and that her many dear friends will stop inviting her.

Jewish kosher kitchens have strict rules about not mixing meat and dairy. There are rules about how long to wait before eating the other kind of food and how to manage the kitchen to keep things separate. When affordable, households have two sets of almost everything, including two sinks, two refrigerators, and two dishwashers. Utensils, pots, pans, cooking surfaces, plates, flatware, dishpans, and sponges, towels, and pot holders are kept separate and cannot be used if they have touched meat and dairy products, kosher and treif (nonkosher) food. If they have touched, a certain level of heat conduction (450 degrees) or soaking them in water for several days is necessary to restore them to a kosher state. Families that do not have the luxury of two sets of items follow the guidelines for washing and storing items that require more work and attention by all family members.

Hinduism

In India, Brahmin Hindus have two types of Hindu meals, *kaccha* (uncooked and unripe) and *pakka* (ripe and cooked) (Kwon & Tamang, 2015). As *kaccha* foods are prone to contamination, there are strict rules for cooking, serving, and eating this type of food (Kwon & Tamang, 2015). Care must be taken with meals that are prepared for being eaten from a large bowl with others using a hand, as well as the hand taking food from the bowl so as to avoid being *jootha* or *Uchchhishta* (contaminated) (Kwon & Tamang, 2015). Some foods have social importance for celebrations, especially during festivals and social occasions. *Lassi* is a traditional yogurt beverage made from *dahi* that is popular in summer and is made especially during the *Holi* and *Shivarathri* festival seasons. *Enduri pitha* is a spiced rice and cheesecake and is prepared during the *prathamastami* festival, during which people pray for the life and prosperity of their eldest child by the mother and other female relatives (Mohapatra, 2013; Sarkar, Lohith Kumar, Dhumal, Panigrahi, & Choudhary, 2015). A practice in orthodox Hinduism is for meals to be eaten in segregated spaces, and for elderly male members of the family being served first, while Hindu female family members eat afterward (Kwon & Tamang, 2015).

Lakshmi's family enjoys kaccha meals, but she dreads making them out of fear that she has not properly stored the food and that it is contaminated. Kaccha khatta is popular with her kids, and even though she has dried and stored the ingredients according to the proper guidelines, she has a nagging doubt about whether they are edible. She compulsively smells and visually checks the items and sometimes asks family members if they think the food is safe. Sometimes, if she sees an unidentifiable speck of something, she will throw the food away.

She is also tasked with helping to prepare food for Hindu festivals and performs the same compulsive behaviors of checking and asking others reassuring questions about her food quality. Lakshmi will typically be the last one to eat, often after all the women have gone, to make sure she has been appropriately respectful and to make sure others have had enough to eat.

Cleanliness and Handwashing before Meals

In times when keeping good hygiene was more difficult, washing hands before eating became a strong recommendation for preventing illness. Nonetheless, many people are not in the habit of doing so and do not appear to suffer any consequences.

In Judaism, the act of washing the hands brings holiness to the mundane. The ritual for handwashing before meals served with bread consists of pouring water from a cup or glass over the right hand twice and then twice over the left hand, repeating this sequence three times. While washing, the following blessing is recited: "Blessed art Thou, O Lord our God, King of the Universe, who has sanctified us with Thy commandments and has commanded us concerning the washing of the hands." Hands are dried with a towel, and then the person is ready to eat the meal.

Even though Jewish laws are specific about when handwashing before eating is required, Shifteh washes her hands before every meal according to the instructions for when bread is served. She becomes unsure if she performed the steps with the right number of repetitions and will start over until she is sure. At times she asks a family member to watch her as a way of avoiding uncertainty, but because she has OCD, she rewashes her hands anyway until she feels "right." Meanwhile, her family is waiting for her to finish in order to start eating.

References

Agte, V., & Chiplonkar, S. (2007). Linkage of concepts of good nutrition in yoga and modern science. *Current Science, 92*, 956–960.

al-Bukhari, S., & Uddin, M. M. (2020). *Sahih al-Bukhari (All Volumes in One Book)* (Vol. 3). n.p.: Mohee Uddin Publishing.

Allen, M., Dickinson, K. M., & Prichard, I. (2018). The dirt on clean eating: A cross sectional analysis of dietary intake, restrained eating and opinions about clean eating among women. *Nutrients, 10*(9), 1266.

BBC. (2008). *Fasting.* Retrieved from https://www.bbc.co.uk/religion/religions/mormon/customs/fasting.shtml

Bell, R. (1985). *Holy anorexia.* Chicago, IL: University of Chicago Press.

Bratman, S. (2017). Orthorexia vs. theories of healthy eating. *Eating and Weight Disorders, 22*(3), 381–385. doi:10.1007/s40519-017-0417-6

Cena, H., Barthels, F., Cuzzolaro, M., Bratman, S., Brytek-Matera, A., Dunn, T., . . . Donini, L. M. (2019). Definition and diagnostic criteria for orthorexia nervosa: A narrative review of the literature. *Eating and Weight Disorders, 24*(2), 209–246. doi:10.1007/s40519-018-0606-y

Forcen, F. E. (2013). Anorexia mirabilis: The practice of fasting by Saint Catherine of Siena in the late middle ages. *American Journal of Psychiatry, 170*(4), 370–371. doi:10.1176/appi.ajp.2012.12111457

Gardner, E. (1908). St. Catherine of Siena. In *The Catholic Encyclopedia.* New York, NY: Robert Appleton Company. Retrieved from http://www.newadvent.org/cathen/03447a.htm

Griffin, J., & Berry, E. (2003). A modern day holy anorexia? Religious language in advertising and anorexia nervosa in the West. *European Journal of Clinical Nutrition, 57*, 43–51. doi:10.1038/sj.ejcn.1601511

Gupta, L., Khandelwal, D., Singla, R., Gupta, P., & Kalra, S. (2017). Pragmatic dietary advice for diabetes during Navratris. *Indian Journal of Endocrinology and Metabolism, 21*(1), 231–237. doi:10.4103/2230-8210.196009

Jones, C., & Ryan, J. D. (2006). *Encyclopedia of Hinduism*. New York, NY: Infobase Publsing

Kannan, S., Mahadevan, S., Seshadri, K., Sadacharan, D., & Velayutham, K. (2016). Fasting practices in Tamil Nadu and their importance for patients with diabetes. *Indian Journal of Endocrinology and Metabolism, 20*(6), 858–862. doi:10.4103/2230-8210.192921

Koven, N. S., & Abry, A. W. (2015). The clinical basis of orthorexia nervosa: Emerging perspectives. *Neuropsychiatric Disease and Treatment, 11*, 385–394. doi:10.2147/NDT.S61665

Kwon, D., & Tamang, J. (2015). Religious ethnic food. *Journal of Ethnic Foods, 2*. doi:10.1016/j.jef.2015.05.001

Mohapatra, J. (2013). *Wellness in Indian festivals & rituals*. Bloomington, IN: Partridge Publishing.

Moroze, R. M., Dunn, T. M., Holland, J. C., Yager, J., & Weintraub, P. (2015). Microthinking about micronutrients: A case of transition from obsessions about healthy eating to near-fatal "orthorexia nervosa" and proposed diagnostic criteria. *Psychosomatics, 56*(4), 397–403.

Pearce, J. M. (2004). Richard Morton: Origins of anorexia nervosa. *European Neurology, 52*(4), 191–192. doi:10.1159/000082033

Pearson, A. M. (1996). *Because it gives me peace of mind: Ritual fasts in the religious lives of Hindu women*. New York: State University of New York Press.

Pittock, A. (2014). *How are anorexia nervosa and spirituality connected, and what implications does this have for treatment?* Royal College of Psychiatrists. Retrieved from https://www.rcpsych.ac.uk/docs/default-source/members/sigs/spirituality-spsig/alexandra-pittock-anorerxia-nervosa-and-spirituality.pdf?sfvrsn=e9002559_2

Raphaely, T. (2015). *Impact of meat consumption on health and environmental sustainability*. Hershey, PA: IGI Global.

Sarkar, P., Lohith Kumar, D. H., Dhumal, C., Panigrahi, S. S., & Choudhary, R. (2015). Traditional and ayurvedic foods of Indian origin. *Journal of Ethnic Foods, 2*(3), 97–109. doi:10.1016/j.jef.2015.08.003

Sharma, R. (2014). *The Hindu ritual where wives fast for their husbands: A close-up look at the full moon festival of Karwa Chauth*. Retrieved from https://international.la-croix.com/news/religion/the-hindu-ritual-where-wives-fast-for-their-husbands/180

Shridhar, K., Dhillon, P. K., Bowen, L., Kinra, S., Bharathi, A. V., Prabhakaran, D., . . . Ebrahim, S. (2014). Nutritional profile of Indian vegetarian diets—The Indian Migration Study (IMS). *Nutrition Journal, 13*, 55. doi:10.1186/1475-2891-13-55

Tremelling, K., Sandon, L., Vega, G. L., & McAdams, C. J. (2017). Orthorexia nervosa and eating disorder symptoms in registered dietitian nutritionists in the United States. *Journal of the Academy of Nutrition and Dietetics, 117*(10), 1612–1617. doi:10.1016/j.jand.2017.05.001

Vandereycken, W., & Deth, R. V. (1994). *From fasting saints to anorexic girls: The history of self-starvation.* London, UK: Athlone Press.

Zickgraf, H. F., Ellis, J. M., & Essayli, J. H. (2019). Disentangling orthorexia nervosa from healthy eating and other eating disorder symptoms: Relationships with clinical impairment, comorbidity, and self-reported food choices. *Appetite, 134*, 40–49.

CHAPTER EIGHT

"Deadly" Sinning: Sexual Obsessions, Mental Adultery, Violence, and Death

"You have heard that it was said 'You shall not commit adultery'; but I say to you, that everyone who looks on a woman to lust for her has committed adultery with her already in his heart."

Matt. 5:27–28

Versus:

"Do not be disturbed about bad thoughts; it is one thing to have them and quite another to consent to them."

St. Francis de Sales

Previous chapters have outlined the nature of obsessions consisting of taboo thoughts and committing deadly sins provoked by overactivity in the moral center of the brain. The types of symptoms included in this discussion are classified as belonging to the specific OCD dimension of repugnant obsessional sexual, religious, and violent obsessions (Abramowitz et al., 2010) that people with OCD endure just by having the disorder.

Sexuality and sexual functioning are among the key elements for well-being that can become dysfunctional through different medical and mental health problems (Chou, Cottler, Khosla, Reed, & Say, 2015). In OCD, 17–57% of OCD patients reported experiencing problems with their sexuality (Kendurkar & Kaur, 2008; Thakurta, Dhar, Sarkar, Ray, & Mallick, 2016). People with OCD were found to have a higher degree of sexual disgust than those with other anxiety disorders (Van Minnen & Kampman, 2000; Vulink, Denys, Bus, & Westenberg, 2006). Prevalence of sexual and religious obsessions was assessed in different cultures. In the United States, 30% of people with OCD had sexual or religious obsessions (Ruscio, Stein, Chiu, & Kessler, 2010). A finding of an Iranian study was that 30% of the sample reported having blasphemous thoughts (Ghassemzadeh et al., 2002). In Egypt, 60% of people with OCD had religious and contamination obsessions (Okasha, Saad, Khalil, el Dawla, & Yehia, 1994). It is unclear if these findings reflect accurate or underestimated prevalence rates due to the limited number of places reporting on these symptom types.

Sexual obsessions can be especially difficult for people with OCD because they often overidentify with the content and mistakenly assume that they define their sexual desires. People with intrusive sexual, violent, or scrupulosity obsessions experience a "feared self" even though their symptoms are ego-dystonic. The "feared self" represents a perception that their symptoms indicate the potential for being bad, immoral, harmful, or insane (Aardema & O'Connor, 2007; Aardema et al., 2013).

Individuals with sexual obsessions experience a high degree of guilt, shame, hopelessness, and depression and often—mistakenly—consider themselves deviant, disgusting, or evil (Ghassemzadeh, 2018). As we have learned, the search for definitive clarity about whether one's soul is in jeopardy due to obsessive thoughts is impossible. We have also learned that OCD always generates taboo content of obsessions, and those with intrusive sexual thoughts feel they are sinning by having them.

Sexual obsessions cause a feeling of disgust or being in a state of "mental pollution" in OCD and are met with high urges to perform washing and cleaning rituals (Cougle, Lee, Horowitz, Wolitzky-Taylor, & Telch, 2008; Ghassemzadeh et al., 2017). Many cultures subscribe to washing and cleaning behaviors as ways to eliminate the distress associated with the disgust caused by the obsessive thoughts (Ghassemzadeh et al., 2017). Further, disgust sensitivity has been found to inhibit sexual functioning for people with OCD and scrupulosity contamination symptoms (Pozza et al., 2020).

A participant in a doctoral thesis that studied scrupulosity and Catholicism explained how a priest responded to his confession about having engaged in sexual exploration as a child. "The clergy stressed hell and damnation. My only rest from a tortured mind was sleep. I felt filthy and dirty and different. I believe (sic) that God has done his duty to punish me. Not once did a priest utter a kind word. I became bitter toward the clergy yet in complete awe of them [because of their vow of celibacy]" (Cobb, 2014b, p. 76).

Rules around showering are common for people with OCD who experience disgust about their genital areas. Normally, people get wet, shampoo, lather up, and rinse. It is a space where people say they have creative ideas because showering is a mindless activity conducive to relaxing and letting the imagination flow. Some scrupulous people will avoid washing their genital areas altogether due to contamination avoidance (especially of the rectal area), whereas others will wash them as the final step. In that case, it is common for people to wash their hands first before and after washing their genitals.

People can also be sensitive about sex-related vernacular words and body parts. Hearing others using "vulgar" language to talk about sexuality triggers urges to mentally ritualize by thinking "proper" words or handwash. Scrupulous people may revert to using safe or childish language when referring to these body parts. Sadly, people often develop a negative relationship with and become disconnected from their genital areas and treat them as if they were foreign objects.

Sexual obsessions can take many forms, including a fear of being attracted to children, engaging in a forbidden sexual activity, and bizarre sexual images. OCD patients might experience intrusive images of sexual organs, imagine themselves performing unwanted and unacceptable sexual acts, or have persistent doubts about their own sexual or gender identity. Some of the experienced thoughts, images, and urges may take the form of doubtful questions, such as, "What if I have an affair with that person?" "What is stopping me from exposing my genitals to that person on the subway platform?" or "What if I lose control and act out sexually?" Most often, it is difficult for people to explain these obsessions even to a therapist because of shame, concern about being judged, worries that the obsessions will be considered ego-syntonic, or concern that explaining them will cause the therapist to feel, disgust even if she doesn't show it (Abramowitz, 2009; Hyman & Pedrick, 2010).

The construct of TAF-M, referred to in previous chapters, is the belief that immoral thoughts are immoral actions. TAF-M plagues sufferers who live in a subjective state of disgrace and shame. They judge themselves harshly because the content of these ego-dystonic taboo thoughts often involves pedophilia, rape, pornographic images, animals, adultery, and disturbing sexual images. Some may consider natural sexual responses to be lustful and that they lead to a loss of control over behaviors such as masturbation; flirting; and being aroused by sexual scenes on TV and movies, in books, or in other media entertainment. Even a simple distraction like playing video games can expose sufferers to characters that are often portrayed as sexually provocative, and playing them becomes a profane act.

Certainly, having sexual obsessions in houses of worship feels sinful. People describe having sexually graphic images of the religious icons they see before them in places of worship. The images can consist of the person performing sexual acts with them, calling them profane names, or having decidedly sacrilegious thoughts. Instead of being open to the spiritual and communal atmosphere, sufferers feel tortured and often drop out of attending. Further, people are horrified to learn that their exposure tasks will consist of purposefully having these thoughts and images for the treatment to be successful. Chapter 12 explores how clergy helps people with OCD manage their fears of committing sins or rejecting God.

Sexual and Reproductive Bodily Functions, Sexual Ideation, and Physiological Responses

A challenging issue surrounding sexuality for the scrupulous is "autosexuality" (masturbation). Though there is nothing in the Bible that specifically addresses masturbation, many religions have prohibitions against it. Historically, "spilling" semen was considered sinful in Judeo-Christian faiths because it is wasting the substance intended for procreation. Engaging in it is also committing the deadly sin of lust.

> Rather, clothe yourselves with the Lord Jesus Christ, and do not think about how to gratify the desires of the flesh. (Rom. 13:14)

Paul lived a secular life until he got married and became a Jehovah's Witness. He suffers from severe obsessive guilt about having masturbated in the past as well as having "fornicated" by having had sex outside of marriage. When not yet a Jehovah's Witness, he used to shower after having masturbated to wash off the self-disgust. Now he washes his hands to purify his soul when he has intrusive thoughts and images about these past behaviors. He fears he cannot be forgiven and lives in a constant state of shame and disgrace; he fears being condemned on Judgment Day.

Nocturnal emissions (wet dreams) occur naturally and unintentionally and result in a state of moral, spiritual, or physical contamination for male scrupulosity sufferers. When this happens, the urge to shower excessively, launder all the linens and clothing that are out in the open, and pray can consume the entire day. In Islam, the man is obligated to perform *ghusl* because he is considered to be in a *junub* state of impurity (Ghassemzadeh, 2018).

In Judaism, during menstruation women are considered to be in an unclean state and sexual activity is suspended. In order to resume sexual relations with their husbands after menstruation, Jewish women purify themselves through the mikvah (ritual bath) and wait for seven days after until all traces of blood are gone. Women with scrupulosity may be too afraid to have intercourse due to obsessive doubt about being physically and spiritually pure. They also fear contaminating their husbands and may avoid sex in spite of their husbands' protests.

Fantasies are normal cognitive events and are part of one's imaginative sexuality. They may be graphic or scripted scenes of sexual encounters that would never be acted upon or past sexual experiences that can enhance sexual arousal but also cause feelings of guilt or shame (Kinsey, Pomeroy, & Martin, 1948; Leitenberg & Henning, 1995).

Although no studies have been found on this topic, we can assume that, just like with any other cognitive processes, the content of sexual fantasies would be the same for people with and without OCD. In OCD, however, normal sexual fantasies become sinful and disgusting images or thoughts that the person tries to suppress. The obsessions may consist of taboo scenarios, including religious figures, or sexually explicit vulgarities that are not sexually arousing, interfere with daily functioning, and are said to be more difficult to treat than other types of intrusive sexual thoughts (Gordon, 2002).

Another difference between sexual fantasies and sexual obsessions is that there are differing physiological systems that produce arousal. Sexual arousal is a response by the parasympathetic nervous system, whereas anxiety is activated by the sympathetic nervous system (Tindle & Tadi, 2020). However, there appears to be some confusing interaction between the two systems that affects how people with OCD interpret these sensations. Reports have suggested that anxiety may facilitate sexual arousal due to overlapping bodily sensations that occur during their respective arousals (e.g., increased heart rate, sweating, racing thoughts) (Barlow, 1986; Kane et al., 2019). People with pedophilia obsessions have described this triggering sensation as a "tingle" and misinterpret it to mean they are sexually aroused by children.

Sexual fantasies also create cognitive and emotional reactivity in people with OCD who may believe they are harmful or "deviant," depending on the nature of the fantasy. As such, unwanted physiological and emotional reactions such as lust, disgust, anger, guilt, and shame complicate how people with OCD respond to these experiences. Trying to suppress the thoughts appears to increase the frequency of the obsessions and can lead to depression and difficulties in concentrating (Gordon, 2002).

Sexual Orientation, Identity, and Homosexual Obsessions

Homosexual obsessions do not characterize a person as being homophobic. In fact, being homophobic is a common moral obsession for which the sufferer feels guilty because she is an accepting person. The distress people have with these obsessions has to do with uncertainty, fear that others may perceive them as homosexual, or fear that their symptoms indicate latent homosexual desires. As is the case for all obsessions, there is no test to prove it one way or the other.

Straight and gay people may obsess about whether they are really of the other sexual orientation. Compulsions include pushing the thoughts away, analyzing them, somatic checking for signs of physiological arousal, seeking reassurance from others, or internet surfing for signs that one might be gay, straight, transgender, or queer. It can be complicated when people have binary sexual fantasies or feelings that are common in normal, healthy sexuality (Coimbra-Gomes, 2020).

The lifetime prevalence of homosexual obsessions ranges from 8% to 12% (Pinto et al., 2008; Williams & Farris, 2011). It is likely that this is an underestimation due to a level of shame or embarrassment in disclosing this symptom.

A differential assessment of gay obsessions, however, may be indicated in some cases. OCD sufferers may be at a time in their lives when they begin questioning their sexual identity. One complicating feature about why this type of sexual ideation is problematic may be due to the person not wanting to be gay and the effort made to resist the thoughts. Assessing whether there is a real attraction to a person of the same sex may indicate that the feelings and thoughts are ego-syntonic but that the person has not come to terms with accepting being gay.

Sexuality and Religion

It is fairly common for teenagers to struggle with issues of sexual morality. "Something about scrupulosity does not click until the person starts to develop sexual feelings in conjunction with the mandate to confess these sexual urges" (Cobb, 2014a, p. 71). Learning how to manage new sexual thoughts and feelings can be challenging, depending on the learned attitudes about the body (carnality) and what to do with it. Those with latent or active OCD can develop scrupulosity or moral perfectionism if they internalize a negative message about sexuality and sexual feelings, as well as questions about sexual identity. Youthful activities such as going to shopping malls, parties, and participating in extracurricular activities begin to be avoided. In its extreme, social media and other screen entertainment can also be triggering. The consequences of becoming socially isolated can lead to missing important developmental and maturational events.

Father Santa was introduced in Chapter 6 and is the editor of the *Scrupulous Anonymous* newsletter. Many people write in with questions about whether certain aspects of physical attraction and sexuality are sinful. On the question of modesty and lust, one person asked:

> Is there still a requirement to practice "custody of the eyes"? Today's clothing and swimwear attire make me feel surrounded by temptation. I avoid the beach, swimming pools, and all other places where I know there will be temptation. (Santa, 2020)

Father Santa's response was:

> There is a huge difference between a spiritual practice such as modesty and choosing to live a way of life that becomes more and more isolating every day. It is not spiritually or psychologically healthy to isolate, no matter what the reason. I would suggest that you find someone to help you find balance in your perception so you can enjoy the freedom of living that is required and necessary to be healthy. (Santa, 2020)

A college professor from Scotland wrote:

> I grew up with a distorted conscience on sex. What if this is a sin? What if it isn't? I flitted from book to book looking for answers. I found none. Confessions were fitful and an ordeal. Because of sexual exploration at an early age, which was no more than a response to anatomy, I suffered horrific guilt. The clergy stressed hell and damnation. My only rest from a tortured mind was sleep. I felt filthy and dirty and different. I believe (sic) that God has done his duty to punish me. Not once did a priest utter a kind word. I became bitter toward the clergy yet in complete awe of them. (Cobb, 2014b, p. 69)

Pedophilia Obsessions

Pedophilia obsessions are extremely distressing and ego-dystonic for people. Readers should understand that, like all obsessions, the content of the intrusive thoughts is irrelevant. People who are upset about having them are not people at risk for acting on them. They typically avoid being around children. They avoid public places and family gatherings because they are ashamed of having the intrusive thoughts, and they want to avoid any chance that they would, on impulse, do something inappropriate.

Pablo is an Evangelical born-again Christian. He obsesses about being a pedophile because of an alleged incident that happened twenty years ago. He was at a friend's house and, while he was using the bathroom, the friend's young daughter came in while he was buckling up his pants. His obsessive fear is that he didn't realize the girl might have been there before he was fully dressed. Worse than that, he obsessed that maybe he wanted it to happen and that he is attracted to young girls. Along with being mortified, his biggest fear was that his eternal salvation was at risk. He was afraid of being eternally separated from God and his loved ones after death. In the back of his mind, he always held a plan to turn himself over to the police. Parenthetically, another obsession Pablo has is that whenever he wants something to go his way, or that he could have an advantage by doing something easier, he is bargaining with the devil by being lazy.

While in confession, he told the priest in great detail what he had done wrong in order to make sure he was given the appropriate penance. Pablo started repeating himself just in case the priest had been distracted while he was confessing. The priest interrupted him and ended the confession.

Pornography Viewing

By any measure, pornography would be considered violating virtuous conduct. And yet, many religious people engage in it, even those with scrupulosity. An investigation into internet pornography searches and pornographic website subscriptions of heterosexual males found that the rates of viewing pornography were higher in more religious communities (Edelman, 2009; MacInnis & Hodson, 2015). People with higher religiosity considered their use of pornography to be addictive, compulsive, and causing higher psychological distress (Abell, Steenbergh, & Boivin, 2006; Bradley, Grubbs, Uzdavines, Exline, & Pargament, 2016), presumably due to guilt over having been overtaken by the deadly sin of lust.

Experiential avoidance has also been found to be a mediator of scrupulosity and pornographic viewing, mostly for men but also women (Borgogna & McDermott, 2018). Experiential avoidance is the attempt to control uncomfortable internal experiences and negative emotions (Chawla & Ostafin, 2007). It has been suggested that thoughts about pornography use in scrupulous males may lead to more pornography viewing from the rebound effect of using thought suppression as a coping strategy (Borgogna, Isacco, & McDermott, 2020; De Jong & Cook, 2021). Attempts at not thinking certain thoughts result in *having* the thoughts, which is how people with OCD reinforce their obsessions. Efforts at experiential avoidance also result from the disconnect between sufferers' religious and moral identities and pornography and wanting to avoid the shame and guilt they experience from doing so (Volk, Thomas, Sosin, Jacob, & Moen, 2016).

> Conflict between religious values and engaging in behavior considered to be a vice causes feeling of guilt and shame (self-loathing). (Gilliland, South, Carpenter, & Hardy, 2011)

A study examined whether the role of religious primes is a factor in in pornography viewing and OCD (De Jong & Cook, 2021). Because obsessive individuals consider these thoughts immoral, obsessions often trigger shame (Weingarden & Renshaw, 2015). The three religion-related primes are religious agents, such as God or angels; the spiritual/abstract prime, which includes the divine and sacred; and institutional/concrete prime, which includes behavioral practices such as performing rituals and reading scripture (De Jong & Cook, 2021). The study found that the religious prime was associated with increased shame regarding one's pornography use, but only among individuals who were high on both organizational religiosity and handwashing rituals; in turn, increased shame was associated with greater perceived compulsivity. The religious/sex prime, relative to neutral, was associated with increased shame, but only among individuals who were high on both organizational religiosity and ordering. In turn, increased shame was associated with greater perceived compulsivity. The religious prime, relative to neutral, was associated with increased shame, but only among individuals who were high on both organizational religiosity and checking; in turn, increased shame was associated with greater perceived compulsivity. Additionally, among individuals high on organizational religiosity and checking, the religion/sex prime also caused increased shame and, in turn, greater perceived compulsivity.

Relationship OCD, Mental Adultery/Betrayal

There are two types of relationship OCD (R-OCD) (Doron, Derby, & Szepsenwol, 2014). One type of R-OCD is relationship-focused and the other is partner-centered. Relationship-focused OCD involves obsessive doubts about whether their partner is the "right one," worries that the partner also wonders if he is the "right" person, and whether the relationship itself is "right." Partner-centered OCD involves other obsessive doubts about the suitability of the partner's personality as well as other attributes such as the person's attractiveness, sociability, morality, intelligence, and emotional stability (Melli, Bulli, Doron, & Carraresi, 2018). The traits of R-OCD do not consist of jealousy, concern about infidelity, or stalking behavior.

People with OCD know that these doubts do not reflect the state of the relationship or how they really feel about their partner, and they feel shame for having obsessive doubts or guilt for imposing the doubts on their partner as well as potentially putting the relationship at risk. The partner may not understand the doubts are OCD-driven and may often feel rejected (Koolwal, Agarwal, Manohar, Koolwal, & Gupta, 2020).

Obsessive perfectionism is another factor that causes doubts about the relationship or the partner (Melli et al., 2018) as the not-right-feeling can be mistaken for dissatisfaction. Compulsive questioning, reassurance-seeking, and comparison of the partner are behaviors that affect the quality of the relationship, and at times can actually destroy the relationship. Other compulsions are mental reviewing of interactions, constant assessing of feelings and emotional connection to the partner, and comparing the partner to past partners. Reassurance-seeking behaviors, including confessing doubts to the partner, are other common compulsions performed as attempts to gain certainty. Another type of relationship OCD, unrelated to the ones already described, relates to past regrets about previous relationships. "Did I lose the love of my life?" or "How badly did I hurt that person when I broke up with him?"

Sharon is a divorced Protestant woman and is unforgiving about having violated her wedding vows. She considers the story of Naomi and Ruth as an example of ideal fidelity of which she has fallen short:

> *And she said, Behold, thy sister-in-law is gone back unto her people, and unto her gods: return thou after thy sister in law. And Ruth said, Intreat me not to leave thee, or to return from following after thee: for whither thou goest, I will go; and where thou lodgest, I will lodge: thy people shall be my people, and thy God my God: Where thou diest, will I die, and there will I be buried: the LORD do so to me, and more also, if ought but death part thee and me.* (Ruth: 16–17)

Sharon's obsessive rigid and literal interpretation of this biblical relationship made it difficult for her to forgive herself for divorcing her husband, even though she maintains it was the best decision under her personal circumstances. Her decision about the marriage was based on guilt and obligation to marry her boyfriend, as well as her assumption about others' expectations that it was "meant to be." Sharon was unable to stop punishing herself by restricting her food intake, which, unfortunately, led to binge-eating episodes.

Harming and Violent Obsessions

Obsessions about harming others or oneself is one of the more common OCD symptoms (Rasmussen & Eisen, 1992). Again, the ego-dystonic thoughts and images that agonize people who are the last to ever act on them cause self-stigmatization. They also cause people to isolate themselves because they worry that their presence puts their loved ones at risk. Others try to endure in spite of their torment.

This kind of OCD is often misunderstood and misdiagnosed. People with sexual, violent, and harmful obsessions, who are not yet diagnosed, may mistake them as real intentions that pose being a risk to others. People with intrusive thoughts about harming children were reported to disclose their thoughts after reaching a crisis point, not because they realized they had OCD, but because they were afraid they were capable of acting on them and wanted to ensure that children were safe (Vuong, Gellatly, Lovell, & Bee, 2016). They may delay getting help due to their fear of how health professionals will react, including the fear of being identified as criminals (Robinson, Rose, & Salkovskis, 2017).

A study of mental health clinicians' attitudes toward people with intrusive harming and sexual obsessions showed they would be more likely not to accept them as patients due to their misjudging people who have these OCD symptoms (Steinberg & Wetterneck, 2017). Another study assessed the accuracy of an OCD diagnosis made by a primary care physician who read a case example of a friend disclosing certain types of obsessions. The findings reported 85% misidentification rates for homosexuality, 80% for aggression, 71% for pedophilia, and 38% for religion (Glazier, Swing, & McGinn, 2015).

The practice of circumcision can cause harmful obsessions. Parents with OCD may fear that the procedure will be done incorrectly or cause permanent physical and emotional harm. Deontological guilt results from the conscious decision to put the child in harm's way or that they will be traumatized. Doubts set in about whether to carry out a long-held religious practice for the benefit of the boy's health.

Here is a glimpse of the daily life of someone with harmful obsessions and scrupulosity.

Raisa is a busy Orthodox Jewish mother of five. She suffered from having images of grinding up glass and putting it in her family's food. She had images of putting glass in the butter and stopped serving it. When her family wanted to use it, she would look for shiny particles before allowing it. Soon it extended to family and friend gatherings. To keep people safe, she kept checking to see if there was anything shiny wherever they were.

Her skin felt "prickly" due to excessive handwashing. Her explanation for that sensation was that she was being careful by washing away tiny shards of glass that might be on her hands. Her obsessions were especially bad when she was angry, an emotion she found to be unacceptable. She also had other contamination obsessions, but focusing treatment on her scrupulosity symptoms would help alleviate those symptoms as well as they are all based on guilt, fear of sinning, and fear of God.

Her worst fear, though, was that God was out to get her. Ever watching, ever present, He waited for her to make a lethal mistake. Her obsessive fear of upsetting God caused even more rituals in the form of "prayers." Other obsessive thoughts were, "Did I care enough when my uncle died?" "Did I give my pregnant friend toxoplasmosis from my cat?" "Did my pheromones cause someone to rape?" "Will God punish me by not letting me have another baby?" Even though Jews don't believe in the devil, she the obsessive thought "Will I have made a pact with the devil to become pregnant again?" Raisa's treatment is described in Chapter 12.

Hit and Run

"Oh no! That bump I drove over might have been a person!" Not only do people with scrupulosity fear causing harm to others but they also worry that they could kill somebody. Many people avoid driving around parks, near schools, or on busy streets. They are triggered by bicyclists and joggers. They feel compelled to do their due diligence by going back and checking the area where they were triggered. They won't see any emergency vehicles or evidence of an accident, but they still don't feel they have sufficiently examined the environment around where they think it happened. They may be tempted to call the police as a checking/reassurance ritual but know that is an offense. They will turn on the local news or check the next day's newspaper for any reported hit-and-run accidents. They may get up from bed during the night because they can't sleep and go back over the area again. They lose their confidence in performing what is typically an automatic function.

References

Aardema, F., Moulding, R., Radomsky, A. S., Doron, G., Allamby, J., & Souki, E. (2013). Fear of self and obsessionality: Development and validation of the fear of self questionnaire. *Journal of Obsessive-Compulsive and Related Disorders, 2*(3), 306–315.

Aardema, F., & O'Connor, K. (2007). The menace within: Obsessions and the self. *Journal of Cognitive Psychotherapy, 21*, 182–197. doi:10.1891/088983907781494573

Abell, J. W., Steenbergh, T. A., & Boivin, M. J. (2006). Cyberporn use in the context of religiosity. *Journal of Psychology and Theology, 34*(2), 165–171. doi:10.1177/009164710603400206

Abramowitz, J. S., Deacon, B. J., Olatunji, B. O., Wheaton, M. G., Berman, N. C., Losardo, D., . . . Hale, L. R. (2010). Assessment of obsessive-compulsive symptom dimensions: Development and evaluation of the Dimensional Obsessive-Compulsive Scale. *Psychological Assessment, 22*(1), 180–198. doi:10.1037/a0018260

Barlow, D. H. (1986). Causes of sexual dysfunction: The role of anxiety and cognitive interference. *Journal of Consulting and Clinical Psychology, 54*(2), 140–148. doi:10.1037/0022-006X.54.2.140

Borgogna, N., Isacco, A., & McDermott, R. (2020). A closer examination of the relationship between religiosity and problematic pornography viewing in heterosexual men. *Sexual Addiction & Compulsivity, 27*(1–2), 23–44. doi: 10.1080/10720162.2020.1751361

Borgogna, N., & McDermott, R. (2018). The role of gender, experiential avoidance, and scrupulosity in problematic pornography viewing: A moderated-mediation model. *Sexual Addiction & Compulsivity, 25*(4), 319–344.

Bradley, D. F., Grubbs, J. B., Uzdavines, A., Exline, J. J., & Pargament, K. I. (2016). Perceived addiction to internet pornography among religious believers and nonbelievers. *Sexual Addiction & Compulsivity, 23*(2–3), 225–243. doi:10.1080/10720162.2016.1162237

Chawla, N., & Ostafin, B. (2007). Experiential avoidance as a functional dimensional approach to psychopathology: An empirical review. *Journal of Clinical Psychology, 63*(9), 871–890. doi:10.1002/jclp.20400

Chou, D., Cottler, S., Khosla, R., Reed, G. M., & Say, L. (2015). Sexual health in the International Classification of Diseases (ICD): Implications for measurement and beyond. *Reprod Health Matters, 23*(46), 185–192. doi:10.1016/j.rhm.2015.11.008

Cobb, K. F. (2014a). *Understanding scrupulosity: Psychopathological and Catholic perspectives* (Master's). Iowa City: The University of Iowa.

Cobb, K. F. (2014b). *Understanding scrupulosity: Psychopathological and Catholic perspectives* (Master of Arts). Iowa City: The University of Iowa.

Coimbra-Gomes, E. (2020). Ego-dystonic stance-taking in sexual orientation obsessive-compulsive disorder (SO-OCD). *Journal of Obsessive-Compulsive and Related Disorders, 27*, 100576. doi:10.1016/j.jocrd.2020.100576

Cougle, J., Lee, H., Horowitz, J., Wolitzky-Taylor, K., & Telch, M. (2008). An exploration of the relationship between mental pollution and OCD symptoms. *Journal of Behavior Therapy and Experimental Psychiatry, 39*(3), 340–353. doi:10.1016/j.jbtep.2007.08.007

De Jong, D. C., & Cook, C. (2021). Roles of religiosity, obsessive–compulsive symptoms, scrupulosity, and shame in self-perceived pornography addiction: A preregistered study. *Archives of Sexual Behavior, 50*(2), 695–709. doi:10.1007/s10508-020-01878-6

Doron, G., Derby, D. S., & Szepsenwol, O. (2014). Relationship obsessive compulsive disorder (ROCD): A conceptual framework. *Journal of Obsessive-Compulsive and Related Disorders, 3*(2), 169–180. doi:10.1016/j.jocrd.2013.12.005

Edelman, B. (2009). Markets: Red light states: Who buys online adult entertainment? *Journal of Economic Perspectives, 23*(1), 209–220. doi:10.1257/jep.23.1.209

Ghassemzadeh, H. (2018). Scrupulosity, sexual ruminations and cleaning in obsessive-compulsive disorder: Novel insights from cognitive perspectives. In D. Geeraerts, D. Divjak, & J. R. Taylor (Eds.), *Cognitive linguistics research* (pp. 293–310). Berlin, Germany: De Gruyter.

Ghassemzadeh, H., Mojtabai, R., Khamseh, A., Ebrahimkhani, N., Issazadegan, A. A., & Saif-Nobakht, Z. (2002). Symptoms of obsessive-compulsive disorder in a sample of Iranian patients. *International Journal of Social Psychiatry, 48*(1), 20–28. doi:10.1177/002076402128783055

Ghassemzadeh, H., Raisi, F., Firoozikhojastefar, R., Meysamie, A., Karamghadiri, N., Nasehi, A. A., . . . Ebrahimkhani, N. (2017). A study on sexual function in Obsessive-Compulsive Disorder (OCD) patients with and without depressive symptoms. *Perspectives in psychiatric care, 53*(3), 208–213. doi:10.1111/ppc.12160

Gilliland, R., South, M., Carpenter, B. N., & Hardy, S. A. (2011). The roles of shame and guilt in hypersexual behavior. *Sexual Addiction & Compulsivity, 18*(1), 12–29. doi:10.1080/10720162.2011.551182

Glazier, K., Swing, M., & McGinn, L. K. (2015). Half of obsessive-compulsive disorder cases misdiagnosed: Vignette-based survey of primary care physicians. *Journal of Clinical Psychiatry, 76*(6), e761–e767. doi:10.4088/JCP.14m09110

Gordon, W. M. (2002). Sexual obsessions and OCD. *Sexual and Relationship Therapy, 17*(4), 343–354.

Hyman, B., & Pedrick, C. (2010). *The OCD workbook: Your guide to breaking free from obsessive-compulsive disorder* (3rd ed.). Oakland, CA: New Harbinger.

Kane, L., Dawson, S. J., Shaughnessy, K., Reissing, E. D., Ouimet, A. J., & Ashbaugh, A. R. (2019). A review of experimental research on anxiety and sexual arousal: Implications for the treatment of sexual dysfunction using cognitive behavioral therapy. *Journal of Experimental Psychopathology, 10*(2). https://journals.sagepub.com/doi/full/10.1177/2043808719847371

Kendurkar, A., & Kaur, B. (2008). Major depressive disorder, obsessive-compulsive disorder, and generalized anxiety disorder: Do the sexual dysfunctions differ? *Primary Care Companion to the Journal of Clinical Psychiatry, 10*(4), 299–305. doi:10.4088/pcc.v10n0405

Kinsey, A. C., Pomeroy, W. B., & Martin, C. E. (1948). *Sexual behavior in the human male*. Philadelphia, PA: W. B. Saunders Co.

Koolwal, A., Agarwal, S., Manohar, S., Koolwal, G. D., & Gupta, A. (2020). Obsessive–compulsive disorder and sexuality: A narrative review. *Journal of Psychosexual Health, 2*(1), 37–43. doi:10.1177/2631831819896171

Leitenberg, H., & Henning, K. (1995). Sexual fantasy. *Psychological bulletin, 117*(3), 469.

MacInnis, C. C., & Hodson, G. (2015). Do American states with more religious or conservative populations search more for sexual content on Google? *Archives of Sexual Behavior, 44*(1), 137–147. doi:10.1007/s10508-014-0361-8

Melli, G., Bulli, F., Doron, G., & Carraresi, C. (2018). Maladaptive beliefs in relationship obsessive compulsive disorder (ROCD): Replication and extension in a clinical sample. *Journal of Obsessive-Compulsive and Related Disorders, 18*, 47–53. doi:10.1016/j.jocrd.2018.06.005

Okasha, A., Saad, A., Khalil, A., el Dawla, A., & Yehia, N. (1994). Phenomenology of obsessive-compulsive disorder: A transcultural study. *Comprehensive Psychiatry, 35*(3), 191–197. doi:10.1016/0010-440x(94)90191-0

Pinto, A., Greenberg, B. D., Grados, M. A., Bienvenu, O. J., 3rd, Samuels, J. F., Murphy, D. L., . . . Nestadt, G. (2008). Further development of YBOCS dimensions in the OCD Collaborative Genetics study: Symptoms vs. categories. *Psychiatry Research, 160*(1), 83–93. doi:10.1016/j.psychres.2007.07.010

Pozza, A., Marazziti, D., Mucci, F., Grassi, G., Prestia, D., & Dèttore, D. (2020). Sexual arousal in obsessive-compulsive disorder with and without contamination/washing symptoms: A moderating role of disgust sensitivity. *Journal of Nervous and Mental Disease, 208*(9), 694–700. doi:10.1097/nmd.0000000000001184

Rasmussen, S. A., & Eisen, J. L. (1992). The epidemiology and differential diagnosis of obsessive compulsive disorder. *Journal of Clinical Psychiatry, 53*(Suppl.), 4–10. Retrieved from http://www.ncbi.nlm.nih.gov/pubmed/1564054

Robinson, K. J., Rose, D., & Salkovskis, P. M. (2017). Seeking help for obsessive compulsive disorder (OCD): A qualitative study of the enablers and barriers conducted by a researcher with personal experience of OCD. *Psychology and Psychotherapy, 90*(2), 193–211. doi:10.1111/papt.12090

Ruscio, A. M., Stein, D. J., Chiu, W. T., & Kessler, R. C. (2010). The epidemiology of obsessive-compulsive disorder in the National Comorbidity Survey Replication. *Molecular Psychiatry, 15*(1), 53–63. doi:10.1038/mp.2008.94

Santa, T. M. (2020). The care of the soul. In T. Santa (Ed.), *Scrupulous anonymous* (Vol. 57, pp. 1–4). Liguori, MO: Liguori Publications. Retrieved from https://scrupulousanonymous.org/wp-content/uploads/2020/07/0820_SA_Web.pdf

Steinberg, D. S., & Wetterneck, C. T. (2017). OCD Taboo thoughts and stigmatizing attitudes in clinicians. *Community Mental Health Journal, 53*(3), 275–280. doi:10.1007/s10597-016-0055-x

Thakurta, R. G., Dhar, O. P. S. P., Sarkar, S., Ray, P., & Mallick, A. K. (2016). Prevalence and nature of sexual dysfunctions in OCD in a tertiary medical college. *Eastern Journal of Psychiatry, 17*(2), 120–130.

Tindle, J., & Tadi, P. (2020). Neuroanatomy, parasympathetic nervous system. In *StatPearls*. Treasure Island, FL: StatPearls Publishing.

Van Minnen, A., & Kampman, M. (2000). The interaction between anxiety and sexual functioning: A controlled study of sexual functioning in women with anxiety disorders. *Sexual & Relationship Therapy, 15*, 47–57. doi:10.1080/14681990050001556

Volk, F., Thomas, J., Sosin, L., Jacob, V., & Moen, C. (2016). Religiosity, developmental context, and sexual shame in pornography users: A serial mediation model. *Sexual Addiction & Compulsivity, 23*(2–3), 244–259. doi:10.1080/10720162.2016.1151391

Vulink, N. C., Denys, D., Bus, L., & Westenberg, H. G. (2006). Sexual pleasure in women with obsessive-compulsive disorder? *Journal of Affective Disorders, 91*(1), 19–25. doi:10.1016/j.jad.2005.12.006

Vuong, T. M., Gellatly, J., Lovell, K., & Bee, P. (2016). The experiences of help-seeking in people with obsessive compulsive disorder: An internet study. *The Cognitive Behaviour Therapist, 9*. Retrieved from https://www.semanticscholar.org/paper/The-experiences-of-help-seeking-in-people-with-an-Vuong-Gellatly/f94697e5f02fa062a585083cabb464b67414fea8

Weingarden, H., & Renshaw, K. D. (2015). Shame in the obsessive compulsive related disorders: A conceptual review. *Journal of Affective Disorders, 171*, 74–84. doi:10.1016/j.jad.2014.09.010

Williams, M., & Farris, S. G. (2011). Sexual orientation obsessions in obsessive–compulsive disorder: Prevalence and correlates. *Psychiatry Research, 187*(1–2), 156–159.

CHAPTER NINE

Saving the Planet: Scrupulous Hoarding and Green Guilt

Social and cultural problems change over time. People become involved in issues that affect the quality of life in the community. Certain social issues have never been solved such as world hunger, war, poverty, and the many unintended consequences of industrialization (i.e., effects on the environment, class divisions, etc.). Many idealists will take these social problems on as social justice efforts through vocational or volunteer work. Driven by altruistic tendencies, they feel a sense of reward for contributing to the greater good. The pattern for the scrupulous or moralous is adopting an all-or-nothing approach that often ends in burnout and guilt about dropping out of the cause they are trying to support. Scrupulous hoarding and "green guilt" are examples of extreme behaviors that are motivated by obsessiveness more than altruism.

Hoarding Disorder

Hoarding disorder (HD) was once considered a subtype of obsessive-compulsive disorder (OCD) as they have many overlapping beliefs and behaviors. It is now classified as its own disorder under the obsessive-compulsive spectrum disorder category in the DSM-V (American Psychiatric Association, 2013) with a prevalence range of 3–10% (Postlethwaite, Kellett, & Mataix-Cols, 2019).

Cognitive and behavioral challenges shared by both disorders are problems with decision-making, rigid thinking, disorganization and overorganization, overimportance of items, perfectionism, and not-just-right-experiences (NJREs).

Sam's office, while neat and tidy, is overorganized due to his trouble conceptualizing how to decide what paperwork goes where. When an item could fit into more than one category, he made copies and put them into individual folders. Instead of one file for insurance, he made individual files for car, medical, dental, and homeowner's insurance. Though this seemed like a perfect system, he had to add more filing cabinets and shelving, which ended up filling the "white space," meaning all the surfaces and areas were taken up with more and more boxes. On the other hand, Terry's home office is messy and disorganized, with dozens of dusty, unsorted files dating back more than a decade. When new mail and paperwork arrive, she puts them in the office to be looked at "later." When she becomes aware of the files piled on the floor and those on top of the desk, which are no longer visible, she becomes too overwhelmed to know where to start making decisions about how to organize them.

What distinguishes OCD and HD is that OCD is ego-dystonic whereas HD is ego-syntonic. People with OCD experience their obsessions as distressing and not in line with their identity and perform compulsions to reduce their distress. People who acquire and save items report experiencing positive emotions such as pleasure, safety, and comfort (Shaw et al., 2017), which subsequently reinforces collecting behaviors (Grisham & Barlow, 2005). On the other hand, people who hoard also have negative emotional reactivity associated with difficulties with discarding and acquisition (Shaw et al., 2017). People who hoard also overidentify with their possessions, feel a meaningful connection with them, and have little to no insight that they have a problem (Frost et al., 2018). Some people report that discarding any hoarded item is tantamount to losing a part of themselves. A psychologist has reported that hoarders tell him things like, "If I throw too much away, there'll be nothing left of me" (Smail, 2014).

A link between hoarding behaviors, scrupulosity, and moral emotions has been identified in clinical practice and in research findings. Some reasons offered for this connection include a sentimental and personal attachment to items, avoiding waste due to the potential practical use to the person or others in the future, being economical by buying multiple items on sale, reducing the ecological carbon footprint on the environment, and fulfilling the role of being good stewards of the earth. Their beliefs about the maximum usage of possessions have a prosocial quality in an age of environmental concern.

Some hoarders may have the trait known as pathological altruism (Oakley, Knafo, Madhavan, & Wilson, 2011) or empathic overdrive (Whitton, Henry, Grisham, & Rendell, 2012). They have a pattern of hoarding pets or animals because they feel compelled to provide shelter and take on the role of caretaker. They feel that "adopting" them is virtuous behavior. In reality, the amount of animals they collect makes it impossible to provide nurturing care (Frost, Patronek, & Rosenfield, 2011). Animal hoarders often live in squalid conditions and lack the ability to provide even minimal standards of nutrition, sanitation, and veterinary care. They often fail to acknowledge the deteriorating condition of the animals (including disease, starvation, and even death) and the household environment (severe overcrowding, very unsanitary conditions) as well as the negative effect of the collection on their own health and well-being and on that of other household members (Patronek, 2001) and (HARC, Animal Hoarding Research, at http://www.tufts.edu/vet/cfa/hoarding.html).

Evolutionary Biology

From an evolutionary standpoint, hoarding and OCD appear to originate from instinctive nesting behaviors (Taylor, 2017). Some OCD symptoms exhibit survival and preservation instinctual behaviors such as cleaning/washing for hygiene purposes, checking for safety reasons, and religion/morality to cope with existential anxiety (Aouizerate et al., 2004). Research conducted by neuroscientists explains that hoarding behaviors evolved from an overactivity of the adaptive instinct to save important items (Smail, 2014). Hoarding behavior has also been considered to be an evolutionary response to fears of deprivation and insecurity about having enough essential survival resources, which promotes compulsive checking behaviors meant to keep track of the level of supplies (Green, 1967). Terms such as "cocoon" and "bunker" have been used by people who hoard to describe their living environment (Frost & Steketee, 2010).

Feelings of guilt and shame are emotional reactions often resulting from a sense of wasting or mistreating objects (Frost, Steketee, & Tolin, 2012). These emotions stem from evolutionary and cultural forces, and they are experienced as intuitive judgments about morality (Haidt, 2001).

Another factor that may explain hoarding behavior is a reduced sensitivity to disgust and the ability to tolerate the deteriorating condition of things that would be reflexively aversive to others (Mataix-Cols et al., 2004).

Scrupulosity and Material Hoarding

Randy Frost, professor and academic researcher at Smith College, and colleagues have used the term "material scrupulosity" as a set of rigid and exaggerated beliefs about having a sense of moral obligation for the care, safety, and maximization of the use of possessions to prevent waste (Frost et al., 2018). When people feel they have fallen short of doing so, they experience feelings of guilt and believe that they have morally and personally failed to do their due diligence. The visual and emotional results of "rescuing" the items can range from mild to severe clutter and are evidence of having taken personal responsibility for the items' value (Frost et al., 2018).

The Measure of Material Scrupulosity (MOMS) assesses an individual's sense of morality around their reasons for hoarding (Frost et al., 2018). The measure is not only valuable for assessment; how each item is phrased helps inform clinicians about the mindset, thoughts, and emotional processes of people who suffer from this problem. The measure is helpful in teaching what questions to ask during the assessment process, although it does not provide a severity scale.

The following list is the items included in the MOMS:

1. I feel guilty about throwing things away.
2. I feel a sense of duty to my possessions.
3. I feel guilty about things I have wasted in the past.
4. My sense of duty toward my possessions interferes with my ability to enjoy things I would like to.
5. It is my responsibility to make sure objects are not wasted or destroyed.
6. Being unprepared (not having things I need) is a serious mistake.
7. I feel like a morally good person when I rescue objects from being wasted.
8. Even when I know I won't use something, I feel guilty about throwing it away.
9. I keep broken things because it feels morally wrong to waste them, even though I know I won't fix them.

Biblical Stewardship

Humanity's role as stewards of nature is referenced all the way back to Genesis: "And the LORD God took the man, and put him into the garden of Eden to dress it and to keep it" (Gen. 2:15). Over time, the religious and moral obligation to maintain the natural world has become more challenging as industrialization and technology have overrun natural habitats. The environmental movement and the crisis of climate change have affected the social mindset toward being more responsible consumers, but as is typical, even people with OCD as well as people who hoard take this responsibility to the literal extreme.

One rationale for scrupulous or moral hoarding may stem from the biblical lesson on the responsibility of humanity to be good stewards of the earth.

> And God blessed them. And God said to them, "Be fruitful and multiply and fill the earth and subdue it, and have dominion over the fish of the sea and over the birds of the heavens and over every living thing that moves on the earth." (Gen. 1:28)

Some religious beliefs hold God has instilled in people the responsibility for caretaking the earth and should be mindful of the influence human behavior has on the environment. The present research focuses on the religious stewardship belief and belief in a controlling god. Human stewardship and a controlling god are commonly endorsed in many religions, especially Abrahamic religions. The belief in a controlling god suggests that God is the agent (e.g., lord or master) who exerts powerful control over the world and intervenes in the affairs of humans (e.g., Isa. 40:23; Rom. 9:15–16; Qur'an 16:70).

Stewardship refers to the roles of humankind as stewards who are responsible to take care of the world created by a god. For example, Christianity highlights God's ownership of the world and all living things and his command for humans to look after it (e.g., Gen. 2:15; Lev. 25:23; Psalm 24:1). (). Similar teachings also appear in Islam, emphasizing that humans are *khala'ifa* (successors and stewards) upon the earth that Allah created (e.g., Qur'an 6:165; 2:60) (Saniotis, 2012).

Research suggests that belief in an external controlling god decreases a sense of personal control over outcomes (Kay, Gaucher, Napier, Callan, & Laurin, 2008). Accordingly, people may view that a god is in charge of all the matters in the end, including environmental problems. When misdeeds are attributed to external rather than internal factors, the wrongdoers are less likely to be blamed and may feel relatively free from environmental responsibility (Cullen, Link, Wolfe, & Frank, 1985; Stroessner & Green, 1990). One study showed that people whoconsidered god as authoritarian and controlling,were associated with lower perceived importance of preserving nature and animals (Johnson et al., 2017). When people hold beliefs in external sources of control, such as belief in fate (Chan & Tam, 2021) and belief in scientific progress (Meijers & Rutjens, 2014), they also hold weaker pro-environmental orientations. These findings suggest that belief in potent external determinants often undermines pro-environmental motivation.

Based on the reasoning that stewardship belief and belief in a controlling god have contrasting implications for human responsibility to the world, it is suggested that environmental guilt is a psychological mediator that unifies the opposing effects involving stewardship belief versus belief in a controlling god. Guilt is an emotion that primarily results from a sense of responsibility for harmful actions (Ellsworth & Smith, 1988; Wohl, Branscombe, & Klar, 2006; Zeelenberg & Breugelmans, 2008) and a key element within many religions used as a motivational tool for the religious to maintain their spirituality and morality in particular (Narramore, 1974). Importantly, research shows that environmental guilt is an important emotional driver of proenvironmental actions (Ferguson & Branscombe, 2010; Tam, 2019). A study that examined the role of the sense of personal stewardship versus the belief in a controlling god predicted that environmental guilt occurs in opposing ways. It found that having a stewardship belief positively reinforced the sense of guilt that motivated the subjects to tend to the health of the earth, while less guilt was found in those with a belief in a controlling god negatively affected), elief that a god controls and determines theevents in the world according to his plan) and this guilt, in turn, predicts individuals' pro-environmental support (see for the hypothesized model). The present research advances an understanding of how religiosity influences proenvironmentalism by focusing on the roles of stewardship beliefs and beliefs about god's control. Stewardship is about human responsibility to the world designated by a god, promoting proenvironmental attitudes and behaviors, stewardship belief positively, whereas belief in a controlling god negatively, predicted environmental guilt, which, in turn, predicted greater proenvironmental support (Eom, Tok, Saad, & Kim, 2021). Environmental guilt, in turn, predicted greater behavioral commitment to environmental sustainability.

In both articles, relevant bible verses were included to bolster the arguments, such as, "They will neither harm nor destroy on all my holy mountain, for the earth will be full of the knowledge of the LORD as the waters cover the sea" (Isa. 11:9) for the stewardship condition and "The day is yours, and yours also the night; you established the sun and moon. It was you who set all the boundaries of the earth; you made both summer and winter" (Psalm 74:16–17) for the controlling god condition.

We provided support for a mediation model where stewardship belief positively predicted environmental guilt, whereas belief in a controlling god negatively predicted environmental guilt—which, in turn, predicted greater pro-environmental support (Eom, Tok, Saad, & Kim, 2021).

Natural Disaster Preparation

Natural disasters are catastrophic and can be traumatic. People often want to know why they happen or what caused them. Some Christian faiths believe in the prophecy that the catastrophic events are a sign of the belief in end-times prophesy (eschatology) (Burley, 2017). Some believers consider their occurrences as a sign of God's displeasure with and punishment for people who sin, that the righteous will be protected from harm during these events, and have a plan for survival. People's fear of death may become more present in their lives and interfere with focusing on the control they have in the present.

A thesis written about what views religious organizations have toward natural disaster preparedness (Hesse, 2012). The study found that Latter Day Saints, Jehovah's Witnesses, Orthodox Jews, and Lutherans encourage readiness efforts on the part of individuals rather than on the group (Hesse, 2012). Some religious organizations focus on how families should secure survival items in their homes and others focus more on providing material and social support for their religious communities and beyond.

Along with the anxiety about the uncertain future or the end-times, the anxiety for those Christians and people of other faiths with scrupulosity is likely to be many levels higher and can become the focus of obsessive fears. Traits such as an excessive sense of responsibility, obsessive sense of obligation to protect others, and fear of death drive the scrupulous and moral perfectionists into saving themselves and others as their mission.

The followers of the Church of Jesus Christ of Latter-Day Saints (LDS) have a tradition of storing enough food, water, emergency supplies, and money in their homes to last for at least three months and up to a year for the good of the family and others in the community (Bruner, 2020; https://www.churchofjesuschrist.org/study/manual/gospel-topics/food-storage?lang=eng). "Organize yourselves; prepare every needful thing" (Book of Mormon, Doctrine and Covenants, 88: 119. P. 173). By being prepared with a basic supply of food, water, and monetary savings, a family can survive short-term and long-term adversities while being a resource to others in their community (Bruner, 2020; Morris, 2019).

Jehovah's Witnesses are encouraged to be ready for disasters because they believe the end of the world is approaching. They claim that Jesus said events were going to happen towards the end and that they need to be prepared. Some congregants have advice for what to have ready and began marketing "go bags" that the items are put in, including the bible, and there is a website that provides instructions (https://www.jw.org/en/library/magazines/awake-no5-2017-october/disaster-steps-that-can-save-lives/#link0).

Mormons Who Hoard

The author of a magazine article, who is a Latter-Day Saint, described how the practice of storing housing and food items has generated a cottage industry of do-it-yourself instructions for food preservation and building storage space (Coppins, 2020). On a website known for its "boards," the LDS offers ideas for food storage (https://www.pinterest.com/pin/322993223133629541/).

Moral Emotions

> "I have a duty to reduce, reuse, recycle, and maintain my vigilance about keeping the smallest environmental carbon footprint as possible."

In 1976, Congress passed the Resource Conservation and Recovery Act to increase recycling and to promote conservation efforts to control the increasing level of material waste (United States Environmental Protection Agency, 1976). It is believed that the slogan "reduce, reuse, recycle" was born at this time. In 1971, Oregon instated the first "bottle bill" that instated a ten-cent returnable deposit when the bottle was redeemed (https://www.oregon.gov/deq/recycling/Pages/Bottle-Bill.aspx). Since then, the movement to preserve the environment and control climate change has grown exponentially and increasingly justifies behaviors for conscientious hoarders.

The term "green guilt" characterizes the uncomfortable feeling that some people experience when they believe that they could and should be doing more to preserve the environment than they are (Jensen, 2019). "Ecoguilt" is another emotion felt "when you could have done something for the environment, but consciously made the decision not to" (https://eco18.com/feeling-the-green-guilt/).

Uta's scrupulosity and contamination OCD has her in a bind. Because of her fear of germs, she takes long showers at night to wash off all the dirt from the day. She feels guilty about how much water she is using and tries to make them shorter, but her anxiety is too high. When she is finished, she makes sure to shut the water off so it doesn't drip. When she feels unsure, she turns the water on again and forces the handle to shut tight. If she is having a bad day, she will repeat this action until she feels "right." She does the same things with the sink faucets. On several occasions, she has shut them with such force that they have broken off.

An interesting development in the industrial sector intended to better control carbon emissions was the ability to purchase voluntary carbon offsets by investing in renewable energy, energy efficiency, forest protection, and other projects that either reduce emissions or sequester planet-warming CO_2 as "pollution penance" (Kotchen, 2009, p. 29). Kotchen compares this transaction to the purchasing of indulgences by Christians in the Middle Ages, which provided the ability to buy a way out of religious guilt but did not necessarily reduce the problem behaviors (Kotchen, 2009).

A survey of households was conducted about factors that contributed to feelings of green guilt (Viscusi, Huber, & Bell, 2011). Guilt about the unnecessary use of plastic was reported by 78% of the respondents, 72% reported guilt for wasting food, 57% for wasting products, and 36% for excessive energy consumption use (Viscusi et al., 2011). Plastic bags, plastic containers, and plastic items of all kinds overfill the drawers, cabinets, and pantries of "green guilt" hoarders.

Erica was furious when she saw a plastic straw in the trash. She summoned her family and wanted to know who the culprit was. Her family, not unfamiliar with these inquisitions, looked at her blankly as she lectured them on the virtues of reusing or repurposing items like these. In fact, she was saving straws to use in a sculpture idea she had in mind.

Similar to deontological guilt, "anticipation guilt" is motivated by the urge to be helpful in order to prevent feeling negative emotions and was found to mediate the relationship between environmental concerns and recycling (Erlandsson, Jungstrand, & Västfjäll, 2016). Similarly, a study on anticipated emotions found that the intention of making a pro-environmental act produced a positive anticipated emotional state compared to anticipating one's negative emotional state from inaction (Schneider, Zaval, Weber, & Markowitz, 2017).

Hoarding behaviors have also been found to be motivated by guilt and moral concerns over how wasteful behavior contributes to a larger "contaminating" carbon footprint that negatively impacts the environment. Moral beliefs, moral reasoning, and moral emotions have been associated with hoarding and scrupulosity, especially around the issue of waste (Nelson, Abramowitz, Whiteside, & Deacon, 2006). Wasteful behaviors have been considered moral transgressions even if the items are unusable and impractical (Nelson et al., 2006). Emotions appear to reinforce saving behaviors even if the person is unable to rationalize any practical purpose for keeping them.

Though living "green" is a healthy lifestyle, higher environmental consciousness and behaviors lead to feeling more green guilt. Even people with OCD who don't hoard obsessively think, "Am I being 'green' enough? Do I abide by the standards set to reduce, reuse, and recycle?" These factors contribute to the development of dysfunctional beliefs about identity, responsibility, memory, and control over personal possessions, which, in turn, result in negative emotional reactions such as sadness, anxiety, guilt, shame, and anger when possessions are discarded (Steketee & Frost, 2013). For some people, the acquisition of new possessions results in temporary relief from negative emotions and short-term exhilaration or heightened self-esteem (Lawrence, Ciorciari, & Kyrios, 2014a).

Rowan's house and yard are cluttered with items he has saved and "rescued" over the years. The yard is an eyesore for neighbors, who only see it as a place filled with weatherworn and neglected trash. Rowan does not seem to be aware of how the yard appears to others, and even if he did, he would say that the higher order is not to add to landfills. He believes that there may be uses for them later, such as the flatcar tires that are leaning on the side of the house, the rusty and broken lawnmower he dragged in from the sidewalk that he has never used, and the swing set he found for his grandchildren, who are grown and gone. He has piles of returnable bottles he has taken home from being out in the community.

Emotional Issues

People who hoard and are scrupulous experience intense emotions. Even though hoarding behaviors are experienced as ego-syntonic and feel pleasure from finding and collecting things, people also suffer from emotions such as anxiety, anger, sadness, disgust, regret, guilt, and shame from hoarding behaviors (Steketee & Frost, 2013). People who hoard sense that their negative emotions signal that keeping items is the right thing to do and that not doing so would be committing an immoral act (Lit, 2017). Likewise, the positive feelings experienced from acquiring new items the cycle of compulsive acquisition (Kyrios, 2013).

An emotional and moral dialectic is held when the person who hoards has both positive feelings for safekeeping the items and, at the same time, have feelings of guilt and shame due to the negative effect these behaviors have on the family (Lawrence, Ciorciari, & Kyrios, 2014b; Lit, 2017). Some of the consequences for families include being emotionally affected by the pathological disorder of the environment, being overwhelmed by limited mobility around the house due to the volume of items that take up space, and a lack of socializing within the house, such as children not being able to have play dates in their homes due to shame and embarrassment about what the house looks like. In the most extreme cases, there are also concerns about health and safety.

There is a tendency to feel guilty about throwing away gifts and other items given by other people. The person feels he is betraying those who gave the gifts and the sentiments the person had in choosing and giving the objects. The person may feel the behavior means he doesn't care about that person anymore. He has a fear that the giver has an expectation that the gift will be kept permanently to be cherished forever.

Now an empty nester, Lena's family has convinced her to sell her house and downsize into a two-bedroom condo. Among many other things, she has saved all her three children's greeting cards since they were babies. They take up several bins in the basement, and she has them organized in perfect chronological order. She is heartbroken about the thought of not having them as a complete set of special occasion memories. She feels guilty about throwing them away because she worries her children will think those memories aren't important, even though they have pleaded with her throughout the years to let them go. When her son sat with her to begin dehoarding the house, rather than dumping them into the trash can, she felt the need to tell the story of every card. They worked for an hour while her son abided Lena's tearful recounting the memories of the five cards she was willing to throw away.

Cognitive Issues—Thought-Action Fusion

HD and OCD share the distorted cognitive domains of the overimportance of thoughts, inflated responsibility, TAF-M, and perfectionism (Frost & Steketee, 2010). Other shared cognitive features involved are a style of rigid moral reasoning (Lit, 2017) and dichotomous moral thinking and rule-following about right and wrong, resulting in overwhelming feelings of guilt and shame (Frost & Steketee, 2010; Mancini & Gangemi, 2015).

People who hoard seem to either be so used to the environment that they don't notice how chaotic it is or are too overwhelmed and in denial about it. Some other cognitive issues that contribute to the problem arise from deficits in processing information, memory, decision-making, and organization due to the accumulation of clutter and the chaotic appearance of living spaces that are said to add to the difficulty of discarding and inhibit the effective organization of possessions (Timpano, Smith, Yang, & Çek, 2014).

Personality Traits

Obsessive-compulsive personality disorder (OCPD) has traits common with or that coexist with scrupulosity and hoarding, such as moral perfectionism, cognitive rigidity, and issues around the need for control (Lit, 2017). Conscientiousness, one of the identified traits in the five-factor model (FFM) of personality domains, consists of competence, order, dutifulness, achievement-striving, self-discipline, and cautious deliberation (Costa & McCrae, 1995). Overconscientiousness has been considered a maladaptive trait in OCPD (Samuel & Widiger, 2011). The healthy aspects of conscientiousness become overvalued in OCPD wherein competence becomes (a) pathological striving toward perfection; (b) orderliness as an obsession with cleanliness and order; (c) dutifulness as an obsession with attaining moral behavioral standards; (d) achievement as an obsession with achievement and perfection in work-related tasks; (e) self-discipline as doggedness, evinced by single-minded, rigid determination; (f) cautiousness as ruminative deliberation; and (g) a tendency to overthink and stall action to avoid unwanted or uncertain outcomes (Samuel & Widiger, 2011).

Being scrupulous and rigid about matters of morality and having difficulty throwing things away are two other diagnostic features of OCPD (American Psychiatric Association, 2013), and all have been found to be significantly correlated (Mataix-Cols, Baer, Rauch, & Jenike, 2000; Siev, Steketee, Fama, & Wilhelm, 2011). Perfectionism, over-responsibility, and the need for control are also common in all three problems (Frost & Steketee, 1998).

Making mistakes is unacceptable. For the scrupulous, being perfect and avoiding mistakes eliminates the possibility of committing sins. With hoarding, the sense of material stewardship, maintaining complete sets of collected items, and preserving items of sentimental value are rigid rule-based feelings and behaviors. People with OCPD mistrust others to take care of the task at hand and burden themselves to make sure it is done in the "right" and "perfect" way. As a result, indecisiveness and procrastination interfere with solving problems due to a need to make the "right" and perfect choice, as if there was only one. People fear they may regret their decision of discarding items. Once a decision is set in motion, some people always feel that the other decision was probably the better one.

Other Contributing Factors and Concerns

Creativity

Some people who hoard have an "eye" for the aesthetic value of an object. This desire can manifest in creative reuse of discarded items that are found on the street or elsewhere, finding a good home a "good home" for found items, and having an intention of donating found and saved items. The result is an overly laborious and perfectionistic process to get rid of virtually anything that can be "used to their full potential and not wasted" (p. 148) and for making sure they come to no harm (Tolin, Frost, & Steketee, 2013).

Pierre rents storage space after receiving an ultimatum from his husband, Juan, that he will start throwing things away if any more stuff comes into the apartment. Juan was aware of Pierre's tendency to collect items put out in the trash for making art pieces. Pierre has an eye for items that would hang well for making mobiles. Pierre called this behavior "rescuing abandoned artwork." Pierre has sold several items and feels it is a virtue to see the beauty that others don't. Before their marriage, Pierre had a room with his overflowing art supplies. Since living together, the designated space in the den where Pierre works began running out of room and started to seep into the rest of the common space.

Juan tries to be supportive and is a fan of Pierre's work, especially when it brings in some income. Pierre always has a good reason for the items he brings home. Part of the problem is that he has more ideas than time to complete them. Any semblance of order is lost to the volume of items piled on top of each other. It is unclear if Pierre even remembers what is underneath, but he insists he needs all of what he has collected.

Although it is not the best solution, they agreed to rent a storage space for Pierre to keep his collected items and other accessories he uses for making his art because his stuff was encroaching on the last livable space in the apartment. A date was set for the move and Pierre was overwhelmed by how to start organizing so many things. After reading some material on how to sort through clutter, a "keeping" pile, a "maybe" pile, and a discard pile were set up. Pierre began reminiscing about where he found the items and ideas about what he is going to do with them. Whenever he picked something up and had to make a decision about what to do with it, he not only felt bad about the loss of its potential beauty but he also felt guilty about adding to it in the discard pile, essentially adding it to a landfill.

Fear of Loss of Memories or Information

Fear of losing one's memories by discarding objects speaks to how much they are a part of the person's identity. Even though they may not have remembered, seen, or needed the items, they have a sense of loss and grief.

Information and personal correspondence are so readily and easily available on the internet. People who want information, especially if they have OCD, conduct thorough searches of an item and then have so much information that they become paralyzed about deciding what to keep and want to save all of it. The fear is that what is not saved will be the most valuable.

Work and personal emails are also a source of excessive saving. Along with the fear that something important will be lost, personal emails have sentimental value and are incorporated as a part of people's identities. Spam and unwanted emails are left in the inbox because people feel the need to read each of them, just like saved hard copies of newspapers and magazines, for fear of information loss. As there are too many to read and take care of, the inbox only gets bigger and more overwhelming.

References

American Psychiatric Association. (2013). *Diagnostic and statistical manual of mental disorders* (5th ed.). Washington, DC: Author.

Aouizerate, B., Guehl, D., Cuny, E., Rougier, A., Bioulac, B., Tignol, J., & Burbaud, P. (2004). Pathophysiology of obsessive-compulsive disorder: A necessary link between phenomenology, neuropsychology, imagery and physiology. *Progress in Neurobiology, 72*(3), 195–221. doi:10.1016/j.pneurobio.2004.02.004

Bruner, R. (2020, August 28). *What all Mormons should know about food storage.* Retrieved from https://www.learnreligions.com/food-storage-why-what-how-2159413

Burley, M. (2017). Dislocating the Eschaton? Appraising Realized Eschatology. *Sophia*, 56, 435–452. doi:10.1007/s11841-016-0534-0

Chan, H. W., & Tam, K. P. (2021). Do people's assumptions about the social world matter? The effects of social axioms on environmental attitude and efficacy beliefs. *Journal of Environmental Psychology, 75*, 101598.

Coppins, M. (2020). The stockpile of food in my garage. *The Atlantic.* Retrieved from https://www.theatlantic.com/politics/archive/2020/03/stockpile-food-my-garage/608290/

Costa, P. T., & McCrae, R. R. (1995). Domains and facets: Hierarchical personality assessment using the revised NEO personality inventory. *Journal of Personality Assessment, 64*(1), 21–50. doi:10.1207/s15327752jpa6401_2

Cullen, F. T., Link, B. G., Wolfe, N. T., & Frank, J. (1985). The social dimensions of correctional officer stress. *Justice Quarterly, 2*(4), 505–533. doi:10.1080/07418828500088711.

Ellsworth, P. C., & Smith, C. A. (1988). From appraisal to emotion: Differences among unpleasant feelings. *Motivation and Emotion, 12*(3), 271–302.

Eom, K., Tok, T. Q. H., Saad, C. S., & Kim, H. S. (2021). Religion, environmental guilt, and pro-environmental support: The opposing pathways of stewardship belief and belief in a controlling god. *Journal of Environmental Psychology, 78*, 101717. doi:10.1016/j.jenvp.2021.101717

Erlandsson, A., Jungstrand, A. Å., & Västfjäll, D. (2016). Anticipated guilt for not helping and anticipated warm glow for helping are differently impacted by personal responsibility to help. *Frontiers in Psychology, 7*, 1475. doi:10.3389/fpsyg.2016.01475

Ferguson, M. A., & Branscombe, N. R. (2010). Collective guilt mediates the effect of beliefs about global warming on willingness to engage in mitigation behavior. *Journal of Environmental Psychology, 30*(2), 135–142. doi:10.1016/j.jenvp.2009.11.010.

Frost, R. O., Gabrielson, I., Deady, S., Dernbach, K. B., Guevara, G., Peebles-Dorin, M., . . . Grisham, J. R. (2018). Scrupulosity and hoarding. *Comprehensive Psychiatry, 86*, 19–24. doi:10.1016/j.comppsych.2018.06.011

Frost, R. O., Patronek, G., & Rosenfield, E. (2011). Comparison of object and animal hoarding. *Depression and Anxiety, 28*(10), 885–891.

Frost, R. O., & Steketee, G. (1998). Hoarding: Clinical aspects and treatment strategies. In M. Jenike, L. Baer, & W. E. Minichiello (Eds.), *Obsessive compulsive disorders: Practical management* (3rd ed., pp. 533–554). St. Louis, MO: Mosby.

Frost, R. O., & Steketee, G. (2010). *Stuff: Compulsive hoarding and the meaning of things*. Boston, MA: Houghton Mifflin Harcourt.

Frost, R. O., Steketee, G., & Tolin, D. F. (2012). Diagnosis and assessment of hoarding disorder. *Annual Review of Clinical Psychology, 8*, 219–242.

Green, A. (1967). Metapsychology of obsessional neurosis. *Revue Française de Psychanalyse, 31*(4), 629–646. Retrieved from http://www.ncbi.nlm.nih.gov/entrez/query.fcgi?cmd=Retrieve&db=PubMed&dopt=Citation&list_uids=5602312

Grisham, J. R., & Barlow, D. H. (2005). Compulsive hoarding: Current research and theory. *Journal of Psychopathology and Behavioral Assessment, 27*(1), 45–52.

Haidt, J. (2001). The emotional dog and its rational tail: A social intuitionist approach to moral judgment. *Psychological Review, 108*(4), 814.

Hesse, D. (2012). *Disaster Preparedness and Response Among Religious Organizations.* Master of Arts, University of Alabama Tuscaloosa.

Jensen, T. (2019). *Ecologies of guilt in environmental rhetorics.* New York, NY: Springer.

Johnson, K. A., Liu, R. L., Minton, E. A., Bartholomew, D. E., Peterson, M., Cohen, A. B., & Kees, J. (2017). US citizens' representations of God and support for sustainability policies. *Journal of Public Policy & Marketing, 36*(2), 362–378.

Kay, A. C., Gaucher, D., Napier, J. L., Callan, M. J., & Laurin, K. (2008). God and the government: Testing a compensatory control mechanism for the support of external systems. *Journal of Personality and Social Psychology, 95*(1), 18.

Kotchen, M. J. (2009). Offsetting green guilt. *Stanford Social Innovation Review, 7*(2), 26–31.

Kyrios, M. (2013). *Psychological models of compulsive hoarding.* In R. O. Frost, & G. Steketee (Eds.), *The Oxford handbook of hoarding and acquiring* (pp. 206–220). Oxford, UK: Oxford University Press.

Lawrence, L. M., Ciorciari, J., & Kyrios, M. (2014a). Cognitive processes associated with compulsive buying behaviours and related EEG coherence. *Psychiatry Research, 221*(1), 97–103. doi:10.1016/j.pscychresns.2013.10.005

Lawrence, L. M., Ciorciari, J., & Kyrios, M. (2014b). Relationships that compulsive buying has with addiction, obsessive-compulsiveness, hoarding, and depression. *Comprehensive Psychiatry, 55*(5), 1137–1145. doi:10.1016/j.comppsych.2014.03.005

Lit, K. (2017). *Moral reasoning and moral emotions linking hoarding and scrupulosity* (PhD dissertation). Nova Southeastern Univeristy. Retrieved from https://nsuworks.nova.edu/cps_stuetd/111

Mancini, F., & Gangemi, A. (2015). Deontological guilt and obsessive compulsive disorder. *Journal of Behavior Therapy and Experimental Psychiatry, 49*(Part B), 157–163. doi:doi:10.1016/j.jbtep.2015.05.003

Mataix-Cols, D., Baer, L., Rauch, S. L., & Jenike, M. A. (2000). Relation of factor-analyzed symptom dimensions of obsessive-compulsive disorder to personality disorders. *Acta Psychiatrica Scandinavica, 102*(3), 199–202.

Mataix-Cols, D., Wooderson, S., Lawrence, N., Brammer, M. J., Speckens, A., & Phillips, M. L. (2004). Distinct neural correlates of washing, checking, and hoarding symptom dimensions in obsessive-compulsive disorder. *Archives of General Psychiatry, 61*(6), 564–576.

Meijers, M. H., & Rutjens, B. T. (2014). Affirming belief in scientific progress reduces environmentally friendly behaviour. *European Journal of Social Psychology, 44*(5), 487–495.

Morris, P. (2019). Temporal and spiritual self-reliance: The Church of Jesus Christ of Latter-Day Saints and development in the South Pacific. *Sites: A Journal of Social Anthropology and Cultural Studies, 16*(1), 70–94.

Narramore, S. B. (1974). Guilt: Where theology and psychology meet. *Journal of Psychology and Theology, 2*(1), 18–25.

Nelson, E., Abramowitz, J. S., Whiteside, S., & Deacon, B. (2006). Scrupulosity in patients with obsessive-compulsive disorder: Relationship to clinical and cognitive phenomena. *Journal of Anxiety Disorders, 20*(8), 1071–1086. doi:10.1016/j.janxdis.2006.02.001.

Oakley, B., Knafo, A., Madhavan, G., & Wilson, D. S. (Eds.). (2011). *Pathological altruism.* New York, NY: Oxford University Press.

Patronek, G. (2001). The problem of animal hoarding. *Municipal Lawyer, 19*(6), 19.

Postlethwaite, A., Kellett, S., & Mataix-Cols, D. (2019). Prevalence of hoarding disorder: A systematic review and meta-analysis. *Journal of Affective Disorders, 256*, 309–316.

Samuel, D. B., & Widiger, T. A. (2011). Conscientiousness and obsessive-compulsive personality disorder. *Personality Disorders: Theory, Research, and Treatment, 2*(3), 161–174. doi:10.1037/a0021216

Saniotis, A. (2012). Muslims and ecology: Fostering Islamic environmental ethics. *Contemporary Islam, 6*(2). Retrieved from https://www.researchgate.net/publication/257695114_Muslims_and_ecology_Fostering_Islamic_environmental_ethics

Schneider, C. R., Zaval, L., Weber, E. U., & Markowitz, E. M. (2017). The influence of anticipated pride and guilt on pro-environmental decision making. *PLoS ONE, 12*(11), e0188781. doi:10.1371/journal.pone.0188781

Shaw, A., Marie, Timpano, K., R., Britton, J., C., Carver, C., S., Doss, B., D., & Levin, B. (2017). *The role of negative and positive emotional reactions in hoarding symptomatology* (Doctoral dissertation). University of Miami. Retrieved from https://scholarship.miami.edu/discovery/delivery/01UOML_INST:AlmaGeneralView/12355321740002976

Siev, J., Steketee, G., Fama, J. M., & Wilhelm, S. (2011). Cognitive and clinical characteristics of sexual and religious obsessions. *Journal of Cognitive Psychotherapy, 25*(3), 167–176. doi:10.1891/0889-8391.25.3.167

Smail, D. L. (2014). Neurohistory in action: Hoarding and the human past. *Isis; An International Review Devoted to the History of Science and Its Cultural Influences, 105*(1), 110–122. doi:10.1086/675553

Steketee, G., & Frost, R. O. (2013). *Treatment for hoarding disorder: Therapist guide.* Oxford, UK: Oxford University Press.

Stroessner, S. J., & Green, C. W. (1990). Effects of belief in free will or determinism on attitudes toward punishment and locus of control. *The Journal of Social Psychology, 130*(6), 789–799. doi:10.1080/00224545.1990.9924631

Tam, K. P. (2019). Anthropomorphism of nature, environmental guilt, and pro-environmental behavior. *Sustainability, 11*(19), 5430.

Taylor, J. (2017). *The role of emotion regulation in compulsive hoarding.* Hawthorn, VIC, Australia: School of Health Sciences, Department of Psychological Sciences Swinburne University of Technology.

Timpano, K. R., Smith, A. M., Yang, J. C., & Çek, D. (2014). Information processing. In *The Oxford handbook of hoarding and acquiring* (pp. 100–119). New York, NY: Oxford University Press.

Tolin, D., Frost, R. O., & Steketee, G. (2013). *Buried in treasures: Help for compulsive acquiring, saving, and hoarding.* New York, NY: Oxford University Press.

United States Environmental Protection Agency. (1976). *Resource conservation and recovery act*. Washington, DC: Author. Retrieved from https://www.epa.gov/rcra

Viscusi, W. K., Huber, J., & Bell, J. (2011). Promoting recycling: Private values, social norms, and economic incentives. *American Economic Review, 101*(3), 65–70.

Whitton, A., Henry, J., Grisham, J., & Rendell, P. (2012, September 13–17)). *Hoarding, excessive responsibility and pathological guilt: Symptoms of empathy in overdrive?* 16th World Congress of Psychophysiology of the International Organization of Psychophysiology (IOP), Pisa, Italy. Retrieved from https://www.researchgate.net/publication/233858909_Hoarding_excessive_responsibility_and_pathological_guilt_Symptoms_of_empathy_in_overdrive

Wohl, M., Branscombe, N. R., & Klar, Y. (2006). Collective guilt: Emotional reactions when one's group has done wrong or been wronged. *European Review of Social Psychology, 17*(1), 1–37. doi:10.1080/10463280600574815

Zeelenberg, M., & Breugelmans, S. M. (2008). The role of interpersonal harm in distinguishing regret from guilt. *Emotion, 8*(5), 589–596. doi:10.1037/a0012894

CHAPTER TEN

Created This Way: Neurobiology and Evolutionary Overview

This chapter provides perspectives on the neurobiological and evolutionary functions of the brain and the moral emotions related to obsessions that were not covered in the previous chapters. The most up-to-date findings have been provided from the ever-evolving developments that enhance our understanding of the interplay between the brain, mind, and emotions involved in the conscience-related aspect of obsessive-compulsive disorder (OCD). Presently, the findings on these neural connections are preliminary as they have yet to be well replicated.

Neurotheology

Neurotheology focuses on identifying the connections between neurological and evolutionary traits that are believed to explain subjective experiences that occur from religious or spiritual practices (Shukla, Acharya, & Rajput, 2013). Though no specific "God spot" has been identified in the brain, evolutionary biology explains that the increasing capacity of the limbic system was conducive to developing a metaphysical consciousness.

The limbic system consists of the frontal cortex (decision-making), hypothalamus (regulates autonomic processes), hippocampus (cognition and memory), amygdala (cognition and emotions), thalamus (sensory and motor), basal ganglia (cognition, emotion, and movement), and cingulate gyrus (older part of the brain's fight or flight function—survival adaptation). It is thought that as the brain evolved, the increased size of the cerebral cortex came to dominate the more primitive function of the limbic system that regulates emotion as well as overtaking the most primitive brain-stem structures of the hypothalamus, which is responsible for regulating the autonomic nervous system (Ashbrook, 1984). The phenomena of religion and God are believed to have emerged out of the competing functions of the prefrontal cortex's rational mind, the subjective emotions expressed by the limbic system, and the fight/flight survival functions of the thalamus.

Debates abound about the causal relationship between biology and theology. Is religion an artifact of brain circuitry, or did God create religion that manifests in the common brain areas? As stated previously, there is an interesting parallel between what can and cannot be quantified by science or religion as proof over one or the other.

Neurobiology

Executive Functioning

Briefly, OCD and moral emotions exist in the prefrontal cortex (PFC), the "brain's brain," where executive functions are processed for goal-directed behavior, decision-making, and judgments (Serpell & Esposito, 2016). Executive functioning is responsible for perception, response selection, working memory, episodic memory, problem-solving, selective attention, self-control, cognitive flexibility, and reasoning (Diamond & Ling, 2020). Clearly OCD causes problems in each of these functions and can cause distractibility, behavioral urges to restore a feeling of moral standing, problems with planning, rigid thinking, and irrational reasoning.

Within the executive functioning system, OCD has been mapped as a cortico-striatal-thalamic-cortical neurocircuit that fires off a sense of threat followed by emotional responses to intangible obsessive triggers (Dougherty et al., 2018). This circuit links areas that have important roles in the executive function and regulation of behavior (Saxena, Bota, & Brody, 2001) and likely mediates OCD symptoms (Chamberlain, Blackwell, Fineberg, Robbins, & Sahakian, 2005). They include cortical and subcortical regions and the white matter tracts that link them (de Salles Andrade et al., 2019).

OCD involves circuits from areas in the frontal cortex. The orbitofrontal cortex is responsible for context-related processing and response inhibition. The dorsolateral prefrontal cortex is where working memory is processed. The anterior cingulate cortex monitors emotions and reward. It is the cingulate gyrus that triggers someone with OCD with the sense that something bad will happen if compulsions aren't performed (Vahabzadeh & McDougle, 2014).

Another identified area is the basal ganglia, which plays a role in executive functioning, behaviors, and emotions (Lanciego, Luquin, & Obeso, 2012). The neural circuits underlying OCD are thought to involve frontal and cingulate cortices, as well as the caudate nucleus and thalamus (Aouizerate et al., 2004), implicating basal ganglia circuitry required for reward-dependent learning (Kreitzer & Malenka, 2008).

The neurotransmitters serotonin, dopamine, glutamate, and gamma-aminobutyric acid are also found to be active in OCD, religion, spirituality, and meditation (Borg, Andrée, Anckarsäter, & Farde, 2003; Newberg, Pourdehnad, Alavi, & d'Aquili, 2003). Interestingly, the findings of Borg and colleagues suggested that those who are more spiritual are biologically more predisposed to anxiety (Borg et al., 2003).

The Conscience

The conscience is more of a construct that captures the moral spirit. This includes the emotions of guilt, shame, sympathy, and empathy (Tangney, Stuewig, & Mashek, 2007). Shame and guilt are emotions felt from having made moral lapses and misjudgments (Shweder et al., 1997). Different neuronal networks have been identified for altruistic and deontological guilt, with the insula selectively being activated during deontological guilt situations (Basile et al., 2011).

The emotion "excessive empathy" was introduced in the previous chapter, and the impact of "empathic stress" was studied to measure the physiological potential it may have in "contaminating" the stress system and compromising our well-being (Engert, Plessow, Miller, Kirschbaum, & Singer, 2014). People with hoarding disorder demonstrate these emotions when discarding sentimental items.

Empathic stress is described as a "full blown physiological stress response" (Engert et al., 2014, p. 192) that arises solely by observing someone else undergoing a stressful situation. When this occurs in someone with OCD, the hypothalamic-pituitary-adrenal axis and overlapping ventral fronto-limbic circuits increase cortisol levels as measured by the Interpersonal Reactivity Index (Engert et al., 2014), which found a relationship between empathy and OCD symptom dimensions (Fontenelle et al., 2009).

Moral emotions, compared to anger and sadness, are active in the brain's prefrontal cortex (Harrison et al., 2012), such as the cingulate gyrus, caudate nucleus, medial frontal cortex, the amygdala, the insula (Saxena & Rauch, 2000), basal ganglia, and the thalamus (Lanciego et al., 2012).

Research on the areas that comprise the prefrontal cortex have mixed findings as to whether there is a specific function for each region, or whether there is a synergistic relationship between them.

Evolutionary Biology

The religious belief developed as a concept to address existential questions, mortality, and fear of the unknown, and it developed rituals as a way to communicate with forces beyond our control. One factor created over the course of evolution was developing pattern-processing capabilities that developed as a result of the expansion of the cerebral cortex, particularly the prefrontal cortex and regions involved in the processing of images (Kapogiannis et al., 2009). The evolving brain created networks responsible for social cognition, language, and logical reasoning (Bulbulia, 2004). Religious cognition likely emerged from a synchronous combination of these several evolutionarily important cognitive processes (Boyer, 2003; Kapogiannis et al., 2009).

A fMRI study suggests that religious belief involves neural networks that process information regarding intent and emotion, abstract semantics, and imagery (Kapogiannis et al., 2009). This process reinforces psychological theories of the evolution of religious belief and magical thinking being adaptive cognitive functions (Culotta, 2009).

Evolutionary biology uses the term "spandrel" for features of an organism arising as by-products, rather than adaptations, that are not necessary for the organism's fitness and survival but came to have a purpose (Gould & Vrba, 1982). Religion can be considered as one of the by-products.

Religion

Common areas shared by religion and OCD include the basal ganglia (BG), prefrontal cortex (PFC), medial frontal cortex (MFC), dorsolateral prefrontal cortex (DLPFC), and the thalamus (Muramoto, 2004). The neurotransmitters serotonin, dopamine, glutamate, and gamma-aminobutyric acid are also found to be active in OCD, religion, spirituality, and meditation (Borg et al., 2003; Newberg et al., 2003). Interestingly, the findings of Borg and colleagues suggested that those who are more spiritual are biologically more predisposed to anxiety (Borg et al., 2003).

Heightened religiosity and OCD may be attributed to the overactivity of the prefrontal cortex which causes rigid and legalistic conformity to rules, customs, excessive concern over oneself and one's existence (excessive self-reflection) that can lead to self-inflated levels of responsibility that provoke excessive guilt consciousness, and interpretations of their obsessions which often result in literal interpretations of religious texts and God's mind (Muramoto, 2004). Genetic research into the role of religion reported that it increases prosocial and altruistic behavior in the dopamine D4 receptor (DRD4) gene (Sasaki et al., 2013) as well as disgust sensitivity (Kang, Kim, Namkoong, & An, 2010).

Morality

One function also developed over time, morality, to keep the social order. A fMRI study examined the neural basis of distorted cognition and morality in OCD patients. It found an increased level of activity in the MFC, the left DLPFC, and middle temporal gyrus (Harrison et al., 2012). The study also found that problems with inhibitory control caused uncontrolled emotional responses in neutral situations and led to an increased tendency toward deontological guilt (Greene, Nystrom, Engell, Darley, & Cohen, 2004). Cognitive rigidity has also been shown to keep people with OCD stuck in their obsessions and compulsions rather than being able to distract their attention away from the uneventful situational trigger (Whitton, Henry, & Grisham, 2014).

Guilt

The feeling of guilt is a complex mental state underlying several human behaviors in both private and social life. Guilt is "an emotional and cognitive function, characterized by prosocial sentiments, entailing specific moral beliefs, which can be predominantly driven by inner values (deontological guilt) or by more interpersonal situations (altruistic guilt)" (Basile, Mancini, Macaluso, Caltagirone, & Bozzali, 2014).

Patients with OCD have abnormal guilt processing and experience intense feelings of disgust for immorality and tend to make deontological judgments in what are perceived to be moral situations based on the surge of neurotransmitters such as glutamate and serotonin (Hosseinzadeh,

Azhdehakosh, & Valibeygi, 2020). An fMRI study found guilt-related clusters of brain activation in the prefrontal, temporal, and parietal regions, mainly in the left hemisphere and the left dorsal cingulate cluster (Nakagawa et al., 2019).

A study found that reading a guilt-inducing script to people undergoing an fMRI procedure increased the cerebral blood flow in the anterior cingulate gyrus, a common area of OCD (Shin et al., 2000). Another fMRI study showed that the medial prefrontal cortices, left posterior and superior temporal sulci, anterior insula, anterior middle cingulate cortex, and the visual cortex areas of the brain were activated when people read a guilty or embarrassing scenario during the brain scan (Goubert et al., 2005). Examining the areas related to altruistic behavior, researchers found that the anterior cingulate becomes activated for affective empathy, and the temporoparietal junction plays a role in cognitive perspective taking, which are precursors of prosocial behavior and social cognition found within and between individuals (Tusche, Böckler, Kanske, Trautwein, & Singer, 2016).

A study of brain density investigated whether white matter structures were involved in feelings of guilt and their association with social and moral cognition. The inferior parietal lobule, prefrontal cortex, and cingulate were areas of interest during an MRI scan during which guilt and rule-breaking situations were provoked. The research team investigated the association between regional white matter structures and feelings of guilt in 1,196 healthy, young students using MRI and the Guilty Feeling Scale, which measures interpersonal and deontological guilt such as hurting friends or breaking rules. The authors showed that the results would be predicted by the Macbeth effect, as described earlier as an obsession with dirt leading to handwashing rituals resulting from guilt (Nakagawa et al., 2019).

A literature review of twenty-one functional and structural imaging studies demonstrated that guilt was more likely to be associated with activity in the ventral anterior cingulate cortex, posterior temporal regions, and the precuneus than were other negative moral emotions such as shame and embarrassment (Bastin, Harrison, Davey, Moll, & Whittle, 2016).

Shame

Shame and guilt are considered "self-conscious emotions" (Tangney & Dearing, 2002) and play an essential role in OCD (Hennig-Fast et al., 2015). OCD participants who were under a shame-inducing condition while having a fMRI scan showed increased activity in the limbic, temporal, hypothalamus, and limbic areas that process excessive shame and guilt (Hennig-Fast et al., 2015). Another study found that shame was associated with activity in the dorsolateral prefrontal cortex, posterior cingulate cortex, and sensorimotor cortex (Bastin et al., 2016).

Disgust

Visceral disgust has been characterized as an adaptive and protective "behavioural immune system" against disease and illness (Curtis, de Barra, & Aunger, 2011). This is likely because moral disgust evolved as a means of social control to maintain appropriate conduct.

Some brain areas that respond to disgust-inducing stimuli are the anterior insular cortex, BG, ventrolateral prefrontal cortex, anterior temporal cortex, insular cortex, medial prefrontal cortex, and visual cortex (Curtis et al., 2011).

The title of a study by Zhong and Ljienquist is *Washing Away Your Sins*. They also found that physical cleansing acts result from the psychological, physiological, and neurological overlap between physical and moral disgust. These behaviors are intended to reduce social or moral disgust to alleviate potential moral condemnation (Zhong & Liljenquist, 2006).

Another article compared altruistic guilt and deontological guilt and found an increased parasympathetic response to physiological symptoms of disgust and increased washing behaviors that were done to reduce the physiological symptoms of disgust (Ottaviani, Collazzoni, D'Olimpio, Moretta, & Mancini, 2019). A pattern of washing and cleaning behavior was also shown to be the reaction in both clinical and nonclinical subjects after being exposed to material that elicited a disgust response (Phillips et al., 2000).

Other studies found the insulae was activated during disgust-inducing stimuli and that washing and cleaning behaviors were performed by those with OCD and deontological guilt (Basile et al., 2014). The same results were found in a nonclinical sample and that the cleaning behaviors served to reduce deontological guilt (D'Olimpio et al., 2013). An fMRI scan of brain activity in OCD patients consistently showed hyperactivity of the insular cortex, which is responsible for disgust processing, when confronted with symptom-triggering stimuli (Viol et al., 2019). The insula was also shown to cause disgust reactivity in OCD patients who were presented with emotionally distressing cognitive stimuli, body sensations, and interoceptive sensory stimuli (Bhikram, Abi-Jaoude, & Sandor, 2017).

TXT>OCD capitalizes on superstitious behaviors and rituals. Unlike superstitious behaviors that have a beginning and an end, OCD rituals are rigid, perfectionistic, and performed to "completion."

Superstitious rituals involve the BG "habit system" in the orbitofrontal cortex and the hippocampus that enables behavioral variability. In OCD, the behaviors become excessive and exaggerated, even though the person with OCD recognizes how irrational the behaviors are (Brugger & Viaud-Delmon, 2010). An OCD study characterized "a limbic memory system" in the medial temporal lobe structures in the hippocampus (Atmaca et al., 2008). This system coordinates subordinate brain circuits that account for controlling inflexible habits and fixed action sequences (Eilam, Zor, Szechtman, & Hermesh, 2006). Another characterization of process is the "syndrome of sensory-limbic hyperconnection," which is characterized by a preoccupation with mystical, religious, and paranormal themes and an exaggerated belief in an extrasensory causation of coincidences (Bear, 1979).

Religion and morality exist in all of humanity. Not all people are religious, but religion exists in all cultures. Not all people have OCD, but it, too, exists in all cultures. Although we all have complex, delicate, and busy brains, slight variations as well as life experiences cause a range of differences, as evidenced by the variety of mental illnesses and their causes. In that too, we share a common humanity.

References

Aouizerate, B., Guehl, D., Cuny, E., Rougier, A., Bioulac, B., Tignol, J., & Burbaud, P. (2004). Pathophysiology of obsessive–compulsive disorder: A necessary link between phenomenology, neuropsychology, imagery and physiology. *Progress in Neurobiology, 72*(3), 195–221. doi:10.1016/j.pneurobio.2004.02.004

Ashbrook, J. B. (1984). Neurotheology: The working brain and the work of theology. *Zygon, 19*(3), 331–350. doi:10.1111/j.1467-9744.1984.tb00934.x

Atmaca, M., Yildirim, H., Ozdemir, H., Ozler, S., Kara, B., Ozler, Z., . . . Tezcan, E. (2008). Hippocampus and amygdalar volumes in patients with refractory obsessive-compulsive disorder. *Progress in Neuro-Psychopharmacology & Biological Psychiatry, 32*(5), 1283–1286. doi:10.1016/j.pnpbp.2008.04.002

Basile, B., Mancini, F., Macaluso, E., Caltagirone, C., & Bozzali, M. (2014). Abnormal processing of deontological guilt in obsessive-compulsive disorder. *Brain Structure and Function, 219*(4), 1321–1331.

Basile, B., Mancini, F., Macaluso, E., Caltagirone, C., Frackowiak, R., & Bozzali, M. (2011). Deontological and altruistic guilt: Evidence for distinct neurobiological substrates. *Human Brain Mapping, 32*(2), 229–239. doi:10.1002/hbm.21009

Bastin, C., Harrison, B., Davey, C., Moll, J., & Whittle, S. (2016). Feelings of shame, embarrassment and guilt and their neural correlates: A systematic review. *Neuroscience & Biobehavioral Reviews, 71*, 455–471. doi:10.1016/j.neubiorev.2016.09.019

Bear, D. M. (1979). Temporal lobe epilepsy—A syndrome of sensory-limbic hyperconnection. *Cortex, 15*(3), 357–384. doi:10.1016/s0010-9452(79)80064-7

Bhikram, T., Abi-Jaoude, E., & Sandor, P. (2017). OCD: Obsessive-compulsive … disgust? The role of disgust in obsessive-compulsive disorder. *Journal of Psychiatry & Neuroscience: JPN, 42*(5), 300–306. doi:10.1503/jpn.160079

Borg, J., Andrée, B., Anckarsäter, M. D. P. H., & Farde, L. (2003). The serotonin system and spiritual experiences. *The American Journal of Psychiatry, 160*, 1965–1969. doi:10.1176/appi.ajp.160.11.1965

Boyer, P. (2003). Religious thought and behaviour as by-products of brain function. *Trends in Cognitive Sciences, 7*(3), 119–124. doi:10.1016/S1364-6613(03)00031-7

Brugger, P., & Viaud-Delmon, I. (2010). Superstitiousness in obsessive-compulsive disorder. *Dialogues in Clinical Neuroscience, 12*(2), 250–254. doi:10.31887/DCNS.2010.12.2/pbrugger

Bulbulia, J. (2004). The cognitive and evolutionary psychology of religion. *Biology and Philosophy, 19*(5), 655–686.

Chamberlain, S. R., Blackwell, A. D., Fineberg, N. A., Robbins, T. W., & Sahakian, B. J. (2005). The neuropsychology of obsessive compulsive disorder: The importance of failures in cognitive and behavioural inhibition as candidate endophenotypic markers. *Neuroscience and Biobehavioral Reviews, 29*(3), 399–419. doi:10.1016/j.neubiorev.2004.11.006

Culotta, E. (2009). On the origin of religion. *Science, 326*(5954), 784–787. doi:10.1126/science.326_784

Curtis, V., de Barra, M., & Aunger, R. (2011). Disgust as an adaptive system for disease avoidance behaviour. *Philosophical Transactions of the Royal Society of London. Series B, Biological Sciences, 366*(1563), 389–401. doi:10.1098/rstb.2010.0117

D'Olimpio, F., Cosentino, T., Basile, B., Tenore, K., Gragnani, A., & Mancini, F. (2013). Obsessive-compulsive disorder and propensity to guilt feelings and to disgust. *Clinical Neuropsychiatry, 10*, 20–29.

de Salles Andrade, J. B., Ferreira, F. M., Suo, C., Yücel, M., Frydman, I., Monteiro, M., . . . Tovar-Moll, F. (2019). An MRI study of the metabolic and structural abnormalities in obsessive-compulsive disorder. *Frontiers in Human Neuroscience, 13*, 186–186. doi:10.3389/fnhum.2019.00186

Diamond, A., & Ling, D. S. (2020). Review of the evidence on, and fundamental questions about, efforts to improve executive functions, including working memory. In J. M. Novick, M. F. Bunting, M. R. Dougherty, & R. W. Engle (Eds.), *Cognitive and working memory training: Perspectives from psychology, neuroscience, and human development* (pp. 143–431). Oxford University Press. doi:10.1093/oso/9780199974467.003.0008

Dougherty, D. D., Brennan, B. P., Stewart, S. E., Wilhelm, S., Widge, A. S., & Rauch, S. L. (2018). Neuroscientifically informed formulation and treatment planning for patients with obsessive-compulsive disorder: A review. *JAMA Psychiatry, 75*(10), 1081–1087. doi:10.1001/jamapsychiatry.2018.0930

Eilam, D., Zor, R., Szechtman, H., & Hermesh, H. (2006). Rituals, stereotypy and compulsive behavior in animals and humans. *Neuroscience & Biobehavioral Reviews, 30*(4), 456–471. doi:10.1016/j.neubiorev.2005.08.003

Engert, V., Plessow, F., Miller, R., Kirschbaum, C., & Singer, T. (2014). Cortisol increase in empathic stress is modulated by emotional closeness and observation modality. *Psychoneuroendocrinology, 45*, 192–201. doi:10.1016/j.psyneuen.2014.04.005

Fontenelle, L. F., Soares, I. D., Miele, F., Borges, M. C., Prazeres, A. M., Rangé, B. P., & Moll, J. (2009). Empathy and symptoms dimensions of patients with obsessive–compulsive disorder. *Journal of Psychiatric Research, 43*(4), 455–463. doi:10.1016/j.jpsychires.2008.05.007

Goubert, L., Craig, K. D., Vervoort, T., Morley, S., Sullivan, M. J. L., Williams, C. A. C., . . . Crombez, G. (2005). Facing others in pain: The effects of empathy. *Pain, 118*(3), 285–288. doi:10.1016/j.pain.2005.10.025

Gould, S. J., & Vrba, E. S. (1982). Exaptation—A missing term in the science of form. *Paleobiology, 8*(1), 4–15. doi:10.1017/S0094837300004310

Greene, J. D., Nystrom, L. E., Engell, A. D., Darley, J. M., & Cohen, J. D. (2004). The neural bases of cognitive conflict and control in moral judgment. *Neuron, 44*(2), 389–400. doi:10.1016/j.neuron.2004.09.027

Harrison, B. J., Pujol, J., Soriano-Mas, C., Hernández-Ribas, R., López-Solà, M., Ortiz, H., . . . Cardoner, N. (2012). Neural correlates of moral sensitivity in obsessive-compulsive disorder. *Archives of General Psychiatry, 69*(7), 741–749. doi:10.1001/archgenpsychiatry.2011.2165

Hennig-Fast, K., Michl, P., Müller, J., Niedermeier, N., Coates, U., Müller, N., . . . Meindl, T. (2015). Obsessive-compulsive disorder—A question of conscience? An fMRI study of behavioural and neurofunctional correlates of shame and guilt. *Journal of Psychiatric Research, 68*, 354–362. doi:10.1016/j.jpsychires.2015.05.001

Hosseinzadeh, M., Azhdehakosh, E., & Valibeygi, A. (2020). Moral judgments in obsessive-compulsive disorder: A narrative mini-review. *Neuroscience Research Notes, 3*, 11–22. doi:10.31117/neuroscirn.v3i1.39

Kang, J. I., Kim, S. J., Namkoong, K., & An, S. K. (2010). Association of DRD4 and COMT polymorphisms with disgust sensitivity in healthy volunteers. *Neuropsychobiology, 61*(2), 105–112.

Kapogiannis, D., Barbey, A. K., Su, M., Zamboni, G., Krueger, F., & Grafman, J. (2009). Cognitive and neural foundations of religious belief. *Proceedings of the National Academy of Sciences, 106*(12), 4876–4881. doi:10.1073/pnas.0811717106

Kreitzer, A. C., & Malenka, R. C. (2008). Striatal plasticity and basal ganglia circuit function. *Neuron, 60*(4), 543–554. doi:10.1016/j.neuron.2008.11.005

Lanciego, J. L., Luquin, N., & Obeso, J. A. (2012). Functional neuroanatomy of the basal ganglia. *Cold Spring Harbor Perspectives in Medicine, 2*(12), a009621. doi:10.1101/cshperspect.a009621

Muramoto, O. (2004). The role of the medial prefrontal cortex in human religious activity. *Medical hypotheses, 62*(4), 479–485. doi:10.1016/j.mehy.2003.10.010

Nakagawa, S., Takeuchi, H., Taki, Y., Nouchi, R., Kotozaki, Y., Shinada, T., . . . Kawashima, R. (2019). Mean diffusivity related to rule-breaking guilt: The Macbeth effect in the sensorimotor regions. *Scientific Reports, 9*, 1–8. doi:10.1038/s41598-019-48654-8

Newberg, A., Pourdehnad, M., Alavi, A., & d'Aquili, E. (2003). Cerebral blood flow during meditative prayer: Preliminary findings and methodological issues. *Perceptual and Motor Skills, 97*(2), 625–630. doi:10.2466/pms.2003.97.2.625

Ottaviani, C., Collazzoni, A., D'Olimpio, F., Moretta, T., & Mancini, F. (2019). I obsessively clean because deontological guilt makes me feel physiologically disgusted! *Journal of Obsessive-Compulsive and Related Disorders, 20*, 21–29.

Phillips, M., Marks, I., Senior, C., Lythgoe, D., O'Dwyer, A., Meehan, O., . . . McGuire, P. (2000). A differential neural response in obsessive-compulsive disorder patients with washing compared with checking symptoms to disgust. *Psychological Medicine, 30*, 1037–1050. doi:10.1017/S0033291799002652

Sasaki, J. Y., Kim, H. S., Mojaverian, T., Kelley, L., Park, I. Y., & Janušonis, S. (2013). Religion priming differentially increases prosocial behavior among variants of the dopamine D4 receptor (DRD4) gene. *Social Cognitive and Affective Neuroscience, 8*(2), 209–215.

Saxena, S., Bota, R. G., & Brody, A. L. (2001). Brain-behavior relationships in obsessive-compulsive disorder. *Seminars in clinical neuropsychiatry, 6*(2), 82–101. doi:10.1053/scnp.2001.21833

Saxena, S., & Rauch, S. L. (2000). Functional neuroimaging and the neuroanatomy of obsessive-compulsive disorder. *Psychiatric Clinics of North America, 23*(3), 563–586.

Serpell, Z. N., & Esposito, A. G. (2016). Development of executive functions: Implications for educational policy and practice. *Policy Insights from the Behavioral and Brain Sciences, 3*(2), 203–210. doi:10.1177/2372732216654718

Shin, L. M., Dougherty, D. D., Orr, S. P., Pitman, R. K., Lasko, M., Macklin, M. L., . . . Rauch, S. L. (2000). Activation of anterior paralimbic structures during guilt-related script-driven imagery. *Biological Psychiatry, 48*(1), 43–50. doi:10.1016/s0006-3223(00)00251-1

Shukla, S., Acharya, S., & Rajput, D. (2013). Neurotheology—Matters of the mind or matters that mind? *Journal of Clinical and Diagnostic Research: JCDR, 7*(7), 1486–1490. doi:10.7860/JCDR/2013/5409.3181

Shweder, R. A., Much, N. C., Mahapatra, M., Park, L., Brandt, A., & Rozin, P. (1997). Morality and health. In A. Brandt & P. Rozin (Eds.), *Morality and Health* (pp. 119–169). New York, NY: Routledge.

Tangney, J. P., & Dearing, R. L. (2002). *Shame and guilt*. New York, NY: The Guilford Press.

Tangney, J. P., Stuewig, J., & Mashek, D. J. (2007). Moral emotions and moral behavior. *Annual Review of Psychology, 58*, 345–372. doi:10.1146/annurev.psych.56.091103.070145

Tusche, A., Böckler, A., Kanske, P., Trautwein, F.-M., & Singer, T. (2016). Decoding the charitable brain: Empathy, perspective taking, and attention shifts differentially predict altruistic giving. *Journal of Neuroscience, 36*(17), 4719–4732.

Vahabzadeh, A., & McDougle, C. J. (2014). Obsessive-compulsive disorder. In L. M. McManus & R. N. Mitchell (Eds.), *Pathobiology of human disease* (pp. 2512–2521). San Diego, CA: Academic Press.

Viol, K., Aas, B., Kastinger, A., Kronbichler, M., Schöller, H. J., Reiter, E.-M., . . . Schiepek, G. K. (2019). Erroneously disgusted: fMRI study supports disgust-related neural reuse in obsessive-compulsive disorder (OCD). *Frontiers in Behavioral Neuroscience, 13*, 81. doi:10.3389/fnbeh.2019.00081

Whitton, A. E., Henry, J. D., & Grisham, J. R. (2014). Moral rigidity in obsessive-compulsive disorder: Do abnormalities in inhibitory control, cognitive flexibility and disgust play a role? *Journal of Behavior Therapy and Experimental Psychiatry, 45*(1), 152–159.

Zhong, C.-B., & Liljenquist, K. (2006). Washing away your sins: Threatened morality and physical cleansing. *Science, 313*, 1451–1452. doi:10.1126/science.1130726

CHAPTER ELEVEN

Treatment and Relief: Behavior Therapy and Cognitive Strategies

"The opposite of a scrupulous person is not an unscrupulous person, but a person of faith."

Kilpack, 1956

"A scruple is cured by ignoring it."

O'Flaherty, 1973

In vivo exposure and response prevention (ERP) is the gold standard behavioral treatment for obsessive-compulsive disorder (OCD), regardless of symptom type, severity of episode, and duration of illness. Conscience-related issues are often overlooked and thought to be more difficult to treat due to the sensitive nature of the obsessive content (Riley, 2003). The focus of therapy sessions can get easily derailed when time is spent analyzing the person's religious or moral intentions (often obsessively) rather than addressing the thoughts and behaviors as OCD "by-products." The goal of treatment is to validate how distressing the obsessive fears are to the person, while providing psychoeducation throughout the course of treatment about how her obsessions are target the clinical symptoms of OCD, will help to restore her own sense of faith, spirituality, morality, and self-trust. Emphasizing to the patient that consistent ritual prevention while facing the obsessive fear constitutes healthy leaps of faith will result in normalizing her overactive brain system.

This chapter will assist in helping clinicians assess symptoms, create behavioral plans, and identify treatment factors that may interfere with achieving the maximum treatment outcome for a stable recovery. The case materials presented in this chapter are from examples already introduced throughout the text. Chapter 12 will provide clergy formulations about how the problem is understood and addressed. Those who address it as a religious failure can cause a profound spiritual crisis, whereas those who understand it as a clinical issue can help restore confidence and trust both in faith and in the treatment process.

Below is a testimony from a scrupulosity sufferer:

> Given that the work of ERP is intensely painful, yet gradually empowering, it is a fertile field for spiritual growth. I found that performing ERP forced me to confront certain inescapable truths about the human condition: finitude, the inevitability of doubt and ambiguity, and the fact that real faith requires trust and risk. Instead of offering to God my obsessive rituals, I began offering to God my willingness to bear the ambiguity and to undergo the exposure. As the ERP began to lower my anxiety reactions to triggers, I felt more in control of my life and my faith. Having gone through it myself, I believe that a person with scrupulosity undergoing ERP with well-trained support from a mental health professional and a spiritual director cannot help but mature spiritually. (https://www.ocdmassachusetts.org/2014/06/25/ocd-scrupulosity-spiritual-direction-through-the-stages-of-recovery/)

Another OCD sufferer who completed a residential program at the OCD program where I work attended the symptom-specific scrupulosity and moral perfectionism group that I have run for over twenty years. One of the most valuable aspects of group work is creating a safe space for those who have conscience-related OCD symptoms to hear and share how they have been affected by this type of OCD. Along with the content of the group, people gain a more objective perspective and learn that the compassion they feel for others is the same compassion they can feel toward themselves.

The patient who attended the "scrup group" related that the experience of seeing that he was not the only one struggling with these issues was very powerful. He learned that there was actually a name for the problem he was struggling with, that he could now explain to other people the kind of hell that he had been going through, and that there was treatment for it. The scrupulosity group helped him realize that the less he let scrupulosity take over, the more faithful he felt. "Every ritual resisted is an act of faith," is a common adage I offer the group; he said it was a phrase that was enlightening, and he used it to optimize his treatment.

For one of his exposures, he went to a church, put up his middle finger, and said, "F— you, God," not as a blasphemous act but as an act of faith that God understood what he was doing and why he was doing it. He related that trusting the treatment by stepping in the dark helped him trust his true faith more than listening to the OCD that was constantly nagging in his ear.

Clinical and Treatment Issues

Sexual and religious obsessions have been categorized under the domain of "unacceptable obsession thoughts" (Abramowitz et al., 2010). These symptoms have been found to be more treatment resistant (Alonso et al., 2001) and have poor treatment outcomes (Mataix-Cols, Marks, Greist, Kobak, & Baer, 2002).

The following is a list of factors for the clinician to be mindful of during the assessment and treatment process. These items will not be explored in depth but will help identify issues that can be potentially helpful for or interfering with treatment.

- Make a safe space for the patient to be open. He may be embarrassed or afraid that discussing "religious" symptoms may betray his religion (TAF) or that the therapist will be judgmental or offended
- The issue of trust and mistrust of the therapist is an ongoing challenge due to the level of fear and "risk" people feel they are taking in ERP treatment. "You are not understanding enough or qualified to help me with my fears about God and my salvation." Treatment requires that they do the opposite of what the OCD is demanding. It is important to provide feedback that it will be natural for patients to look for faults or imperfections in the therapist to avoid facing the difficult challenges required for effectively conquering their fears.
- Trust and mistrust of clergy consulted for guidance or who may be part of the treatment team is also a challenge. "You lack experience with the psychological/psychiatric nature of my problem." Obsessive doubt and fear will creep in when clergy advises total obedience to their guidance and to that of the therapist.
- Provide psychoeducation and support for the problem by citing accounts from saints and other notables who suffered with scrupulosity as examples of how they practiced the same ERP approach to gaining control of their symptoms.
- Inform patients that selective bible quoting to validate their obsessions is a form of distortion, as they are not considering the entire context of the situation in which it was said.

- Redirect patients when there is too much talking and not enough doing the treatment tasks. Talking is an easy way for the patient and therapist to get distracted from the anxiety they may both be feeling in the exposure situation, and no progress will have been made. It is important that the therapist be aware of her own discomfort in conducting the exposures as it is difficult to watch people struggle. ERPs done correctly will result in treatment gains, one ERP after the other.
- The same is true for too much thinking. It interferes with focusing on the challenge of the moment, a sort of a mental checking out. If thinking helped cure OCD, it would have already worked.
- Overanalyzing the thoughts or thinking into the future is also a mental ritual that interferes with focusing on the exposure challenge. Redirection back to the reality of the moment is essential.
- Avoid trying to reason with the patient and the obsessions. Though there is always a kernel of truth to the obsession, it has reached an irrational or unreasonable level. There is always a probability that something negative could happen, but this is not because the person has the thought or didn't do the ritual. Having OCD does not change the laws of probability—they remain the same, just as they are for people without OCD.
- Focusing on religious or moral issues will be adding fuel to the fire. It is important to validate the person's experience and sense of values, but while in the throes of an OCD episode and exposure task is not the time to have a meaningful discussion on these topics.
- Guilt is an underlying clinical factor that is often overlooked due to the focus on overt symptoms, which is another reason why assessing the function of rituals is so important. Regardless of symptom type, asking what interferes with resisting rituals often results in sufferers saying they would feel guilty if something bad happened (e.g., "If I didn't wash my hands, I could cause someone to get sick").
- It is important to understand and respect religious, moral, and cultural diversity. What may seem like obsessions and compulsions to some may actually be traditions shared in their religious, cultural, or social groups. That is why understanding the function of the ritual is important.
- However, if the patient is rigidly adhering to the letter of the law, rather than the spirit, it will be important to address the excessiveness of her behavior compared to how others observe the tradition.
- Language is important. Phrases such as "I can't," "I have to," "OCD makes me," and similar statements are not true but rather are obsessive beliefs and feelings. As soon as possible, teach that using those words rule out the idea of choice. People can choose normal behavior, even if it doesn't feel right at first. Helpful reframes include "It is hard for me to," "I feel like I have to," and "I can choose to," which will promote cognitive flexibility.

- People-pleasing behaviors and perfectionism may be missed as good adherence and compliance in treatment. OCD typically takes its toll on people's self-esteem, and they may want to please the therapist to gain approval. What may appear to be good treatment adherence may actually be someone trying to be the perfect patient to avoid perceived criticism by the therapist or to perform perfectly rather than be willing to make mistakes. This is a symptom of the disorder, and patients should be encouraged to "make mistakes" so that they benefit from the true outcome of the exposure rather than trying to control the process.
- Try to deal with expectancy issues about what is "supposed" to happen during exposures by helping the person to be open to the process rather than thinking about the outcome.
- Another form of perfectionism in treatment occurs when patients are never satisfied with the established, agreed-upon exposure task. There may be an expectation that it will be the perfect one, which may cause disappointment when doubts and the "not-right" feeling sets in. Therapists can begin chasing the "right" exposure along with the patient so that it targets the precise fear. Because the therapist and patient already identified the exposure task from having reviewed the options, staying the course and supporting the patient to stick with the current plan until it is clear that sufficient habituation to the situation has occurred.
- People often overidentify with their symptoms. They mistake their obsessions as defining who they are, instead of seeing their intrusive thoughts as by-products of a clinical disorder.
- Poor insight is problematic as the person will overestimate the probability of the feared consequences happening. One strategy is the use of acceptance as applied in pain management. "You have the fear (pain), now what?" Planning how to organize life around the thoughts can improve functionality.
- Experiencing strong emotions that are primary, not secondary, to OCD or anxiety may add an additional treatment challenge. Dialectical behavior therapy skills are helpful in coping with the additional stress of ERP work for those who have problems with distress tolerance and regulating affect.
- Some patients morally object to taking medication because they consider it a form of "cheating." The rigidity around this aspect of the disorder handicaps them from taking advantage of an effective treatment tool which may very well be the thing that helps them gain better control of their thinking help them realize their judgment during their OCD episode may have been compromised by trying to be morally pure.
- Personality traits, a diagnosed personality disorder, strong emotions, or emotional avoidance may create challenges that require adaptations to how the treatment is delivered. Understanding the key elements or structure of these factors will help guide how to include and negotiate appropriate

coping strategies for the types of experiential responses the person may have. It may not be apparent at the outset of treatment, but intervening as soon as possible can help prevent those issues from taking over or help keep the patient from dropping out of treatment.

- Assessing how family and friends accommodate the OCD and helping them understand that those behaviors are essentially ritualizing with the patient is an important aspect of successful treatment. The intention of supporting people is usually to try to be helpful. They often have trouble tolerating the distress the OCD has taken on their loved ones, may feel frustrated in the way it has overtaken the functioning of the household, and be upset or angry about the wedge the OCD has put in their relationship. Providing psychoeducation about the role of accommodation often results in loved ones being able to let go of guilt and find relief about being able to say no to the demands of the OCD while still loving the person.
- Patients may have consulted clergy who may not be psychologically minded and are not educated about scrupulosity. Clergy responses to the obsessive thoughts of being sinful and sacrilegious may have caused deep feelings of shame and guilt for being offensive to God. Some people may have recovered from this experience, but for others, it will take persistence and work to help them sort out the difference between intentional and unintentional intrusive thoughts, disengage from trying to find meaning about themselves in them, and understand that their obsessions do not identify who they are as people.
- Countertransference is a psychoanalytic term for the therapist's unconscious emotional experiences in response to the patient's issues (Freud, 1910). OCD therapy is typically conducted with empirical, behavioral, cognitive, or solution-focused approaches. Other factors contributing to this dynamic may occur if the therapist is of a different religious faith, an atheist, an agnostic, or areligious, or has had negative experiences in religious settings or teachings. The therapist may be unaware that this dynamic exists in the therapy relationship, and it is unclear if it affects the course or outcome of treatment. However, this unconscious process on the part of the therapist may be unconsciously felt by the patient. When negative religious countertransference becomes conscious, the therapist can more objectively discuss the patient's religious beliefs and practices within the appropriate clinical context (Griffith, 2006). Healthy management of countertransference contributes to better therapy outcomes (Hayes, Gelso, & Hummel, 2011).

Assessment

During the assessment phase, it is important to understand what function the rituals play in response to obsessions. If someone reports symptoms of contamination, she may say she washes her hands to get the germs off. Asking "What would happen if you didn't wash your hands?"

would reveal that she would be afraid of causing others to get sick and be guilty of negligent behavior. This type of question is worth asking regardless of symptom type.

A survey of the patient's OCD symptoms is the first step in assessing the overall picture of active symptoms and their accompanying level of distress. Most patients have more than one obsession and accompanying behaviors. The Yale-Brown Obsessive-Compulsive Checklist (Bonchek, 2009) or the Dimensional Obsessive-Compulsive Scale (available for download at http://www.jabramowitz.com/uploads/1/0/4/8/10489300/docs.pdf) (Abramowitz et al., 2010) are reliable measures of symptom assessment. The Yale-Brown Obsessive-Compulsive Scale (Y-BOCS) measures symptom severity and is also available for download (https://pandasnetwork.org/wp-content/uploads/2018/11/y-bocs-w-checklist.pdf) (Bonchek, 2009).

The Dimensional Obsessive-Compulsive Scale (DOCS) consolidated obsessions into four categories: contamination, responsibility for harm or bad luck, symmetry/incompleteness/exactness, and unacceptable thoughts (Abramowitz et al., 2010). It includes assessing factors such as avoidance and expands the parameters beyond the number, range, or different types of obsessions and compulsions (Abramowitz et al., 2010). Scrupulosity was included in the unacceptable thoughts category.

After the original DOCS was introduced, scrupulosity was considered to have properties that were different from the other unacceptable thoughts dimension and has been added as its own subscale (DOCS – scrupulosity/religion) (Wetterneck et al., 2021). As such, clinicians now have a validated tool to assess aspects of scrupulosity that can be included in treatment plans.

The Scrupulosity Checklist was developed by James Ciarrocchi, who was a Jesuit priest before becoming a psychologist. It serves as a structure for assessing scrupulosity symptoms, though it is not a validated or published measure. It helps determine if the patient identifies the function of her religious rituals as alleviating guilt or to cope with religious-related obsessions.

The Pennsylvania Inventory of Scrupulosity-Revised (PIOS-R) is a validated two-factor measure of scrupulosity symptoms (Olatunji, Abramowitz, Williams, Connolly, & Lohr, 2007). The factors consisted of Fear of Sin and Fear of God (see Appendix E). A severity cutoff of 24/60 was found to reliably classify patients with clinically significant scrupulosity among a sample of residential level of care patients, indicating that the PIOS-R is a useful and appropriate measure for use in evaluating scrupulosity in patients with severe OCD (Shapiro, Krompinger, Gironda, & Elias, 2013).

In order to plan the order of exposure work according to level of challenge, the Subjective Units of Distress Scale (SUDS) is used to rate the level of anxiety each item provokes on a 0–100 scale. Some patients may report not being in distressing situations because they have effectively avoided them through self-isolation. It is also important that the level of anxiety is based on being in the situation but not performing any compulsions. Then a ranked order hierarchy is designed as the road map for the treatment plan. Examples of hierarchies will be provided further into the chapter once other preliminary treatment factors are discussed.

If, during the initial assessment, symptoms of scrupulosity begin to emerge, the next session should delve further into the role religion plays, if any, in the person's life. It is recommended that the clinician be culturally aware of normal practices and sensitive to religious beliefs that may seem archaic. Assessing the thoughts and beliefs of a person with moral perfectionism is important to ensure the work targets ego-dystonic cognitions while respecting those that reflect someone's true values.

Providing psychoeducation about how the treatment is conducted and why it works neurochemically will help the person understand why it would be recommended that he do the opposite of his obsessive fear. Explaining the rationale for scrupulosity exposures is not to commit sins, but to put his faith forward to accept the clinical importance of doing so. Chapter 12 provides information about how clergy supports exposure and response prevention therapy.

Rowan's initial Y-BOCS score was 34/40 (40 being the highest) , and his PIOS score was 50/60 (60 being the highest), both of which are in the severe range. He was diagnosed with OCD in the fourth grade and said there was a long history of OCD in his family. His obsessions were being separated from God, selling his soul to the devil, the need to know that he is saved and will see loved ones in heaven, blasphemous images, sexual words and images, and fear of going to hell. He came from a strict Christian home and was taught about evil forces that would tempt him. He also questioned his intention of thought, wondering if he really meant the obsessive thoughts he was having, and if so, was he going to act on them? A frequent obsessive thought was, "What if God's grace . . . ?" for which he ruminated about all possible negative conditions to fill in the blank and was paralyzed by indecision because he could never know for sure.

The most troubling obsession for him was his fear of being a pedophile. He related an incident that occurred over twenty years ago when he was at a friend's house and was buckling up his pants after having used the bathroom. His friend's five-year-old daughter walked in on him, and he fears he may have exposed himself to her. He is haunted by the idea that maybe he did it on purpose and that he likes young girls. He tries to resist the image of the event but has it all the time. He has always held out the possibility of contacting the police or turning himself in at some point in time.

Rowan quit his job because OCD began interfering with his productivity. He had trouble focusing on his work tasks, and his rituals began eating up time he should be spending on his clients' financial portfolios. At home, he avoids using his contaminated computer because he used to watch pornography on it. He no longer uses the internet or social media, avoids playing video games because the female characters look sexy (and gaming is an indulgent waste of time), avoids watching movies or TV, stopped reading books due to potentially sexually arousing content, and avoids making eye contact with women in public because it might mean flirting and cheating on his wife. He does not allow his son to read Harry Potter or science fantasy books, as they dabble in the occult. When he allows himself to "indulge" his talent for sketching, he makes sure to be in the "right" and moral mindset to make sure the devil is not controlling him.

Rowan came to treatment very skeptical and ambivalent. He was motivated by wanting some relief from the mental, spiritual, moral, and emotional anguish he has been enduring. He worried that the secular treatment will conflict with his faith's philosophy and values and that making progress in treatment meant that he should no longer pay his penance and would no longer care about his bad behavior. He reported being afraid when a "not-right feeling" and feelings of uncertainty set in, even when he knew, rationally, that the treatment recommendations did not jeopardize his salvation.

Treatment Planning

Having created the fear hierarchy, it is important to plan exposures that are challenging enough to make progress but not too challenging which might result in the patient being overwhelmed and discouraged. Beginning with a triggering situation at a SUDS level of 60/100 is a good measure by which the therapist can assess how the patient did during the challenge and set it as the daily "homework" task. Have the patient structure his daily exposure practices by carving out sixty to ninety minutes of designated time in his schedule. The plan can be modified if the task was too easy or hard. Once the task is formalized into the plan, it will stay in place until, ideally, the peak SUDS level habituates to a manageable (±40/100) level and that the rituals are essentially eliminated. Habituation can be characterized as neurobiological boredom. The *most* common reason for lack of habituation is the performance of rituals. A functional analysis that breaks down the sequence of behaviors during the triggering event will help identify overt or covert rituals that the patient may not have been aware of performing. The plan should be modified to include response prevention strategies for behaviors. If the absence of identifying new rituals does not account for the lack of progress, please refer to the list provided earlier for other complicating or interfering factors that are preventing progress.

Reassurance seeking and questions that arise when patients want the therapist to make decisions for them are best managed by consistently asking the patient to put the thoughts into statements. This way, the therapist is setting limits on obsessive doubts and helping the patient take responsibility for making decisions based on her own judgment. When questions persist, remind her that there are no perfect decisions and that mistakes are inevitable and that the feared consequences are often out of proportion to the actual risk posed by the decision. Asking what is the worst that could happen and how probable that outcome helps put the situation into a more realistic context. Exaggerating the feared outcome can bring some light and humor into the mood, but only when the therapist has a good sense of whether it would be an appropriate intervention. Obsessive doubts in the form of "How will I know?" "I can't," "If only," "Yeah but," "What if?" followed by "But then what if," and more "what ifs" can be met with "Who knows," "Right, there is no certainty," and "Can you live with the doubt?" in order to put those questions on extinction.

It is best not to answer obsessive questions directly, as the results of trying to use logic is the same as trying to provide reassurance: it never works. Instead, validate the patient's concern and reidentify the problem as an obsessive need for certainty and to feel "right." As OCD is a doubting disease, it is important to reinforce the goal of learning to live with uncertainty and the "not-right" feeling. This may need to be repeated as the obsessive need for answers might override the feedback you are initially presenting.

It is important to remember that focusing on the content of obsessions is obsessing with the patient. Using the "broken record" technique found in assertiveness training for how to stay on track will help disengage from paying too much attention to the thoughts. This may necessitate a kind but firm approach. If, in spite of the redirection you are providing to refocus on the therapeutic process, you continue to be met with resistance, it may be necessary to disengage from the process and offer to return to planning treatment when the person is more ready to face the fear. When asked, the patient may report that he has had other obsessions in the past, and this will be an important teaching moment to ask why he is no longer worried about those thoughts and if it is possible that the current obsession will eventually pass just like the others did. The simple mindset and approach to treatment is to face the fear, resist any urges to fix or change distressing anxiety or emotions, let the brain run its course, and experience habituation. It takes courage and patience as it takes consistent practice, and the change will not likely occur overnight, although some people do experience habituation quickly—most likely when they are fully engaged in the exposure and fully resist urges to ritualize.

Imaginal Exposure

Not all obsessive triggers can be replicated in real life, especially for violent, sexual, scrupulous, and moral types of OCD. In circumstances where the exposure can't be conducted directly *in vivo*, imaginal exposure is an effective, albeit indirect, intervention (Foa, 2010). Imaginal exposure, or script writing, is the process of facing the obsessive fear by writing in great detail how the feared consequences have actually come true and what happens as a result. Sometimes the theme of the script targets uncertainty and the never knowing if the feared consequence has happened or will ever happen. Patients will describe how they are functioning with doubt and the ways it is affecting their quality of life or their self-concept.

It is essential that the patient understand that the function of the script is to fully confront the fear and experience any provoked anxiety and emotions to emerge and tolerate them until they have run their course without performing rituals or avoidance behaviors. Many patients do not realize that they have been avoiding uncomfortable emotions such as anger, guilt, and sadness and that the exposure will help them learn that, like anxiety, they are temporary and will pass.

The scripts should be written in the first person and in the present tense as if the event is actually happening. During the writing process, the use of descriptive language about how the event is unfolding while the person is allowing the physiological signs of anxiety and emotions they are experiencing in the moment will lead to habituation to the obsessive feared outcome. The script ends when the patient has taken the event to its complete endpoint (i.e., "I am in jail and my family has forsaken me," "I am burning in hell," etc.). The script writing should not be rushed or completed in one session. It may be recommended that other feared scenarios for the same obsession type be conducted. If someone is afraid of doing immoral acts, such as stealing or cheating on taxes, a separate script should be written for those triggers.

Recording the scripts, listening to them repeatedly, and reading them out loud enhances the cognitive and emotional benefits of the exposure. Imaginal exposure can be convenient as a stopgap measure for addressing obsessions that may occur during recovery. While no outcome studies have measured the long-term effect of imaginal exposure, using it as soon as possible for "lapses" in response prevention may help to prevent relapses. In addition, the combination of in vivo and imaginal exposure appears to be more effective than either alone and was found to produce clinically significant and lasting benefits to people with OCD (Berman, Summers, Weingarden, & Wilhelm, 2019).

Islam

According to the ninth-century scientist Abu Zayd al-Balkhi, distorted cognitions and irrational catastrophic thinking of an anticipated future harm is now identified as a primary factor that drives the compulsive behaviors of *Waswâs* (OCD scrupulosity) (Badri, 2013; Keshavarzi, Khan, & Syed, 2018). Hooman Keshavarzi, Fahad Khan, and Syed, Beena developed a treatment modality known as Traditionally Islamically Integrated Psychotherapy (TIIP) for Waswâs that seeks to restore the *I'tidal* (balance) of the *aql* (cognitions), *nafs* (behaviors), *ruh* (spirit), and *ihsaas* (emotions), which are identified as the elements of the human psyche (Keshavarzi et al., 2018). They treated *Waswâs al-Qahri* with forgiveness and prayers, and a modified form of Islamic focused-centered therapy.

Another Muslim treatment combined the religious text with psychological therapy for a patient who excessively washed until she felt perfectly pure before praying while teaching about the behaviors being performed for OCD contamination symptoms (Rassool, 2018). A passage from Prophet Muhammad's (SAW) teachings was presented: "'There is a dirty road between me and the Mosque (so my clothes/shoes/feet become soiled).' The Prophet asked 'Is there a cleaner road after it? 'The answer was yes and The Prophet said: 'This (road will wipe out the effect) of that'" (Sunan Abi Dawud, Hadith: 387, Sunan Ibn Majah, Hadith: 533 and Musannaf ibn Abi Sahybah, Hadith: 621).

Exposure Plans

The recommended exposures for treating scrupulosity, moral perfectionism, and obsessive guilt may seem extreme if taken out of context. We must remember that the way to combat OCD clinically is to do the opposite in a way that does not violate faith practices or commit immoral actions (i.e., a kosher Jew would never be asked to eat a cheeseburger). Building a relationship of trust is crucial because the person will be questioning the exposure recommendations until she has had enough practice to feel relief and think more clearly. Clinicians should do their homework in getting to know the faith practices of the person's religion so that the exposures are respectful and effective. Clergy who understand the nature of the problem support the practice of ERP even when it may appear inappropriate to the uninformed. The next chapter will provide information about helpful and unhelpful clergy responses to the problem.

Rowan's case entails many of the classic scrupulosity concerns involved in OCD for Christians and will be developed more than the other cases to avoid repetition. His fear hierarchy in Table 11.1 is an abbreviated version for the sake of space.

Table 11.1 Rowan's Treatment Plan

SUDS 0/100	Trigger	Obsessive Fear	Ritual	Exposure and Response Prevention
100	Sexual images of friend's daughter	Losing salvation*; being sent to hell; not repentant	Quoting scripture; excessive apologizing; excessive praying	Purposely hold image of girl in mind; look at pictures of girls in family magazines
98	Thinking about incident with friend's daughter in bathroom	Being a pedophile; being sent to hell	Prituals; mental reviewing/ checking of event	Write imaginal detailed scenario of the event as if it is happening now
98	Being around young girls	Being sexually aroused; being a pedophile; hell	Avoids going to public places	Go to public park
95	Making easy choices; taking shortcuts	Making pact with the devil; hell	Mental ritual to assure God of his intentions; avoid making decisions	Do what's easy or efficient on purpose
90	Intrusive thoughts about past mistakes	End times are coming without soul being pure; separated from God and family for eternity	Prituals for forgiveness and salvation until thoughts subside; makes pact to stay clear of spiritual and moral risks	Write imaginary script about that being true and what will happen

(continued)

Table 11.1 *(continued)*

SUDS 0/100	Trigger	Obsessive Fear	Ritual	Exposure and Response Prevention
90	Not having proper mindset for prayer	God won't accept prayer, denying his faith	Mental checking and making self-reassuring statements	Pray once in spite of not feeling complete
87	Feeling pleasure	Having spiritually compromised by gaining benefit from evil	Self-imposed punishment; confessing; avoidance	Engage in a fun or avoided leisure activity
85	Wanting to engage in leisure activities: sketching; reading comic books; doing magic card tricks; playing video games with sexy female characters	Being selfish; may lead to sexual arousal; fear of making "nefarious" choices and becoming evil	Avoids doing them because he might be "playing with the devil"	Work on sketching neutral images or images that are a bit more challenging
85	Wanting to look something up on the internet	Seeing improper or sexual material and giving into sinful urges	Avoids using his computer altogether; uses phone instead	Look up and read sketch artists or card game tricks
80	Playing games of chance	Winning means having bargained with the devil	Avoids doing them	Intentionally make pacts with the devil to win
80	Obsessing about salvation	Going to hell	Does prituals; calls father who reassures him	Accept uncertainty/ not knowing; assume salvation has been lost

(continued)

Table 11.1 *(continued)*

SUDS 0/100	Trigger	Obsessive Fear	Ritual	Exposure and Response Prevention
75	Wanting to hold girlfriend's hand	Being lustful and sexually aroused	Avoids physical contact	Interlock pinkies and increase holding fingers as is manageable
75	Feeling angry, stressed, or frustrated about unexpected glitches during work	Making pact with devil to have things go his way	Prituals done for forgiveness; punishes self for unacceptable feelings	Allow emotions to flow naturally while resisting urges to confess or apologize for them
70	Feeling tired at work and wanting to do a task the easy way	Temptation to take shorts cuts means cheating	Being over thorough and excessive checking of work	Move fluidly through task and review once when finished
70	Fear of losing salvation in treatment	Losing salvation in treatment	Reading accounts of saints and notables with scrupulosity—started as psychoeducation but became reassurance ritual	Read about infamous religious notables while resisting mental checking or praying rituals
65	Wanting to watch PG or PG-13 movies or TV shows	Enjoyment leads to sinful behavior	Avoids watching any movies or screen activities	Watch Harry Potter movie; play video game on phone

*Losing salvation and not being repentant are obsessive fears that carry through each item on the hierarchy.

Rowan's initial exposure plan started in the mid-level SUDS range. Rowan agreed to watch a Harry Potter movie and play a game on his phone while on the train for work every day. He then increased the challenge by doing card tricks with others. At this point, Rowan's pastor attended two therapy sessions. It was unclear how much he really understood about OCD, but he was supportive of treatment and counseled Rowan about the importance of being a part of the religious community and connecting with others of his affiliation. He also counseled Rowan to accept uncertainty, let go of ruminating, and come to terms with the parameters of his religious obligations.

Rowan began reading about saints and historical figures who had scrupulosity (see Chapter 2) as a means of increasing his awareness that "good" people have suffered the relatively same OCD episodes with ego-dystonic obsessions. Instead, after having read several cases and listening to his analyses fraught with arguments and doubts about his case being different, it became clear that the motivation behind the reading wasn't for learning but for seeking reassurance. It became evident because he was not taking what he read and applying it to his treatment but continued with his rigid thoughts and beliefs that kept him stuck in treatment. He tried to structure a safe way of responding to his obsessions and secondary emotions in a formulaic manner that had a set rule for what to think or do for his triggers.

Factors discussed with Rowan that were affecting treatment and recovery success and his actions:

- Accept cognitive flexibility and open-mindedness
  - While reading John Bunyan's case, he learned that he could hold two views at the same time as a helpful dialectic.
- Insight
  - Became more open to feedback about how his consistent thoughts, fears, and behaviors are manifestations of OCD and not in line with the practice of his faith.
- Healthy and unhealthy faith practices and moral living
- Inclusion of his pastor as a person of support during and after treatment
  - Came for two sessions; was supportive of treatment; suggested the problem be understood in the context of a family and community problem and have proper confidence; reiterated the problem not being religious.
- Increase leisure and participation in community
  - Rowan reported increasing trust in acting on his initial "intention" (gut feeling) when deciding to engage in something pleasurable instead of obsessively analyzing the decision or avoid doing it. He agreed to resume watching movies he is interested in seeing even though they may include some sexual material. He resumed his two favorite activities, swimming

and rock climbing, even though it meant risking being around attractive women and sexually aroused.

- Rowan agreed to talk with his pastor about how to manage his sexuality while engaging in social/community activities.

Other elements that were addressed for successful treatment included discouragement of asking obsessive questions to tolerate uncertainty and for the therapist to indicate to Rowan when he was asking reassurance questions that would be left unanswered. Sometimes Rowan wasn't sure if the questions he was asking were obsessive. In order to learn the difference, the therapist suggested that Rowan check his sense of urgency and timing. If the need for an answer was an immediate need to know, or even if it was a legitimate question, he should delay asking the question to see if the urgency was OCD-driven or not. By waiting for the not-right feeling to pass, he could then discern whether to let it go or if it was a reasonable question to ask.

A discussion was held that focused on the need for Rowan to commit to accepting how effective treatment is conducted and that adhering to the treatment plan meant engaging in normalized behavior. He had still been making behavioral decisions secondary to his obsessive thoughts and emotions rather than taking the leap of faith to challenge his fear to engage in the tasks that he, himself, identified as being consistent with his values. Rowan agreed to recommit himself to treatment and be proactive in triggering his obsessive fears. He was reminded that neither God nor faith were being challenged in treatment and that the OCD had highjacked his ability to practice it in a meaningful way.

In vivo exposure was conducted, during which he sketched in a spontaneous manner instead of achieving the "right" mindset and feeling first. His fear was that this would put him in a vulnerable position that would leave room for the devil to take over. He reported his initial SUDS level as 75/100 but was less anxious as the session went on. Rowan admitted that he had the idea of selling his work on a craft website or creating his own business because of the high quality of his work. His homework assignment was to investigate what steps were necessary to put this in motion.

Rowan continued to overidentify with the emotions experienced due to OCD triggers and ritualized by figuring it out until he felt "right." The previous session reviewed several examples of how he had trouble managing the direction to do what he wanted instead of trying to find a way to make it right first. Feedback was provided about the apparent disconnect between how treatment is done and resistance to engage with it effectively. Rowan stated he wanted to work toward being more flexible and to follow treatment guidelines.

Rowan continued to report having ups and downs and that attending church on Sunday was triggering and difficult due to his obsessive thoughts. Aside from that, he reported having reduced his rituals and an increase in normalized functioning. He stated he is resisting "why" questions as a way to resist mentally analyzing or reviewing his obsessive thoughts. He agreed to write out repeatedly the phrase "I might be a bad person" over and over while resisting the urge to do mental rituals. He was instructed to stop every half of a page or so and read the phrase out loud with meaning to enhance the exposure. If he was ready, he could also write out other triggering phrases or sentences that show up as obsessions. He could also write about how how he is a bad person because he did not stop his sister-in-law from getting abortions, about how it was his fault that he contributed to stopping the pregnancy, and how he'll likely go to hell because of it.

At this point Rowan's Y-BOCS score was 23, which put him in a moderate range. Even though there were more symptoms that needed addressing, he felt he reached a plateau and decided to end treatment. He did say that he would keep meeting with his pastor for counseling and try to work on what he learned in treatment.

Transferring Responsibility to God

Psychiatrist, author, and blogger, Ian Osborn, experienced a bout of OCD scrupulosity while in medical school. In his book, *Can Christianity Cure Obsessive-Compulsive Disorder?: A Psychiatrist Explores the Role of Faith in Treatment*, he recommends surrendering one's suffering and sorrow to God, who will take care of it through faith and trust (Osborn, 2008).

Muslim

Ali is a fifty-one-year-old Muslim father of three. He had subclinical OCD symptoms until his last child was born, when he had a full-blown episode. His obsessions were around the fear of being a pedophile, offending Allah, and causing harm to others by not being careful enough. His compulsions consisted of washing and cleaning in order to be worthy to Allah, cleaning, shaking out and checking his prayer mat so as not to offend Allah, stopping and repeating prayers when he had intrusive images of children, and seeking reassurance from his family about whether he did something wrong. He avoided praying at the mosque, going to family gatherings, and going to public places for fear that there may be children there.

Ali's hierarchy and treatment plan is shown in Table 11.2.

Table 11.2 Ali's Treatment Plan

SUDS	Obsessive Fear	Triggering Situation	Ritual	Exposure	Response Prevention
10	Offending Allah Prayers won't count	Praying	Prays for forgiveness Reassures self/Allah thoughts aren't intentional Mental reviewing details: said prayers perfectly/correctly Repeating prayers just in case Seeks reassurance from Imam	Pray fluidly without stopping/repeating Think thoughts are intentional	Resist urges to think reassuring thoughts
10	Being a pedophile	Being around children in public	Avoids going to places such as restaurants, mall, park	Go to public places and sit increasingly closer to where children are	Go out to nearby park and each time be closer to where they are playing (without looking creepy)
10	Offending Allah	Performing wudū	Excessive washing orifices	Adhere to religious guidelines about washing	Resist urges to rewash and keep moving
9	Offending Allah	Laying out prayer mat	Checks to make sure clean/no dirt Repeatedly wipes off with wet wipe	Roll out mat with eyes level to the wall	Skip purposeful checking of mat

(continued)

Table 11.2 *(continued)*

SUDS	Obsessive Fear	Triggering Situation	Ritual	Exposure	Response Prevention
7.5	Being a pedophile	Being intimate with wife Intrusive thoughts while having sex	Fixes bad thoughts with "good" ones Interrupts or stops having sex Having sex with less frequency	Allow obsessive thoughts to be thereHave obsessive thoughts on purpose	Resist responding to the thoughts mentally with self-reassurance; let the uncertainty be there by saying "maybe I am, maybe I'm not."; retrigger the thoughts if mental rituals were performed
6.5	Being a pedophile	Family gatherings	Keeps "safe" distance from children Visual checking/ self-monitoring Seeks reassurance from family after getting home	Go to the next event and stay for at least thirty minutes	Resist urges to leave the room when child(ren) come in; interact with them when you feel ready

Table 11.3 Raisa's Treatment Plan

SUDS	*Obsessive Fear	Triggering Situation	*Ritual	Exposure	Response Prevention
100	Killing family swallowing glass	Preparing food	Visual checking food and cookware *handwashing	Serve meal with glassware; break a light bulb	No checking after setting the table; clean up glass casually without checking to see if nothing shines
95	Causing rape	Vaginal odor especially during menses	Olfactory checking; changing clothes and laundering them right away; avoiding being in public	Run errands in contaminated clothes	Keep same clothes on all day; no checking or changing menstrual pad before leaving the house
90	Glass in clothing	Doing laundry	Checks during each step of the process; rewashes if something dropped on the floor	Put laundry in washer and dryer in fluid manner and then walk away	No checking appliances before or after using them; no handwashing before or after
85	Tiny shards of glass	Hands feel prickly	**Handwashing; visual checking	Use hand lotion to moisturize hands	No visual checking or feeling for sharpness
80	Causing injury	Setting glassware on table; opening/shutting windows	Have other people do these tasks; excessive checking; use plastic cups and plates		
80	Caused bleeding; stepped on blood and bringing into the house	Seeing unidentifiable red spots	Checks/smells her and family's clothes; visually checks skin; takes shoes off when entering house; checks bottom of shoes	Go out into the community, look for red spots, deliberately step on them	Wear shoes into the house and walk through the rooms

(continued)

Table 11.3 *(continued)*

SUDS	*Obsessive Fear	Triggering Situation	*Ritual	Exposure	Response Prevention
80	Sinning	Sexual arousal	Pushes thoughts and feelings away		
75	Bringing glass or other contaminants into the house	Coming in from outside	Checking bottom of her and her kids' shoes; taking shoes off before entering the house		
70	Causing harm	Seeing shiny things	Checking the environment from one room to the next; checking toys		
70	Harming parents	Grandparents babysitting	Giving rules for what they can and can't do or touch	Let grandparents watch son however they want	No rulemaking or giving rules; no reassurance seeking; no checking environment for shiny reflections
70	Poisoning family	Cleaning kitchen and bathroom with chemical products	Washes the surfaces after cleaning with household products; excessive handwashing after use	Use products as directed on the label	Walk away once items are cleaned with product; no handwashing

*All obsessive fears listed included being punished by God, and rituals were suspended until obsessions were under better control.

**Handwashing rituals were performed for every trigger including counting while washing each hand, each wrist, sometimes up to the elbow, back to washing each finger and hand again. If there were any doubts about the rituals not being thoroughly completed, she would go back and repeat the process.

Source: Author.

Jewish

The description of Raisa's treatment in Table 11.3 is tailored toward her glass and somatic obsessions. The fear of God's retribution and being an immoral person underlies all of her obsessive fears and motivation for ritualizing.

Inhibitory Learning

Inhibitory learning is a variation of ERP, which is a behavioral approach that is designed for people to develop the ability to tolerate internal experiences of fear, disgust, and uncertainty rather than habituation through ERP (Elsner, Jacobi, Kischkel, Schulze, & Reuter, 2022). The goal is not to reduce anxiety but rather to become more accepting of it as an uncomfortable but tolerable physiological state. The desired outcome is that people with OCD are better equipped to accept the anxious and emotional reactions to their obsessions than to make efforts to avoid or suppress them. People using inhibitory learning may also experience habituation as a secondary benefit.

Researchers have proposed that anxiety disorders result from rigid efforts at avoiding or controlling the experience of anxiety and fear rather than by the presence of anxiety and fear in and of themselves (Forsyth, Eifert, & Barrios, 2006). Inhibitory learning exposure therapy would assist with tolerating fear, disgust, and uncertainty. For someone with scrupulosity, the exposure to look at Satanic symbols or images would allow for the person to have his obsessive thoughts. Even thought people of his faith would regard purposefully looking at explicit sexual pictures as sinful, it is clearly not a sin to have an unwanted thought, to refrain from fighting it, and to allow God to take responsibility for it.

The inhibitory learning components are expectancy violations, deepened extinction, occasional reinforced extinction, elimination of safety cues, variability of exposure settings, affect labeling, and reconsolidation (Craske, Treanor, Conway, Zbozinek, & Vervliet, 2014; Jacoby & Abramowitz, 2016).

Expectancy violations play a major role in adapting to discomfort and distress caused by OCD. Someone with moral perfectionistic obsessions can purposely think "I am a bad person" long enough to see if any moral, sinful, or harmful events have occurredoccasional reinforced extinction, . A study confirmed that the results represent the first evidence for distress-related expectancy violation and confirm preliminary findings for habituation, suggesting that both processes contribute to treatment benefits of exposure to OCD, and both mechanisms appear to be independent (Elsner et al., 2022). Expectancy violations occur when there is a discrepancy between what the person predicts will happen and what actually occurs, which often has an element of surprise; and that the element of surprise is a learning experience to let go of assumptions or expectations (Rescorla, 1988).

Deepened extinction involves combining multiple triggers into the same exposure after exposure work has been done for each trigger in individual sessions (going to a religious service and thinking "I am a bad person").

Occasional reinforced extinction is another expectancy violation strategy accomplished by intermittently pairing a novel neutral condition with one that the person anticipates being triggering. Someone may go to a party and make small talk while not overexplaining as a way to overcome her fear of lying.

Elimination of safety cues means removing what the person would consider behaviors to fall back on if she feels too anxious to handle the exposure. She might have antibacterial wipes in her car that she knows are there and can retrieve in high-anxiety moments. For example, the person agrees not to carry or wear a religious symbol to ward off evil.

Variability of exposure settings or conditions allows the person to generalize her gains from previous practices in single situations by facing her obsessive fears in a variety of settings that she encounters in her daily routines. She can go to the store and buy groceries and return home without hand washing or cleaning off substances that she fears are halal.

Affect labeling is a technique that has the person label his anticipated emotions of entering the feared situation and then identify them while in the actual setting. More often than not, the emotions anticipated are worse that the actual experience of being in the situation, which creates another expectancy violation. Someone might have put off bringing recycling items to the center because of contamination fears, fears of being wasteful, or fears of hitting someone while driving. Once the exposure gest is underway, rather than the experience being dreadful, the person often feels good about accomplishing a goal and being in control of their behavior.

Reconsolidation asks the person to retrieve stored memories for the purpose of changing the neurochemical responses to the content of the memory to that of the new experience. In that way, the emotional response to prior triggers may change from a heightened sense of fear to being in a more neutral responsive state (Nader, Schafe, & Le Doux, 2000). Instead of remembering the anxiety associated with driving by places of worship and holding one's breath, after having practiced this during exposure work, the person no longer feels the need to avoid routes where they are located and can breathe normally without concern of disrespecting the or contaminating the structures.

Coping Statements for Christians with OCD Scrupulosity

The following are helpful coping statements for Christians—and really for people of any faith—provided by Ted Witzig, PhD, to manage dealing with doubt, uncertainty, intrusive thoughts, and how to move forward.

Dealing with Doubt and Uncertainty:

1. Faith is not the absence of feeling uncertain. Faith is going forward through the uncertainty.
2. OCD wants me to believe that uncertainty and doubt are dangerous. Though uncertainty is uncomfortable, it is not dangerous, and I can tolerate it.
3. My faith is what I believe, not what I feel.
4. Feelings are not facts.
5. OCD will always bring up another *What if . . . ?* Trying to nail down all of the What if . . . ? questions will lead me down a path of never feeling good enough or certain enough.
6. I can have faith and still feel uncertain. *Mark 9:24, "Lord, I believe; help thou mine unbelief."*
7. God loves me completely, even when my feelings are uncertain and clouded by doubt.
8. My peace with God is *not* based on my feelings. Rather, as Romans 5:1 says, *"Therefore being justified by faith, we have peace with God through our Lord Jesus Christ"*: Therefore, I am at peace with God because of Jesus, whether my feelings agree or not.

Dealing with Intrusive Thoughts:

1. Even though they feel real, intrusive thoughts (i.e., distressing thoughts or images with violent, sexual, or blasphemous content) say nothing about my true character.
2. The goal of the intrusive thoughts is to shock and scare me, so I try to suppress or "fix" them. My goal is to identify them as "intrusive thoughts" and move on instead of fighting with them.
3. Having an intrusive thought does not make it more likely for me to act on it.

4. God understands that intrusive thoughts are distressing to me. He understands OCD better than anyone!
5. OCD wants me to believe that worry, anxiety, and compulsions will protect me spiritually. That is all part of the trick OCD wants me to believe.
6. OCD wants me to fight with my thoughts and try to control and suppress them. OCD knows that by getting distressed and fighting with the thoughts, I will refill the "gas tank" in the obsessional engine and keep it running.
7. Trying to prevent myself from ever having certain thoughts, images, and feelings only makes them worse.

Tips on Moving Forward:

1. One of OCD's biggest tricks is asking me the question, "What if this fear isn't from OCD and it really is a serious issue?" Whenever this thought (or one similar) comes, I will treat it as OCD and not try to figure it out.
2. I will pray to God for grace and strength to accept/move on from intrusive thoughts without figuring them out and fight doing compulsions, neutralizing, or avoiding.
3. My goal is to "starve" OCD by not giving meaning to intrusive thoughts or doing compulsions.
4. I have two choices: (1) to chase after a feeling of certainty that never comes or (2) to choose to move forward through the uncertainty.
5. My goal is to focus on doing the tasks that I need to be doing in the present moment (studying, cooking, talking to a friend, working) instead of focusing on trying to figure out the uncertainty or fear.
6. I need to focus on the present moment and allow my thoughts to come and go.
7. Trying to figure it all out only makes it worse.
8. God understands that I don't understand.

Source: Ted Witzig (https://accounseling.org/mentalhealth/ocd/coping-statements-for-christians-with-ocd-scrupulosity/).

Another set of guidelines is from a Jesuit priest, Father V. M. O'Flaherty, S. J.

1. An analysis of the ultimate cause of a scruple should start with a breakdown of the mental experience into the following successive parts:
   (a) There must be a trigger.
   (b) The trigger will have the appearance of sin (thus, if sin is not present in the lines, the scrupulosity will insert it between the lines).

(c) An assumption that I have sinned in the incident must come into mind with certainty, and the emotional force arouses alarming fright.
(d) The assumption of sin is followed by mental compulsions to prove that no sin was committed.
(e) The evidence of "sin" is unsatisfactory; argumentation inevitably ends in doubt.
(f) Obsessive evidence of sinning is not convincing.
(g) In the face of ambiguity and uncertainty, anxiety about eternal salvation becomes overwhelming.
(h) An intention of performing a false religious obligation/emotional compulsion arises to settle the doubt about the sin/guilt.
(i) The torturous thought that I cannot help sinning overtakes the mind.
(j) An assurance from my confessor that no sin was committed fails to stifle apprehension of having committed a sin and extremely guilty feelings are unshakable.
(k) Duties and responsibilities start to be overlooked as the effort to settle the scruples becomes the priority.
(l) Continuous examination of conscience brings me to a state of exhaustion which, in turn, is a handicap in settling my doubts about sinning. (O'Flaherty, 1973)

Comments on the Deadly Sins

The deadly sins exemplify the black-and-white nature of the scrupulous person's fear of experiencing pleasure. The sins are pride, gluttony, lust, avarice, envy, wrath, and sloth. Any hint of temptation is managed by doing the opposite virtues. The virtues in order are humility, temperance, self-control, generosity and charity, love, and diligence. The pattern of going from one extreme to the other with OCD is being motivated from fear versus love, meaning the spirit of the action is lost on the literalness of it. Pride is considered the most serious of the deadly sins, and there is a "duty to act contrary to scruples, for one might otherwise sin by pride, self-will and disobedience" (Jone & Adelman, 1952). If a scrupulous person goes from being prideful to humble, there is still an element of pride in being humbly virtuous.

The Catholic blog from the The Littlest Souls, devoted to divine mercy offered advice from the Priestly Fraternity of Saint Peter:

> we must not voluntarily dwell on the thought when it comes, but if we find that we have done so for a brief moment, we should not be discouraged.

> Instead, we should humble ourselves, recommend ourselves to God and to Our Lady, and focus our attention calmly on something else. Why spend our time worrying when we can simply make an act of perfect contrition? (https://littlestsouls.wordpress.com/2013/06/18/perfect-contrition-the-golden-key-of-paradise/).

And finally, a quote from Gilbert Kilpack:

> There are people who, when they catch sight of how far they are from the grand goal of perfection to get the moral fidgets or the spiritual jitters and they become super careful about details as some sort of atonement for their failure or their imperfection. We ought not to suffer in this way, for we are the inheritors of history, the history of the saints by grace who are most disarming at this point; they accept freely and openly their shortcomings, great and small—not resigned to their distance from the goal, but they accept it as the present condition of fact and would rather joke about it than fret about it. (Kilpack, 1956)

References

Abramowitz, J. S., Deacon, B. J., Olatunji, B. O., Wheaton, M. G., Berman, N. C., Losardo, D., . . . Hale, L. R. (2010). Assessment of obsessive-compulsive symptom dimensions: Development and evaluation of the Dimensional Obsessive-Compulsive Scale. *Psychological Assessment, 22*(1), 180–198. doi:10.1037/a0018260

Alonso, P., Menchon, J. M., Pifarre, J., Mataix-Cols, D., Torres, L., Salgado, P., & Vallejo, J. (2001). Long-term follow-up and predictors of clinical outcome in obsessive-compulsive patients treated with serotonin reuptake inhibitors and behavioral therapy. *Journal of Clinical Psychiatry, 62*(7), 535–540.

Badri, M. (2013). *Abu Zayd AlBalkhi's sustenance of the soul: The cognitive behavior therapy of a ninth century physician*. London, UK: International Institute of Islamic Thought.

Berman, N. C., Summers, B. J., Weingarden, H., & Wilhelm, S. (2019). Positive affect and imaginal exposure processes in patients with taboo obsessions. *Journal of Obsessive-Compulsive and Related Disorders, 23*, 100474. doi:10.1016/j.jocrd.2019.100474

Bonchek, A. (2009). *Religious compulsions and fears: A guide to treatment*. New York, NY: Feldheim.

Craske, M. G., Treanor, M., Conway, C. C., Zbozinek, T., & Vervliet, B. (2014). Maximizing exposure therapy: an inhibitory learning approach. *Behaviour Research and Therapy, 58*, 10–23. doi:10.1016/j.brat.2014.04.006

Elsner, B., Jacobi, T., Kischkel, E., Schulze, D., & Reuter, B. (2022). Mechanisms of exposure and response prevention in obsessive-compulsive disorder: Effects of habituation and expectancy violation on short-term outcome in cognitive behavioral therapy. *BMC Psychiatry, 22*(1), 66. doi:10.1186/s12888-022-03701-z

Foa, E. B. (2010). Cognitive behavioral therapy of obsessive-compulsive disorder. *Dialogues in Clinical Neuroscience, 12*(2), 199–207. doi:10.31887/DCNS.2010.12.2/efoa

Forsyth, J. P., Eifert, G. H., & Barrios, V. (2006). Fear conditioning in an emotion regulation context: A fresh perspective on the origins of anxiety disorders. In M. G. Craske, D. Hermans, & D. Vansteenwegan (Eds.), *Fear and learning: From basic processes to clinical implications* (pp. 133-153). Washington, DC: American Psychological Association.

Freud, S. (1910). *The future prospects of psycho-analytic therapy SE* (Vol. 11). London, UK: Hogarth.

Griffith, J. (2006). Managing religious countertransference in clinical settings. *Psychiatric Annals, 36*, 196–204. doi:10.3928/00485713-20060301-03

Hayes, J. A., Gelso, C. J., & Hummel, A. M. (2011). Managing countertransference. *Psychotherapy, 48*(1), 88–97. doi:10.1037/a0022182

Jacoby, R. J., & Abramowitz, J. S. (2016). Inhibitory learning approaches to exposure therapy: A critical review and translation to obsessive-compulsive disorder. *Clinical Psychology Review, 49*, 28–40.

Jone, H., & Adelman, U. (1952). *Moral theology*. Westminster, UK: The Newman Press.

Keshavarzi, H., Khan, F., & Syed, B. (2018). Islamically integrated treatment of obsessive-compulsive disorder scrupulosity (Waswasa) in Muslim patients. In N. T Ali Ayten & M. Z. Halil Eksi (Eds.), *Spiritual counselling and care in health and prison services: Diverse experiences & practices* (pp. 229–251). London, UK: Ensar.

Kilpack, G. (1956). *Scruples* (89th ed.). Wallingford, UK: Pendle Hill.

Mataix-Cols, D., Marks, I. M., Greist, J. H., Kobak, K. A., & Baer, L. (2002). Obsessive-compulsive symptom dimensions as predictors of compliance with and response to behaviour therapy: Results from a controlled trial. *Psychotherapy and Psychosomatics, 71*(5), 255–262. doi:10.1159/000064812

Nader, K., Schafe, G. E., & Le Doux, J. E. (2000). Fear memories require protein synthesis in the amygdala for reconsolidation after retrieval. *Nature, 406*, 722–726. doi:10.1038/35021052

O'Flaherty, V. M. (1973). Therapy for scrupulosity. In R. M. Jurievich (Ed.), *Direct therapy: Twenty-eight American originals* (pp. 221–243). Miami, FL: Miami University Press.

Olatunji, B. O., Abramowitz, J. S., Williams, N. L., Connolly, K. M., & Lohr, J. M. (2007). Scrupulosity and obsessive-compulsive symptoms: Confirmatory factor analysis and validity of the Penn Inventory of Scrupulosity.

Journal of Anxiety Disorders, 21(6), 771–787. doi:10.1016/j.janxdis.2006.12.002

Osborn, I. (2008). *Can Christianity cure obsessive-compulsive disorder? A psychiatrist explores the role of faith in treatment*. Grand Rapids, MI: Brazos Press.

Rassool, G. H. (2018). *Evil eye, jinn possession, and mental health issues: An Islamic perspective*. New York, NY: Routledge.

Rescorla, R. A. (1988). Pavlovian conditioning: It's not what you think it is. *American Psychologist, 43*(3), 151–160. doi:10.1037/0003-066X.43.3.151

Riley, C. (2003). *Scrupulosity when being perfect punishes* [sound recording]. Canfield, OH: Alba House Cassettes.

Shapiro, L. J., Krompinger, J. W., Gironda, C. M., & Elias, J. A. (2013). Development of a scrupulosity severity scale using the Pennsylvania Inventory of Scrupulosity–Revised. *Journal of Obsessive-Compulsive and Related Disorders, 2*(4), 420–424. doi:10.1016/j.jocrd.2013.08.001

Wetterneck, C. T., Rouleau, T. M., Williams, M. T., Vallely, A., La Torre, J. T., & Björgvinsson, T. (2021). A new scrupulosity scale for the dimensional obsessive-compulsive scale (DOCS): Validation with clinical and nonclinical samples. *Behavior Therapy, 52*(6), 1449–1463. doi:10.1016/j.beth.2021.04.001

CHAPTER TWELVE

Clergy Involvement: Soul Crushing or Saving?

> "God promised His mercy to all, and granted to His priests the license of forgiving sins without any exception."
>
> St. Ambrose of Milan, c. 340–397

Even though scrupulosity is a mental health issue, the content of religious obsessions causes OCD to be mistaken as a problem of faith (Kaviani, Eskandari, & Ebrahimi Ghavam, 2015). For many people struggling with mental health issues, the first point of contact is often a member of their clergy (Stanford & Philpott, 2011). About 17–40% of parishioners who seek mental health treatment will only seek help from members of their clergy (Farrell & Goebert, 2008; Hooley, Wang, & Hodge, 2020; Kramer et al., 2007). Clergy are contacted 17% more often than psychiatrists and general medical doctors (Wang, Berglund, & Kessler, 2003), and it is unclear what kind of mental help clergy members offer (Lehman & Steinwachs, 1998).

A large, international home-based study was conducted that examined the role religious advisors play in mental health care according to disorder severity, sociodemographics, religious involvement, and country income groups (Kovess-Masfety et al., 2017). The study found that 12–30% used religious services for guidance, and attending religious services once per week was a predictor of seeking help through clergy (Kovess-Masfety et al., 2017).

Turning to Clergy for Help

It is unclear if those with mental health issues or their clergy are aware that the presenting problem may be an undiagnosed and untreated clinical problem. To many African American Pentecostal clergy members, the etiology of mental illness is considered to be a spiritual problem (Dempsey, Butler, & Gaither, 2016). Muslims were also found to explain that OCD is a manifestation from a *jinn* spirit or whispers from Satan that causes someone to be disconnected from God to a role (Rassool, 2018).

A survey of American Muslims suggested that only 11% would seek therapy, compared to 21% who would seek help from a family member and 19% who would approach religious leaders (Aloud & Rathur, 2009). In the Middle East, the percentage of people who sought help from traditional healers included 60% of Omanis, 59% of Iraqis, 42% of Saudis, and half of the people surveyed in the United Arab Emirates (Salem, Saleh, Yousef, & Sabri, 2009). These authors also found that many patients continued to seek treatment from faith healers even after having sought mental health services (Salem et al., 2009).

Some significant predictors of those with mental health issues who first sought help from clergy were being younger in age; having less than a high school education; having suicidal ideation, plans, or attempts; having panic or depressive disorders; and being married (Wang et al., 2003).

Some obstacles include mistrust, misunderstanding, and lack of interest in collaboration from both clergy and mental health providers. Although feelings of misunderstanding and lack of interest are experienced by people in both professions, mistrust is experienced more by religious leaders (Harris, 2018). The laity in a study was open to seeking a mental health care professional, but often after being referred by their pastor to seek therapy (Bolger & Prickett, 2021). This same study reported that although congregants sought out pastors because of their perceived expertise, pastors expressed concern over their lack of training in pastoral care and their limited ability to attend to their needs (Bolger & Prickett, 2021).

The common goal of each profession is to alleviate the suffering of those who seek physical, spiritual, mental, and emotional relief. In order to bridge the gap between the two fields, minimizing the differences so that when clinicians and clergy collaborate they can recognize how multiple factors can be interrelated to the psychological and spiritual health of individuals (Stanford & Philpott, 2011).

Regional and Racial Utilization of Clergy for Mental Health Support

In practical terms, clergy may also be the only resource when mental health resources are not available, unaffordable, or simply not knowing where else to turn. Clergy become the most available source of support available in the community.

Residents in an area in the southern United States considered the "Bible Belt" turned the clergy for help in coping with emotional problems (Wang et al., 2003). Community members and clergy in certain locations may also be wary of psychiatry or the mental health systems, which may account for why clergy may be the most available resource most consulted for mental health problems (Campbell, 2021).

Residents of the South who sought help also turned preferentially to the clergy, confirming earlier observations that religion is especially important in the "Bible Belt" of the United States for those coping with emotional problems (Wang et al., 2003).

Clergy Attitudes toward Mental Health

Conflicting religious and psychiatric conceptions about the etiology and healing approaches of mental illnesses can affect where and from whom help is sought (Sullivan et al., 2014). Comparably, clergy members who "demonize the biomedical model of mental health treatment" can also delay or interfere with one's desire to seek help (Sullivan et al., 2014, p. 1269).

Pentecostals were found to view mental illness as a result of having sinned, demonic possession, or punishment from God (Mercer, 2013). This supports the view that mental illness is a form of divine punishment (Gray, 2001). Pentecostal clergy may view those with mental illness as having engaged in sinful lifestyles or being morally weak; they may believe sufferers are receiving divine punishment (Dobbins, 2014) as God's attempt at teaching the forsaken person a spiritual lesson (Wesselmann & Graziano, 2010).

Christian clergy who consider mental illness to be a spiritual problem with a spiritual solution view mental illness and psychological concerns as "manifestations of demon possession, evil spirits, or the work of the devil" and tend not to refer parishioners to mental health professionals (Sullivan et al., 2014, p. 1269). They may believe that "a cure may involve exorcism or faith healing" and that the "use of psychotherapy and medication demonstrates a lack of faith" (Sullivan et al., 2014, p. 1276). Instead, they counsel the person to rely on prayer and faith in God to deliver and heal. The study also reported that clergy who did recognize that clinical care was appropriate made referrals to Christian rather than secular mental health providers (Sullivan et al., 2014).

Christian cognitive behavioral therapy (C-CBT) is an integrative approach to therapy that incorporates spiritual and religious components into traditional CBT approaches (Pearce & Koenig, 2013). Christian psychologists are a specialized group whose practice is faith-based and integrate religious and spiritual knowledge with psychological principles and interventions (McMinn, Staley, Webb, & Seegobin, 2010). Clinicians using this framework draw from the parishioner's Christian faith as a foundation to identify, challenge, and restructure maladaptive thoughts, emphasizing spiritual practices as a way to aid the restructuring process (Pearce & Koenig, 2013). Along with respect for faith beliefs, it is important that the psychologist also be culturally informed about how to use scriptures within the cultural context of the person's identity (Pearce & Koenig, 2013). In the case of a practicing Christian with scrupulosity, it would be important that the practitioner have an awareness about the nature and the clinical aspects of the problem and provide evidence-based treatment while providing spiritual and faith support (Pearce & Koenig, 2013).

These psychologists may be a good resource for people who are resistant to more standard psychological approaches to healing. There do not appear to be any studies that have evaluated the outcome of treatment for scrupulosity by Christian psychologists, but it is hoped that they are providing appropriate services for this problem.

Clergy Preparedness

How equipped are clergy to recognize and manage mental health issues? Clergy have reported referring less than 10% of those who approached them with psychological problems to mental health professionals (Mollica, Streets, Boscarino, & Redlich, 1986; Virkler, 1979). Another 50–80% of clergy members reported that counseling training in seminary postseminary continuing education was inadequate (Farrell & Goebert, 2008; Lowe, 1986). Further, many clergy have expressed interest in mental health-related training, and initial studies have found that even brief training can increase clergy members' sense of competence in dealing with mental health issues (Chevalier et al., 2015; Payne, 2001).

In a study of Protestant clergy, the majority reported feeling insufficiently trained or not having the knowledge about how to recognize mental illness (Farrell & Goebert, 2008). Some reported they made referrals to a mental health practitioner of the same faith (Farrell & Goebert, 2008; Wang et al., 2003). The authors pointed out how doing so limited the choices of qualified providers.

Practicing parish ministers and pastors and those who teach in the seminary were interviewed about the demands, procedures, and preparation for counseling, and 45% stated that they received no training on referral criteria (Virkler, 1979).

In a study conducted in an urban African American faith community, ministers reported that people seeking pastoral counseling came by referral from health professionals, were self-referred, or the ministers sought out people they perceived to be struggling (Young, Griffith, & Williams, 2003). The authors also reported that some ministers frequently made referrals to a social worker, hospital emergency services, or a community mental health center. A minority of ministers made direct referrals to pastoral counselors, psychiatrists, psychologists, and institutional chaplains (Young et al., 2003).

A study of Protestants that examined how prepared clergy felt about recognizing and managing mental health issues reported that they did not have sufficient training or knowledge about how to recognize mental illness (Farrell & Goebert, 2008). Clergy, including Seventh Day Adventists and charismatic ministers, who made mental health referrals felt it was important that the professional share the same religious faith as the parishioner (Farrell & Goebert, 2008).

Clergy awareness of the obsessive-compulsive disorder (OCD) subtypes of scrupulosity and moral perfectionism is essential as people who suffer with these symptoms may not be aware that they are actually experiencing symptoms of a disorder. These types of symptoms are often mistaken as problems of faith, morality, or spirituality due to the content of the obsessions (Shapiro, 2014). People with OCD who have blasphemous, violent, or sexual obsessions may confess them to clergy, who might interpret them as sins to be atoned for or give them advice that may be carried out as OCD rituals and not in the spirit of healthy faith practice. When this occurs, sufferers often end up feeling worse about themselves, inadequate, unworthy, and discouraged when the clerical advice did not work.

Positive religious attitudes were found to predict following up on the advice given by clergy (Kovess-Masfety et al., 2017). As such, training and collaboration with mental health professionals can better ensure that the most appropriate interventions are delivered (Oppenheimer, Flannelly, & Weaver, 2004). Likewise, clinicians' understanding of patients' religious and faith beliefs may provide more validating support (Farrell & Goebert, 2008).

Psychosocial, Demographic, and Clinical Factors

Race/Ethnicity/Culture/Class/Socioeconomics

Help-seeking behaviors in racial and ethnic minority communities have been examined and there are several barriers that interfere with utilizing mental health services. For example, the cost of treatment, geographic limitations of access to services, lack of mental health literacy, and cultural differences in health beliefs are some reasons for disparities, inequalities, and underrepresentation in clinical health care settings (Gallo, Marino, Ford, & Anthony, 1995).

One study compared barriers that parents from different ethnic groups face when trying to access specialized OCD services for their children. Several common barriers for both groups included a lack of knowledge of OCD, lack of resources, mistrust in the mental health system, previous negative experiences, lack of time and financial challenges, inconvenient location of services, and bullying. Barriers identified by parents from the ethnic minority groups but not by white parents largely consisted of perceived or real attitudes within their communities. Stigma, discrimination, negative attitudes toward and mistrust of the health care system, and different beliefs about mental health issues were experienced as external factors, while shame and denial were internal experiences of parents that interfered with getting help.

Another study examined reasons for help-seeking avoidance within an African American community. Along with responses similar to those found in the study cited above, others were affordability, impersonal quality of service, therapists' lack of cultural understanding and sensitivity, and fear of being stereotyped by the health care clinicians (Thompson, Bazile, & Akbar, 2004).

Clergy members who were Episcopalian, Lutheran, Methodist, Presbyterian, United Church of Christ, independent (Baptist or general Christian), charismatic (Assemblies of God, Four Square, and Pentecostal), and Seventh Day Adventist were asked about their training in mental health issues; 71% reported feeling inadequately trained to recognize mental illness (Farrell & Goebert, 2008). Nonetheless, they did provide counseling regardless of their level of training or feelings of inadequacy, despite reporting a belief that the most common cause of mental illness is medical. This was reflected in the case vignettes; more than 40% of respondents who admittedly lacked training said they would counsel the individuals described in the vignettes. These dramatic findings demonstrate that many clergy members were not adequately trained to treat mental illness but proceeded with doing so nonetheless. Their "patients" were not being referred to psychiatrists partly because of clergy members' inability to identify serious mental illnesses (Farrell & Goebert, 2008).

In a study conducted with Lutheran pastors, 36% reported recognizing scrupulosity as a mental health problem (Deacon, Vincent, & Zhang, 2013). Of those, 20% had someone with scrupulosity approach them for help, but the 7% of pastors who reported being familiar with ERP treatment made no referrals (Deacon et al., 2013). It is unclear if this accounted by ERP treatment not being locally available or if the parishioners refused the recommendation.

Clergy awareness of scrupulosity and moral perfectionism is essential since people who suffer with these symptoms may not be aware that they actually have a diagnosable and treatable disorder. As stated, these types of symptoms are often mistaken by clergy and sufferers as problems of faith, morality, or spirituality due to the content of the obsessions (Shapiro, 2014).

Seven hundred forty-six nonclinical and twenty-four clinical participants (with a principal diagnosis of OCD) from a wide range of religious affiliations completed questionnaires. In both samples, obsessional thinking was positively associated with scrupulosity but not religious fundamentalism. The relationship between religiosity and moral TAF was significantly moderated by the belief that the universe is ordered and humanity is connected (high religiosity was only associated with high moral TAF when universality was low). These findings suggest that religious individuals with OCD may benefit from enhancing spirituality through consultation with a religious authority or within therapy (Henderson et al., 2022).

Clergy Perceptions of Blasphemous Obsessions

Some religions and clergymen set and glorify impossible moral standards and practices, and also lay great emphasis on the severe forms of celestial punishment ensuing violation of any religious ethic, irrespective of its significance. Even having certain thoughts violates the principles of some religions and can prove to be distressful to people without OCD. Such values and cultures may prove to be conducive to the development of blasphemous and religious-based obsessions and have a morbid fear of even inadvertent violation of religious doctrine (Abramowitz & Jacoby, 2014; Ali, Mujawar, Davis, Chaudhury, & Saldanha, 2021).

The literature on blasphemous obsessions revealed that it may coexist with contamination, doubt, and symmetry obsessions, but it has also been found to be associated with sexual or violent obsessions (Abramowitz & Jacoby, 2014). It was also found that the presence of varying types of obsessions but not compulsions were predictive factors of religious obsessions (Ali et al., 2021).

Jake had explicit blasphemous and violent thoughts about God and was compelled to confess them. The priest interpreted them as sinful acts that needed to be atoned for by the penance given to Jake for the "wrong" reason, since his intrusive obsessions are something he can't control. Unfortunately, Jake repeated the acts of contrition to perfection to ensure being in God's good grace, which would be considered the "right reason," but as they were compulsions, the spirit of a healthy faith practice was completely lost. As a result, when Jake was finished and realized what he was doing, he ended up feeling worse about himself, because he did not fulfill the sacramental obligation in the "right" spirit.

Mental Health and Physician Practitioner Preparedness

Mental and medical health practitioners may overlook or undervalue the important role religion and cultural beliefs play in many of their patients' lives (Swihart, Yarrarapu, & Martin, 2022). In many cases, identifying and supporting patients' religious practices may help their sense of well-being and find meaning in times of medical challenges (Puchalski, 2001). Many mental health practitioners do not identify as being religious (Rosmarin & Pirutinsky, 2020). Psychiatrists are 70% less religious than other physicians and 36% less likely to look to God for strength in stressful times, and religious physicians are less willing than nonreligious physicians to refer patients to psychiatrists (Curlin et al., 2007).

There may be an unconscious bias with evidence-based practitioners, and medication prescribers may be against or not even think about recommending clergy counseling as an additional source of support for healing, perhaps based on their historical experiences with religious teachings or events (Lannert, 1991; Rosmarin, Green, Pirutinsky, & McKay, 2013); this may affect the quality of the therapeutic relationship (Griffith, 2006). There may also be a disconnect between the practitioners' and patients' values and cultures that may create an unhelpful disconnect on the part of the professional (Bergin, 1980). However, a survey of psychologists reported that 82% of psychologists regarded religion as beneficial to mental health (Delaney, Miller, & Bisonó, 2007).

In Islam, Muslims frequently sought help from traditional healers for mental health issues, especially when *jinn* possession (Lim, Hoek, Ghane, Deen, & Blom, 2018) or witchcraft was suspected (Dein, Lewis, & Loewenthal, 2011). Faith healers treated the problem with *ruqyah* (seeking refuge with Allah) by reciting certain verses from the Qur'an, reciting the Qur'an over water, and instructing the individuals to drink it afterward (Dein, 2004). Alternatively, they may recite the Qur'an over water and blow into it; then they tell the sick person to wash with this water (Dein et al., 2011).

Pentecostals consider mental illness as being caused by the presence of demons and that the way to release them is through deliverance by exorcism (Mercer, 2013). There is also a strong belief that the cause of mental illness is not only demonic possession but also sin (Gray, 2001) and engaging in sinful lifestyles, resulting in divine punishment from God (Dobbins, 2014).

Other Pentecostals may believe that they have not received total healing as a result of lacking faith in God and His ability to deliver, or through praying ineffectively (Dobbins, 2014). Thus, those who view mental illness as a manifestation of moral flaws or spiritual weaknesses will be unlikely to seek treatment from secular providers, possibly because mental health providers might not suggest using one's faith in God for healing (Wesselmann & Graziano, 2010). There is also a belief that healing mental health problems can only be done by an intervention from God or by an intermediary (Plunkett, 2009).

Ideally, a team approach that includes a clergy member and a specialized OCD therapist (as well as having a prescribing psychiatrist on board) can help the sufferer achieve a higher level of trust in the treatment process. Establishing trust is one of the first hurdles to overcome for both clergy and therapists due to the person's obsessive doubt about whether she is being completely understood by the (healer), whether the healer is qualified to appropriately guide her. The advantage of having clergy involved is that they can help patients understand how to separate healthy faith from scrupulosity and, in turn, reinforce the "tenets" of behavior therapy/ERP that are effective (Bretzke, 2004). The structure of exposure work can be designed by the feedback provided by the clergy member about the particular religious questions and practices. The patient and therapist will work out the behavioral tasks that will be carried out during ERP sessions followed by daily practice at home. It is essential that clergy redirect repeated question or urges to "confess" the same sins over and over. These are ritualistic interfering that will undermine treatment outcome.

Clergy Interventions

Catholics

Many Catholics are challenged by having been taught as children that bad thoughts are sins, or at least they report believing that was the message. Working out of the literal understanding of this teaching to a more mature level of faith is one of the first challenges in addressing TAF and the content of obsessions. Because of the endless stream of obsessive doubts, the priest should consult with the person in a kind, confident, and firm manner that he assumes responsibility for knowing the correct way to counsel and dispense penance.

As noted in the chapter on history, directions for ministering to Catholics with scrupulosity date back to the fourth century. Climacus said that "no one in the face of blasphemous thoughts need think that the guilt lies within him, for the Lord is the Knower of hearts and He is aware that such words and thoughts do not come from us but from our foes" (Climacus, 1982, p. 79).

As outlined in the following section, the most consistent strategy advised by Catholic leaders in addressing scrupulosity is for parishioners to unquestioningly obey the mandates of the spiritual advisor. The testing of trust will occur throughout meetings with clergy and therapists since the presenting problem is one of doubt, not faith. Many scrupulous Catholics "priest hop" in the pursuit of certainty and reassurance, much like people with health anxiety schedule medical appointments with different doctors when they inevitably doubt the outcome of the consultation. These efforts never provide the desired outcome of relief, even when the priest and doctor are accurate in assessing the problem and prescribing the correct therapeutic interventions.

Other instructions for counseling scrupulous Catholics is for the person to identify his triggers. Next, the person learns it is best not to yield to the temptation to engage in unproductive arguments with what would be normally considered a doubt about a "sinless" sin. For example, a parishioner without OCD who is attending a religious service may notice he wasn't paying attention after realizing he had been off daydreaming. He would refocus his attention on the portion of the service and not give it another thought. Someone with scrupulosity would feel he had sinned because his attention had been diverted to the pleasurable thoughts in his daydream and would confess to or seek reassurance from his pastor. Then the goal is to teach that a way to avoid the scruple is by turning the person's attention to some distracting thought. The "refusal to pay attention to a scruple cures it" (O'Flaherty, 1973); Gilbert Kilpack makes the distinction that the opposite of a scrupulous person is not an unscrupulous person, but a person of faith (Kilpack, 1956, p. 5).

Vincent O'Flaherty, a Jesuit priest and lecturer in medical ethics at Marquette University, wrote the book *How to Cure Scruples* (O'Flaherty, 1966). He defines a scruple as a "feeling" that a sin was committed in a doubtful incident and is pressed into the mind as a false conviction of guilt (O'Flaherty, 1973). He advised people to remember how St. Ignatius alleviated his scrupulosity through his principle to "Do the opposite" (O'Flaherty, 1973, p. 234).

Clergy Guide for Helping the Scrupulous

Scrupulous Anonymous is a newsletter published for Catholics with scrupulosity. These are the very abridged ten commandments for coping with scrupulosity:

1. Understand that scrupulosity can be a temporary condition or a persistent and seemingly unyielding condition, which is most often a manifestation of Obsessive-Compulsive Disorder (OCD); in either case, it is not a punishment from God.
2. Acknowledge your need for help and guidance and accept that you cannot effectively pursue a path of healing and wholeness by yourself.
3. Accept and understand that the presence of fear and anxiety is the condition of scrupulosity and not the indication or warning of the presence of sin.
4. Always remember and never forget that discipline is essential if you wish to become healed.
5. Learn to be very patient with yourself, your confessor and spiritual director, your therapist, and with family and friends.
6. Discover and recognize your success and learn to celebrate your effort.
7. When you fail, or feel that you have taken two steps backward, pick yourself up and try again. Do not give in to feelings of failure.
8. Never underestimate the power of grace.
9. Pray, pray, pray. Try and live a life of thankful praise.
10. Imagine yourself living free from scrupulosity.

The full text is in *Understanding Scrupulosity: Questions, Helps, and Encouragement* (Santa, 2007).

Obsessive Whispers as a Mistaken Call to the Clergy

Some Catholic men with scrupulosity may feel, mistakenly, that becoming a priest is a religious calling. Family members may feel blessed that their relative has entered the seminary to train for the priesthood. Though there are no prevalence rates or reports on this, empirical experience has shown that clergy who present for treatment may have been referred by superiors due to the excessive nature of their religious practice, distress when they cannot perform their rituals, and the apparent disconnect between the spirit of faith practice and the rigid style the novitiate is demonstrating. With early onset scrupulosity, the obsessiveness may have been reinforced as proof of a calling, a sign of zealous devotion, or strong piety.

If a person was ordained, excessive and atypical religious behaviors will eventually emerge. If properly understood, the person may be referred to a pastoral counselor or mental health professional. Questions and doubts about his religious motivation and uncertainty about his self-identity make treatment more complex. The person can then explore the motivation behind what led them to a religious vocation and whether to continue the pursuit or not. It may lead to a crisis in faith with the person's thinking becoming more flexible, but, in the end, he will have a choice rather than a compulsion. Consultation with someone in the religious community may be a necessary adjunct to help mitigate the emotional turmoil in the throes of coming to terms with the OCD and its impact on life.

These are suggested questions when someone may be considering becoming a Catholic priest:

1. Does the idea of becoming a priest keep coming back time and time again, even though you thought you had moved on in your life and forgotten about it?
2. Do you feel called to give more, to be more?
3. Does your relationship with God sustain you, enliven you, invigorate you in such a way that you want to share his truth and love with others?
4. Do you long for more than what "the world" teaches us to strive for—money, sensuality, power, self-indulgence, and comfort at any cost?
5. Do you have a sneaking suspicion that you are on the brink of a major life decision?
6. Does the idea of becoming a priest attract you and at the same time frighten you because you feel "unworthy"? (https://www.hbgdiocese.org/clergy/vocations/vocation-discernment/are-you-called-to-be-a-priest/)

Latter-Day Saints/Mormons

"Look unto me in every thought; doubt not, fear not."

Doctrines and Covenants Scripture 6:36

An approach to counseling Latter-Day Saints/Mormons with scrupulosity is the reframing of doctrine that emphasizes the role of premortal creation, by the Heavenly Father of intelligences of spirit, sons and daughters whom he chose to create as his children (Weir, Greaves, Kelm, Ragu, & Rick, 2014). It is also helpful to reframe God as loving and smiling, as caring about them and being easily pleased (Newquist, 1974).

Given the mistrust that mental health professionals will have a negative attitude toward religion, fear that the therapist will want to convert them, and the belief that therapy is too secular, people have been reluctant to seek help (Weir et al., 2014). It has been proposed that a Latter-Day Saint with scrupulosity will likely be wary of even an LDS therapist until the therapist has passed some sort of client-imposed "secret test" that the therapist is orthodox or faithful enough as a Latter-Day Saint (Broderick, 1992).

John Dehlin, a Latter-Day Saint who went on to become a psychologist, described his experience with scrupulosity while practicing his faith. His scrupulosity had been reinforced by comments his elders made when he went to confess his "sinful" thoughts. In his podcast he described meeting with an elder who told him, "You are so pure. You are the cleanest vessel in the mission. People around you will take note and praise you for your behaviors." He goes on to say that the problem goes undiagnosed because "the person thinks what he is doing is actually right and because everyone around them says you're such a spiritual giant. You're so amazingly righteous!" (Dehlin, 2011). His advice to the bishops and presidents was to "ease up on guilt-based/fear-based consequences and more toward love, grace, softness, compassion, flexibility. Be less literal about the words in the bible" (Dehlin, 2011).

Islam

Borrowing from psychotherapist Najwa Awad of the Yaqeen Institute (https://yaqeeninstitute.org/najwa-awad/clinicians-imams-and-the-whisperings-of-satan/), the following recommendations are provided to promote reliable and sensitive religious, cultural, and psychological guidance in treating Muslims with scrupulosity. Her guidelines utilize contextual teachings from the Qur'an and Hadith that support the treatment of *waswâs al-qahri* (OCD). This is invaluable for people who may be resistant or mistrustful of psychological conceptualizations/formulations and who live in communities where there is stigma and assumptions about Western psychology being contradictory to Islam, or that therapy is only for people who have weak or no faith. Including an imam as a treatment team member will also validate the treatment recommendations, and the imam can clarify issues of religious faith practice and rule out beliefs and rituals that are driven by OCD. The imam can also help develop exposure tasks and ways to restructure cognitive distortions.

This unique professional collaboration with a cultural and spiritual knowledge of Islam and an imam with the psychological understanding of scrupulosity create an ideal practice for treatment and recovery. Proper sensitivity to OCD symptoms as psychological in nature and respect for religious beliefs and practices are qualities conducive to achieving control over the disorder and a more connected spiritual connection to Allah.

An imam can explain the importance of maintaining important values, such as patience (*sabr*), acceptance (*rida*), reliance on God (*tawakkul*), remembrance of God (*dhikr*), and hope (*raja'*) during exposure work. He can also remind scrupulous Muslims of the Islamic rulings of prayer: if one offers a congregational prayer (*solah al-jama'ah*) behind an imam, all of the responsibility for the rites and rituals of the prayer will be absolved. Scrupulous Muslims will be advised to be mindful of their *khusyu* recitations (prayer) and to refrain from praying alone. The authors noted in their report that after a month of daily congregational prayer, the obsessive rituals of a scrupulous person had completely disappeared (Nabil, Sharip, & Thomas, 2019).

Judaism

Within Ultra-Orthodox Judaism, rabbis interpret *halacha* (Jewish law) for synagogue members who seek legal, spiritual, and personal guidance (Huppert, Siev, & Kushner, 2007). The authors conducted a qualitative study on Orthodox rabbis to assess what their understanding of scrupulosity was, what they suggested as helpful interventions, if there were any Torah sources they cite as being relevant to scrupulosity, and what their views were about their collaboration with mental health professionals while providing religious counseling to their scrupulous congregants (Horwitz, Littman, Greenberg, & Huppert, 2019). They found that the rabbis' conceptualizations about the etiology of scrupulosity were that scrupulosity was primarily psychological in nature, rather than religious or spiritual, and that they were receptive to working with therapists to assist those who had sought their counsel (Bonchek & Greenberg, 2009).

A book was written by a Jewish rabbi and a psychologist specifically for addressing OCD and Jewish scrupulosity (Greenwald, 2019). He presented the following guidelines for when scrupulosity has begun to interfere with adhering to halacha:

- Decide on who will be the rabbinic authority and the person to whom all questions will be asked.
- Pray from a *siddur* and that which he has already said he should not repeat in any event. Even if it seems to him for certain that he did not say it properly or that he skipped some words. He is not required to do more than that. One should not try to explain this to a person who is nervous about the matter. Therefore, the person must be told in no uncertain terms and without explanation [not to repeat his words in prayer].

- *Shenayim Mikra v'Echad Targum*—practice of reading the weekly Torah portion (*sedra*) in a prescribed manner is the only specific learning that has an explicit halachic *requirement*. Review it ahead of time. Have a *chavrusa* (reading buddy). Reviewing the sedra with the same method as prayer—if a word is repeated, person has to begin the verse again. If not helpful, increase the "price" by returning to the *Aliyah*. Consistency—allowing exceptions or "*rachmanus*" to take precedent over consistency undermines [the treatment] and is not fair to the sufferer.
- Read a text aloud to your *chavrusa* (reading buddy) and keep going when triggered. Your *chavrusa* should have a few basic questions prepared to see how much the person understood if the urge is to go back and reread.
- For exposure: take milk and meat wrapped in plastic, and put it on the counter. Use both hands directly to touch the items. Make a cup of coffee with milk and then go to the meat cabinet and take out silverware and dishes. Checking for bugs on vegetables; checking eggs for fertilization—check once. (Greenwald, 2019, pp. 110–116)

Hinduism

There are no guidelines given by swamis or priests for addressing scrupulosity in Hinduism. It is safe to assume that the same approach would be offered as for other religions.

Although this reassurance will never work, scrupulosity sufferers could take comfort in accepting that the level of concern they have about their obsessive doubts of faith and reverence is an indication of their faith and reverence. Helping to distinguish whether faithful acts are performed out of love or fear may lead to changes in their relationship to their obsessive thoughts.

References

Abramowitz, J. S., & Jacoby, R. J. (2014). Scrupulosity: A cognitive–behavioral analysis and implications for treatment. *Journal of Obsessive-Compulsive and Related Disorders, 3*(2), 140–149.

Ali, T., Mujawar, S., Davis, S., Chaudhury, S., & Saldanha, D. (2021). Blasphemous thoughts in obsessive-compulsive disorder: A case series. *Indian Journal of Psychiatry, 30*(Suppl. 1), S258–S262. doi:10.4103/0972-6748.328824

Aloud, N., & Rathur, A. (2009). Factors affecting attitudes toward seeking and using formal mental health and psychological services among Arab Muslim populations. *Journal of Muslim Mental Health, 4*, 79–103. doi:10.1080/15564900802487675

Bergin, A. E. (1980). Psychotherapy and religious values. *Journal of Consulting and Clinical Psychology, 48*(1), 95–105. doi:10.1037/0022-006X.48.1.95

Bolger, D., & Prickett, P. J. (2021). Where would you go? Race, religion, and the limits of pastor mental health care in Black and Latino congregations. *Religions, 12*(12), 1062. doi:10.3390/rel12121062

Bonchek, A., & Greenberg, D. (2009). Compulsive prayer and its management. *Journal of Clinical Psychology, 65*(4), 396–405. doi:10.1002/jclp.20558

Bretzke, J. T. (2004). *A morally complex world: Engaging contemporary moral theology*. Collegeville, PA: Liturgical Press.

Broderick, C. B. (1992). *Marriage and the family* (4th ed.). Englewood Cliffs, NJ: Prentice Hall.

Campbell, A. D. (2021). Clergy perceptions of mental illness and confronting stigma in congregations. *Religions, 12*(12), 1110.

Chevalier, L., Goldfarb, E., Miller, J., Hoeppner, B., Gorrindo, T., & Birnbaum, R. J. (2015). Gaps in preparedness of clergy and healthcare providers to address mental health needs of returning service members. *Journal of Religion and Health, 54*, 327–338.

Climacus, J. (1982). *Ladder of divine ascent (Revised)*. Mahwah, NJ: Paulist Press.

Curlin, F. A., Odell, S. V., Lawrence, R. E., Chin, M. H., Lantos, J. D., Meador, K. G., & Koenig, H. G. (2007). The relationship between psychiatry and religion among U.S. physicians. *Psychiatric Services, 58*(9), 1193–1198. doi:10.1176/ps.2007.58.9.1193

Deacon, B. J., Vincent, A. M., & Zhang, A. R. (2013). Lutheran clergy members' responses to scrupulosity: The effects of moral thought–action fusion and liberal vs. conservative denomination. *Journal of Obsessive-Compulsive and Related Disorders, 2*(2), 71–77. doi:10.1016/j.jocrd.2012.12.003

Dehlin, J. (2011, January 22). *Understanding scrupulosity within the LDS church*. Mormon Stories. Retrieved from https://www.mormonstories.org/podcast/scrupulosity-lds-church/

Dein, S. (2004). Working with patients with religious beliefs. *Advances in Psychiatric Treatment, 10*(4), 287–294. doi:10.1192/apt.10.4.287

Dein, S., Lewis, C. A., & Loewenthal, K. M. (2011). Psychiatrists views on the place of religion in psychiatry: An introduction to this special issue of Mental Health, Religion & Culture. *Mental Health, Religion & Culture, 14*(1/2), 1–8. doi:10.1080/13674676.2010.499209

Delaney, H. D., Miller, W. R., & Bisonó, A. M. (2007). Religiosity and spirituality among psychologists: A survey of clinician members of the American Psychological Association. *Professional Psychology: Research and Practice, 38*(5), 538–546. doi:10.1037/0735-7028.38.5.538

Dempsey, K., Butler, S. K., & Gaither, L. (2016). Black churches and mental health professionals: Can this collaboration work? *Journal of Black Studies, 47*(1), 73–87. doi:10.1177/0021934715613588

Dobbins, R. D. (2014). Psychotherapy with Pentecostal Protestants. In P. S. Richards & A. E. Bergin (Eds.), *Handbook of psychotherapy and religious diversity* (pp. 155–178). American Psychological Association. doi:10.1037/14371-007

Farrell, J. L., & Goebert, D. A. (2008). Collaboration between psychiatrists and clergy in recognizing and treating serious mental illness. *Psychiatric Services, 59*(4), 437–440. doi:10.1176/ps.2008.59.4.437

Gallo, J. J., Marino, S., Ford, D., & Anthony, J. C. (1995). Filters on the pathway to mental health care, II. Sociodemographic factors. *Psychological Medicine, 25*(6), 1149–1160.

Gray, A. J. (2001). Attitudes of the public to mental health: A church congregation. *Mental Health, Religion & Culture, 4*(1), 71–79.

Greenwald, Y. R. (2019). *With truth and with love: Emunah, education, and personal growth*. Jerusalem, Israel: Feldheim Publishers.

Griffith, J. L. (2006). Managing religious countertransference in clinical settings. *Psychiatric Annals, 36*(3), 196–201.

Harris, J. (2018). *African American Pentecostal clergy members' perceptions of mental health and their subsequent referral practices* (Doctoral dissertation). Philadelphia College of Osteopathic Medicine, Philadelphia, PA.

Henderson, L. C., Stewart, K. E., Koerner, N., Rowa, K., McCabe, R. E., & Antony, M. M. (2022). Religiosity, spirituality, and obsessive-compulsive disorder-related symptoms in clinical and nonclinical samples. *Psychology of Religion and Spirituality, 14*(2), 208–221. doi:10.1037/rel0000397

Hooley, C., Wang, Y., & Hodge, D. (2020). Clergy-provided mental health services. *Advances in Social Work, 20*(3). Retrieved from https://advancesinsocialwork.iupui.edu/index.php/advancesinsocialwork/article/view/23975

Horwitz, B., Littman, R., Greenberg, D., & Huppert, J. (2019). A qualitative analysis of contemporary ultra-orthodox rabbinical perspectives on scrupulosity. *Mental Health, Religion & Culture, 22*(1), 82–98. doi:10.1080/13674676.2019.1585778

Huppert, J., Siev, J., & Kushner, E. (2007, October). When religion and obsessive-compulsive disorder collide: Treating scrupulosity in ultra-orthodox Jews. *J Clin Psychol, 63*(10), 925–941. doi:10.1002/jclp.20404

Kaviani, S., Eskandari, H., & Ebrahimi Ghavam, S. (2015). The relationship between scrupulosity, obsessive-compulsive disorder and its related cognitive styles. *Practice in Clinical Psychology, 3*(1), 47–60.

Kilpack, G. (1956). *Scruples*. Philadelphia, PA: Pendle Hill.

Kovess-Masfety, V., Evans-Lacko, S., Williams, D., Andrade, L. H., Benjet, C., Ten Have, M., . . . Gureje, O. (2017). The role of religious advisors in mental health care in the World Mental Health surveys. *Social Psychiatry and Psychiatric Epidemiology, 52*(3), 353–367. doi:10.1007/s00127-016-1290-8

Kramer, T. L., Blevins, D., Miller, T. L., Phillips, M. M., Davis, V., & Burris, B. (2007). Ministers' perceptions of depression: A model to understand and improve care. *Journal of Religion and Health, 46*(1), 123–139. doi:10.1007/s10943-006-9090-1

Lannert, J. L. (1991). Resistance and countertransference issues with spiritual and religious clients. *Journal of Humanistic Psychology, 31*(4), 68–76. doi:10.1177/0022167891314005

Lehman, A. F., & Steinwachs, D. M. (1998). Translating research into practice: The Schizophrenia Patient Outcomes Research Team (PORT) treatment recommendations. *Schizophrenia Bulletin, 24*(1), 1–10. doi:10.1093/oxfordjournals.schbul.a033302

Lim, A., Hoek, H. W., Ghane, S., Deen, M., & Blom, J. D. (2018). The attribution of mental health problems to jinn: An explorative study in a transcultural psychiatric outpatient clinic. *Frontiers in Psychiatry, 9*, 89. doi:10.3389/fpsyt.2018.00089

Lowe, D. W. (1986). Counseling activities and referral practices of ministers. *Journal of Psychology and Christianity, 5*, 22–29.

McMinn, M. R., Staley, R. C., Webb, K. C., & Seegobin, W. (2010). Just what is Christian counseling anyway? *Professional Psychology: Research and Practice, 41*(5), 391.

Mercer, J. (2013). Deliverance, demonic possession, and mental illness: Some considerations for mental health professionals. *Mental Health, Religion & Culture, 16*(6), 595–611.

Mollica, R. F., Streets, F. J., Boscarino, J., & Redlich, F. C. (1986). A community study of formal pastoral counseling activities of the clergy. *The American Journal of Psychiatry, 143*(3), 323–328. doi:10.1176/ajp.143.3.323

Nabil, M. R., Sharip, S., & Thomas, N. (2019). Scrupulosity and Islam: A perspective. *Journal of Spirituality in Mental Health, 23*, 255–277. doi:10.1080/19349637.2019.1700476

Newquist, J. (1974). *Gospel truth: Discourses and writings of George Q. Cannon*. Salt Lake City, UT: Deseret.

O'Flaherty, V. M. (1966). *How to cure scruples.* Milwaukee, WI: The Bruce Publishing Co.

O'Flaherty, V. M. (1973). Therapy for scrupulosity. In R. M. Jurievich (Ed.), *Direct therapy: Twenty-eight American originals* (pp. 221–243). Miami, FL: Miami University Press.

Oppenheimer, J. E., Flannelly, K. J., & Weaver, A. J. (2004). A comparative analysis of the psychological literature on collaboration between clergy and mental-health professionals—Perspectives from secular and religious journals: 1970–1999. *Pastoral Psychology, 53*(2), 153–162.

Payne, D. (2001). Holy water not always a blessing. *BMJ (Clinical Research Ed.), 322*(7280), 190–190. Retrieved from https://pubmed.ncbi.nlm.nih.gov/11159605

Pearce, M. J., & Koenig, H. G. (2013). Cognitive behavioural therapy for the treatment of depression in Christian patients with medical illness. *Mental Health, Religion & Culture, 16*(7), 730–740.

Plunkett, D. P. (2009). *Exploring the relationship between religious faith, mental health help seeking attitudes, and preferences for counselor characteristics among Black American churchgoers* (Doctoral dissertation). Western Michigan University, Kalamazoo, MI.

Puchalski, C. M. (2001). The role of spirituality in health care. *Baylor University Medical Center Proceedings, 14*, 352–357.

Rassool, G. H. (2018). *Evil eye, jinn possession, and mental health issues: An Islamic perspective*. London, UK: Routledge. doi:10.4324/9781315623764

Rosmarin, D. H., Green, D., Pirutinsky, S., & McKay, D. (2013). Attitudes toward spirituality/religion among members of the association for the behavioral and cognitive therapies. *Professional Psychology: Research and Practice, 44*(6), 424–433.

Rosmarin, D. H., & Pirutinsky, S. (2020). Do religious patients need religious psychotherapists? A naturalistic treatment matching study among orthodox Jews. *Journal of Anxiety Disorders, 69*, 102170. doi:10.1016/j.janxdis.2019.102170

Salem, M. O., Saleh, B., Yousef, S., & Sabri, S. (2009). Help-seeking behaviour of patients attending the psychiatric service in a sample of United Arab Emirates population. *International Journal of Social Psychiatry, 55*(2), 141–148. doi:10.1177/0020764008093373

Santa, T. M. (2007). *Understanding scrupulosity: Questions, helps, and encouragement* (Rev. ed.). Liguori, MO: Liguori/Triumph.

Shapiro, L. J. (2014). *Understanding OCD: Skills to control the conscience and outsmart obsessive compulsive disorder.* Santa Barbara, CA: Praeger.

Stanford, M., & Philpott, D. (2011). Baptist senior pastors' knowledge and perceptions of mental illness. *Mental Health, Religion & Culture, 14*(3), 281–290.

Sullivan, S., Pyne, J. M., Cheney, A. M., Hunt, J., Haynes, T. F., & Sullivan, G. (2014). The pew versus the couch: Relationship between mental health and faith communities and lessons learned from a VA/clergy partnership project. *Journal of Religion and Health, 53*(4), 1267–1282. doi:10.1007/s10943-013-9731-0

Swihart, D. L., Yarrarapu, S. N. S., & Martin, R. L. (2022). Cultural religious competence in clinical practice. In *StatPearls*. Treasure Island, FL: StatPearls Publishing.

Thompson, V. L. S., Bazile, A., & Akbar, M. (2004). African Americans' perceptions of psychotherapy and psychotherapists. *Professional Psychology: Research and Practice, 35*(1), 19.

Virkler, H. A. (1979). Counseling demands, procedures, and preparation of parish ministers: A descriptive study. *Journal of Psychology and Theology, 7*(4), 271–280.

Wang, P. S., Berglund, P. A., & Kessler, R. C. (2003). Patterns and correlates of contacting clergy for mental disorders in the United States. *Health Services Research, 38*(2), 647–673.

Weir, K. N., Greaves, M., Kelm, C., Ragu, R., & Rick, D. (2014). Scrupulosity: Practical treatment considerations drawn from clinical and ecclesiastical experiences with Latter-Day Saint persons struggling with religiously-oriented obsessive compulsive disorders. *Issues in Religion and Psychotherapy, 36*(1), 1–15.

Wesselmann, E. D., & Graziano, W. G. (2010). Sinful and/or possessed? Religious beliefs and mental illness stigma. *Journal of Social and Clinical Psychology, 29*(4), 402.

Young, J. L., Griffith, E. H., & Williams, D. R. (2003). The integral role of pastoral counseling by African-American clergy in community mental health. *Psychiatric Services, 54*(5), 688–692. doi:10.1176/appi.ps.54.5.688

CHAPTER THIRTEEN

Supplemental Strategies to Augment Treatment Outcome, Relapse Prevention, and Recovery

Though exposure and response prevention (ERP) therapy effectively treats obsessive-compulsive disorder (OCD) symptoms, a person is more than just her symptoms. Because there is no cure for OCD, people typically have residual symptoms that can be more annoying than distressing. Creating a healthy lifestyle and managing stress are the best strategies for maintaining treatment gains and living the best quality of life. Needless to say, these are recommended for anyone who wants to better cope with life's challenges.

However, OCD likes to take advantage of opportunities to make an appearance whenever it can. Life stressors often cause OCD sufferers to be physically, mentally, and emotionally vulnerable for lapses or relapses. Not getting enough sleep, getting sick, and undergoing unexpected life events lowers the mind and body's resistance to stress. Under such circumstances, people often notice an uptick of symptoms that would be addressed via ERP as soon as possible. At the same time, it is essential to maintain the elements of healthy living to prevent a lapse from becoming a relapse. Doing so will also better equip the person to handle the precipitating problem more effectively.

Self-Compassion

Self-compassion (SC) helps mitigate the effects of negative self-judgment and self-criticism. We may have internalized invalidating messages given to us by powerful others in our childhood that we may continue to believe are true. If these messages continue to define us, they interfere with and disconnect us from our genuine selves and perpetuate our suffering.

In this way, SC can go a long way for all of us! The following description of SC is based on Neff's book *Self-Compassion: The Proven Power of Being Kind to Yourself* (Neff, 2011). Neff has identified three components of SC: self-kindness, common humanity, and mindfulness. Rather than motivating us, our tendencies toward self-criticism and judgment only serve to hold us back. SC is useful for anyone with a mental disorder, but especially for the toll intrusive thoughts take on the psyche of people with OCD.

The practice of SC provides immediate rewards as it sets off the "feel good" hormones endorphins, oxytocin, and the parasympathetic nervous system (Lee & James, 2013). When practiced as a daily discipline, as opposed to only during situational events, SC can develop new compassionate patterns in the brain (Werner et al., 2012).

Studies have shown that scrupulosity is correlated with lower levels of self-compassion (Moroń, Biolik-Moroń, & Matuszewski, 2022) and that a lack of self-kindness and poor insight could foster scrupulosity among religious people (Tolin, Abramowitz, Kozak, & Foa, 2001). It was suggested that the opposite of all three self-compassion components lead to negative self-judgment versus self-kindness, isolation versus common humanity, and overidentification versus mindfulness (Moroń et al., 2022). Another study found that isolation, negative self-judgment, and overidentification could also create rigidity and a lack of self-forgiveness for committing sins (Brodar, Crosskey, & Thompson, 2015).

Self-Kindness

The human condition is one of suffering. Self-kindness allows us to be kind to ourselves in the very moments we are struggling the most. We tend to be down on ourselves and ruminate about our mistakes and imperfections. When we begin to become aware of our negative self-talk, we have the chance to change it. As Neff points out, if we talked to our friends the way we talk to ourselves, we wouldn't have many friends. She also states that we wouldn't treat even someone we don't like the way we treat ourselves (Neff, 2001). Paradoxically, if we talk to ourselves in the way we would when supporting a struggling friend, we can accept ourselves just as we are and be compassionate instead of critical. Neff differentiates SC with self-esteem, which is goal and achievement oriented. If we fail to meet our goals, we consider ourselves failures and become demoralized. Self-kindness is not self-indulgence or self-pity.

Self-compassion and self-talk are different than the self-reassurance people may use during an OCD-triggering event. Being kind to ourselves when we are struggling helps keep us motivated and accepting of reality. Self-reassurance is an OCD ritual that tries to convince people that everything is OK and good. People who do this don't really believe it, because its purpose is to reduce the distress they are experiencing from irrational thoughts and physiology.

Another way of practicing self-compassion is to follow the "opposite golden rule": do unto yourself as you do unto others. Treat yourself as kindly and as compassionately as you would if someone you cared about was struggling. Otherwise, what is the quality of your compassion for others if it's not coming from a compassionate self?

Examples of self-compassion statements that may be helpful are listed below, but it is always better for the person to use his own voice and develop his own personal statements that resonate as true:

- Feeling guilty about obsessions:
    - These thoughts are very painful. I don't like them, but I can learn to live with them.
    - My thoughts are not wrong or right. I don't have to judge them or myself.
    - My thoughts come and go, so these will, too.
    - My mind and emotions sense urgency, but it's OK to wait and let this pass.
    - I define who I am, not my thoughts.
- Feeling guilty for having OCD:
    - I won't blame myself or anyone else for having OCD.
    - I have compassion for other people who struggle. I can be kind to myself.
    - Getting better will help alleviate the stress on my family and work.
- Feeling guilty for having ritualized:
    - I don't need to be perfect. I will try to do better next time, and if I don't, I will keep trying.
    - This is not an all-or-nothing process.

    - Ritualizing does not mean I have failed. Sometimes it is very difficult to manage.
- Feeling guilt for not ritualizing:
    - I know this is what I must do to get better.
    - I must trust this process, even when it feels like I should act to protect others.
    - My OCD tells me I am being careless and selfish. I feel that way sometimes, but I am trying to trust that I am not my OCD.

Common Humanity

The role of common humanity is to tap into our primitive need for connectedness at the very times we are tempted to isolate (Neff, 2011). Because we are mammals, we are programmed to need intimate, family, and community relationships. We are also primed for recognizing danger. Our survival depends on the symbiotic relationship between individuals and their group's survival instincts, which are maintained by neurochemical reinforcement. When we are faced with danger or threat, our brains send off the fight, freeze, or flee hormones cortisol and adrenaline (Ranabir & Reetu, 2011). Alternatively, the emotion of love and the need for connection activates the pleasure hormones oxytocin and endorphins (Dfarhud, Malmir, & Khanahmadi, 2014).

By nature, OCD sets off the fear hormones adrenaline and cortisol in triggering situations in which the person feels a sense of threat in the absence of real danger (de Koning et al., 2013). The person can become very self-focused as the need and urgency for safety becomes paramount. In the process, self-isolation can set in and cut off human contact, which is so necessary for survival.

Social isolation appears to be a predictive factor in OCD (Toro, Cervera, Osejo, & Salamero, 1992). When OCD begins to limit a person's functionality and connection to the community, it leads to social and emotional isolation. As mammals we are comforted by and provide comfort to others, although with varying degrees of success. Isolation leads to more isolation, the breakdown of social supports, an erosion of self-worth and confidence, too much thinking time, and diminished quality of life. Staying connected to others helps sustain treatment recovery because it also provides healthy mental distraction while the anxiety runs its course.

Self-Compassion Mindfulness

The self-compassion practice of mindfulness is to be objective and observing of thoughts and emotions rather than overidentifying with them. Some believe that critical self-talk provides motivation to do better and be better, but the research shows that it does the opposite (Neff, 2001). Along with self-kindness, self-compassion mindfulness helps people be more observing of, objective about, and accepting of their thoughts and emotions. Instead of overidentifying with the content of obsessions, the practice of self-compassion mindfulness helps cultivate a mindset of nonjudgmental openness rather than trying to control or avoid them. Like any new skill, it will take practice and discipline to disengage from the intrusive thoughts and see them for what they really are—symptoms of a treatable brain disorder. It can also enable people to let go of emotional responses to past mistakes, memories, and worries about the future. It also allows for compassionate acceptance that uncertainty and struggles are facts of life.

A group intervention with OCD patients who had already been treated with a course of CBT used a compassion-based model to help teach and practice compassion for themselves and for others. The study was designed based on research that fear of guilt (Shapiro & Stewart, 2011), social isolation (Basile, Tenore, Luppino, & Mancini, 2017), and self-criticism (Key, Rowa, Bieling, McCabe, & Pawluk, 2017; Wetterneck, Lee, Smith, & Hart, 2013) are factors that contribute to the development and maintenance of OCD. The study found a reduction in OCD symptoms, depression, fear of guilt, and self-criticism, as well as an increase in common humanity and compassionate self-talk (Petrocchi et al., 2021).

The Practice of General Mindfulness as a Coping Skill: Uses, Misuses, Caveats, and Religious Attitudes

Mindfulness can be understood as the "antithesis of many obsessive mechanisms and phenomena and, in this sense, obsessive syndrome can be defined as a state of mindlessness" (Didonna, 2009, p. 190). Mindfulness-based interventions, with proper use, may help to change and improve patients' internal experiences of distress, TAF, inability to accept intrusive thoughts, doubts about their perceptions of reality, and interpretation bias for private experiences, and promote the ability to stay in touch with intrusive (normal) thoughts without reacting to them in dysfunctional and counterproductive ways (Didonna, 2009).

Socioculturally, the practice of mindfulness has become an accepted practice for managing worry, stress, maladaptive cognitions, and emotions. Although mindfulness does not create the neurobiological changes necessary for successful habituation to an obsessive trigger, it does serve as a good augmentation for coping with having OCD as well as managing residual OCD symptoms and internal distress (Key et al., 2017; Külz et al., 2019). Of note, mindfulness and meditation share the same neural pathways in the dorsolateral prefrontal cortex (DLPFC), an area that has been associated with executive decision-making and attention (Taren et al., 2017).

An eight-week study was conducted using mindfulness-based cognitive therapy (MBCT) as a post-OCD treatment augmentation for people with residual symptoms (Crowe & McKay, 2016). Results showed that MBCT helped reduce OCD, depression, and anxiety symptoms and fostered a less judgmental and nonreactive responses when obsessions were triggered. The authors suggest that with further research, MBCT used as an augmentation to ERP treatment may help to prevent relapses (Crowe & McKay, 2016).

Developing objectivity to reduce judgments about negative internal experiences may be a helpful aspect of mindfulness for experiencing scrupulosity (Fisak, Rodriguez, & Kissell, 2019). Mindfulness-based interventions may also decrease the tendency to engage in thought suppression when experiencing an obsessive trigger (Fisak et al., 2019).

Research has been conducted on the effects of mindfulness on OCD and the findings are mixed. A study conducted using mindfulness-based ERP reported that the intervention did not lead to clinically important improvements in OCD symptom severity at postintervention compared to ERP treatment alone (Strauss et al., 2015). Another study found no changes in an experimental or control group at posttreatment assessment, even though all participants exercising mindfulness found the manual to be useful (Cludius et al., 2015). However, a meta-analysis found that mindfulness-based cognitive therapy had a moderate effect on OCD symptoms in an experimental group compared to the study's control groups (Başkaya, Özgüç, & Tanrıverdi, 2021), and patients in another meta-analytic study reported that patients rated the mindfulness-based intervention to have been better compared to clinician-rated structured interview reports (Chien, Tse, Chan, Cheng, & Chen, 2022). According to one study, appropriate use of mindfulness may be helpful with scrupulosity and religious obsessions by practicing objectivity with scrupulous thoughts that can help reduce engaging in scrupulous thinking (Fisak et al., 2019).

A caveat in using mindfulness during an OCD episode is that people with OCD may misuse it as a cognitive distraction ritual or as experiential avoidance from their obsessive thoughts. Unfortunately, neither approach will produce the true benefit of mindfulness or provide relief from OCD. Another consideration is that some patients and clinicians find mindfulness to be more affectively manageable than ERP, because it does not entail withstanding the peak anxiety levels of distress (Crowe & McKay, 2016; Hertenstein et al., 2012). Since mindfulness is a cognitive-based intervention, it is an easier strategy to teach and practice, but in this way, it serves as an avoidance strategy.

Another concern is that mindfulness may unintentionally be used in a goal-oriented way. When there is an expectation that mindfulness will produce a certain outcome, it defeats the therapeutic process of practicing objectivity and openness to whatever the person's present-focused experience is (Moss & O'Niell, 2003). Another concern has been that that developing a reliance on mindfulness as a way of eliminating anxiety may indicate resistance to fully accepting the experience (Schanche et al., 2020). Instead, mindfulness can create a healthy shift in the relationship to and acceptance of thoughts or actions (Hayes & Wilson, 2003). Lastly, a common problem in OCD is decision-making. Brendel (2015) argues that some people may use found participants used it to avoid critical thinking or confronting difficulties through a form of "nonengagement," the emphasis on present moment for example could become justification for not needing to make behavioral changes, making choices, or making plans (Brendel, 2015).

Certain considerations should be made prior to incorporating mindfulness into an OCD treatment plan:

- What is the purpose of using it? Is it to defuse from thoughts during a more mild Subjective Units of Distress Scale (SUDS) level, or is it to avoid obsessive thoughts?
- Does the clinician and/or the patient prefer to use it instead of ERP, or use it to augment the cognitive, emotional, and physiological benefits of ERP?
- Is it employed during high SUDS levels, or may it be useful when SUDS are at a level of 50 or below?
- Is the OCD episode level of severity in the high range and not yet cognitively accessible to be effective, or is it in the moderate to subclinical level where it can help defuse from the thoughts?
- Is the person using it properly, or is it another effort at thought suppression?
- Is the person incorporating mindfulness into his lifestyle as a stress management tool, or just when triggered?

There is a concept that thoughts and feelings are not facts as they change and come and go, whereas behaviors can be held constant (Fairfax, 2008). This is helpful for supporting response prevention in the face of obsessive triggers so that habituation can occur. It can also help reduce

TAF as the person can help separate the cognitive dysfunctional belief that having blasphemous or other unacceptable thoughts are not the same, as they're causing any effects in reality (Shafran, Thoradson, & Rachman, 1996). As a result, people can change their relationship to their obsessions.

Problematic Uses

"Mindfulness as a Guard" was a characteristic of how this skill can be misused as reassurance, as an avoidance of obsessions, and served as a way of mentally ritualizing (Bond, 2020). The author further stated that "[c]are may be needed when teaching mindfulness to people with OCD to reduce the likelihood of mindfulness being used solely to reduce short term anxiety" (Bond, 2020, p. 180). A woman in this study reported having used mindfulness that became part of her OCD by using it to reduce her anxiety in response to her intrusive thoughts. "I'll still get the spike and then at that moment I have to actually say, 'Go through the list of: you know you didn't do it, no, no way, no senses, nothing else,' which I call self-reassurance, which is much better than asking somebody else" (Bond, 2020, p. 14).

When people try to suppress their thoughts, they experience a rebound effect because the effort they are putting into not having the thoughts *is* having the thoughts (Wegner, Schneider, Carter, & White, 1987), which, in turn, only intensifies the obsessions (Bond, 2020). This was supported in another study that found that when thought suppression was used by people with scrupulosity, they experienced an increase in the frequency and intensity of their obsessions (Fisak et al., 2019).

Religious Attitudes about Mindfulness

There appears to be some resistance in using modern, rather than traditional, approaches to coping with life in some religious communities. Some may consider mindfulness as a being "New Agey," spiritual, or irreverent. In *The Catholic Guide to Mindfulness*, Susan Brinkmann contrasts prayer as relational and toward God with mindfulness being a turning into the self that creates a distance between the self and Creator (Brinkmann, 2017). She also states another reason it is incompatible with prayer and connection to God is because mindfulness originates from Buddhism, which is a philosophy, not a religion (Brinkmann, 2017). Rowan, mentioned in the treatment chapter, was introduced to mindfulness as a coping skill, but he expressed his resistance and fear of using it because he considered this technique as being too secular.

If mindfulness is considered a Buddhist philosophical approach to coping with distress, then by definition, it is secular (Bowen, Bergman, & Witkiewitz, 2015). Some religions may prohibit engaging in mindfulness practices because religious leaders may teach that because of its Buddhist origins, and thus being a secular practice, engaging in it would be considered sacrilegious or even a form of blasphemy (Bowen et al., 2015). Because mindfulness-based interventions may be effective in the treatment of scrupulosity, it may be beneficial to involve the client's religious leader in treatment, as that person can provide support and reassurance that mindfulness can be considered a therapeutic strategy rather than religious. Clinicians who treat OCD should assess their patients' beliefs about the use of mindfulness aside from their scrupulosity in order to be respectful of their traditions.

Conversely, Gregory Bottaro, a Catholic psychologist, supports the use of mindfulness as a way of creating a connection to God by focusing on the present moment and being open to feeling safe and at peace (Bottaro, 2018). He claims that practicing mindfulness in a Catholic context is a way to recognize the dignity bestowed by God and the value of taking care of the self and being self-aware so as to discover more about the person God made (Bottaro, 2018).

An eight-week mindfulness-based cognitive therapy (MBCT) intervention was provided for people with OCD who had already undergone ERP work and had residual symptoms. After taking the course of MBCT, participants showed improvement in OCD symptoms as well as depression, anxiety, and nonjudgmental responses to their internal experiences (Hertenstein et al., 2012). The authors suggested that more research be conducted to assess whether the use of MBCT as an augmentation to ERP may contribute to preventing relapses (Hertenstein et al., 2012).

Cognitive Approaches

You cannot think your way out of OCD. Challenging black-and-white thinking, cognitive distortions, obsessive beliefs, and compulsive behavior is helpful in improving cognitive flexibility by teaching the dialectic that two or more ideas or beliefs can be held at the same time. A few examples are as follows:

- You can have "bad" thoughts and be a good person.
- You can feel angry and not harm others.
- You can be angry and still be loveable.
- You can make mistakes and still be competent.

- Mistakes you make can be forgiven.
- Just because you feel guilty doesn't mean that anything is wrong.

Questions to ask and suggestions for addressing a patient with scrupulosity include the following:

- Can you delay the ritual to get more clarity and distance from the situation and then decide how to address it?
- Rate the degree of the infraction. If it's less than a SUDS level of 55, let it go.
- Does the situation clearly match what you were taught or warrant punishment?
- What is the intention behind your behavior? Is it heartfelt, sincere, and loving? Or is it to alleviate anxiety and obsessive guilt?
- Are you asking too much of God to provide proof, certainty, and reassurance?
- Isn't that the role of faith?
- Doesn't God expect you to do your part, take responsibility, and handle it?
- Rituals = lack of faith.
- Aren't you sacrificing God-given aspects of yourself to the disorder?
- Is what have you lost or given up your true values? Identity? Is that not rejecting God?
- What is best that could happen, rather than the worst?
- How can you be creative when you are set on following the letter of the law and rules?
- What would you think about living this way of life on your deathbed?
- Think in steps, not the whole thing—process is more valuable than the result = faith (in self, in God, in life).
- Be spontaneous and do what you want. Go with your instinct and be done with it.
- Make a decision and stick with it.

Cognitive Distortions and Restructuring in Religious Scrupulosity

Unrealistic and irrational thoughts contribute to OCD suffering. In the case of religious scrupulosity, obsessive fears often produce cognitive distortions that belie religious faith. Kevin Foss, MFT, and Tom Carboy of the OCD Center of Los Angeles created the following responses to cognitive distortions related to scrupulosity.

All-or-Nothing Thinking (Black-and-White Thinking)

- "I had a passing thought about Satan, so I must secretly be a devil worshipper."
- "I mispronounced a few words when I was praying today, so I must have angered God."

Catastrophizing

- "Because I had a thought about sex with someone other than my spouse, God will send me to hell."
- "I accidentally left out a detail at confession earlier this week, so God will surely judge me as unworthy of heaven."

Discounting/Minimizing the Positive

- "Even though I have consistently and earnestly tried to live my life according to my faith, I had that one blasphemous thought, so I must be a terrible person."
- "I volunteer at church every week, but I'm a selfish person because I can't volunteer today."

Emotional Reasoning

- "My prayer wasn't good enough, because I didn't feel totally connected to God."
- "I feel like my donation doesn't count because I don't have a 'giver's heart.'"

Magical Thinking

- "I had a 'bad' thought while praying, so my mother will go to hell unless I repeat my prayers perfectly and without bad thoughts."
- "If I'm late to church, God will punish my children."

Should/Must Thinking (Perfectionism)

- "I should only have pure thoughts."
- "I must follow all religious laws 100% literally."

Selective Abstraction

- "I've heard *The Wizard of Oz* is a wonderful family film, but it includes wizards and witches, so we better not watch it or else the kids and I may go to hell."

- "Bob is a wonderful husband and father who treats me and the kids great, but he is from a different denomination, so I might not get into heaven." (https://ocdla.com/scrupulosity-ocd-religion-faith-belief-2107)

Becoming aware of the moments when the distorted thinking occurs and then identifying what the specific distortions are at play provides opportunities for reframing. Reframing challenges the subjective and emotional assumptions as a way to consider more rational reasons for why a situation has occurred, or to consider that the assumption may or may not be true. A cognitive distortion in scrupulosity may be "that person gave me a dirty look because I had a sexual thought about them." The person can take a more objective stance about the "mind reading" distortion and challenge it by asking whether the person actually noticed her, or how someone could actually know what she's thinking.

Another example would be missing a religious service due to being sick. "I am going to be punished for not adhering to obligation of attending services to show my respect to God." This all-or-nothing thinking could be challenged by asking herself if she thinks she would assume the same would happen to someone else under the same circumstances, thus reducing the double standard between healthy and scrupulous rules about faith practices.

Care should be taken so that the role of cognitive structuring serves its purpose and is not used as mental ritualizing or seeking certainty around one's standing with God.

Acceptance Commitment Therapy

Acceptance and commitment therapy (ACT) is considered a "Third Wave" of cognitive behavior therapy types (Hayes, 2004). This therapy can be effective in helping clients with OCD learn to accept their circumstances for what they are and making a commitment to change what they have control over. In order to use ACT effectively with scrupulous patients, the therapist should be sensitive to the differences between healthy religious and cultural practices and how they have been co-opted by the disorder. Accepting the presence of the obsessions is different than accepting or believing the content of the obsessions.

The same caveat for using ACT as for mindfulness is proposed in that it is not a replacement for ERP work but, rather, to help the sufferer prepare to engage in it. The willingness to accept the thoughts, especially for those resistant to ERP, will create a more conducive mindset for challenging their obsessive fears.

ACT includes skills for affect regulation to manage deontological guilt, interpersonal emotional responses, and the distress of a sense of inflated responsibility rather than the welfare of the other person (Kämpf et al., 2021). Values-based behavior helps guide sufferers to make decisions based on what they truly care about and how they would be living if not for the OCD.

Forgiveness for past mistakes by the sufferer or others helps shift the belief that those mistakes are evidence of being a bad person. They hold their mistakes against themselves due to the obsessive belief that the OCD serves to prevent making more mistakes. As a result, people tend to avoid attending their faith communities so as not to put themselves and others in harm's way. They maintain a double standard that others can be forgiven for their past mistakes, but for them, the OCD has some kind of meaning, expectations, or demands of being perfectly obedient to the "rules." They believe that God forgives others but not them. They hold themselves to perfectionistic standards that cannot be achieved, and can feel like failures for falling short. They live in fear and have extreme difficulty accepting God's or others' forgiveness. And they certainly cannot forgive themselves, which creates a disconnection from the very supports they value in such a way that the cure becomes the problem.

The goal, then, is to adopt self-forgiveness, which has been defined as "a willingness to abandon self-resentment in the face of one's own acknowledged objective wrong, while fostering compassion, generosity, and love toward oneself" (Enright, 1996, p. 115). Another perspective is that self-forgiveness serves to increase motivation to act benevolently toward the self (Hall & Fincham, 2005).

Gratitude

Gratitude is the act of appreciating the positive aspects of life. We can be grateful for even the smallest moments of joy to larger blessings. Awareness of seeing details in nature, a compliment we received, our family, our friends, and connection to that which is larger than ourselves fosters objectivity, reduces taking for granted the aspects of life that keep us going, and sets off endorphins, which can lighten our mood. In fact, gratitude emits endorphins (Tala, 2019). Some people have a gratitude journal wherein they list three or four items a day as an active way to be aware of and thankful for experiences they might otherwise not notice. It helps focus on the external world and be less self-focused.

Group Interventions

The concept of "tricky brain" was described to participants in an OCD therapy group the nature of the evolved human mind, its emphasis on threat, and how this can create unhelpful connections between thoughts, feelings, and behaviors (Petrocchi et al., 2021). As mentioned in the mindfulness section previously, the authors designed an eight-week compassion-focused group to help reduce OCD symptoms, depression, fear of guilt, and self-criticism while increasing common humanity and compassionate self-reassuring skills for those with treatment-resistant OCD (Petrocchi et al., 2021). Some of the issues posed for participants to remember were the genetic nature and heritability nature of OCD, that they did not do anything to "deserve" OCD, and the benefits of changing their negative or critical self-talk to how they would talk to a friend who was struggling (Petrocchi et al., 2021). At the four-week follow-up, the study found that all participants experienced decreases in OCD symptoms. Participants also had reductions in fear of guilt, self-criticism, and using self-reassurance as a ritual (Petrocchi et al., 2021).

Humor

Who doesn't like a good laugh? Finding things funny is one of life's pleasures, but humor also has neurophysiological benefits. Laughter decreases serum levels of cortisol, epinephrine, and growth hormones (Berk et al., 1989; Yim, 2016) and sets off dopamine, serotonin, and endorphins (Yim, 2016). It improves cognitive functions and helps regulate respiration to better tolerate pain and reduce stress hormones, all of which provide improved psychological well-being (Yim, 2016). Laughter is an expression of pleasant enlightenment.

Humor provides the scrupulous sufferer with a lighter mindset and creates mental space to see the situation for what it is. The humor should be used with regard to the obsessions, not toward the person. "Yeah, I'm the greatest sinner of all time!" might be a response that sets off humor chemicals, enabling the person to "get it" and let go of the obsessive fear, at least for the time being.

References

Basile, B., Tenore, K., Luppino, O. I., & Mancini, F. (2017). Schema therapy mode model applied to OCD. *Clinical Neuropsychiatry, 14*(6), 407–414

Başkaya, E., Özgüç, S., & Tanrıverdi, D. (2021). Examination of the effectiveness of mindfulness-based cognitive therapy on patients with obsessive-compulsive disorder: Systematic review and meta-analysis. *Issues in Mental Health Nursing, 42*(11), 998–1009.

Berk, L. S., Tan, S. A., Fry, W. F., Napier, B. J., Lee, J. W., Hubbard, R. W., . . . Eby, W. C. (1989). Neuroendocrine and stress hormone changes during mirthful laughter. *American Journal of Medical Science, 298*(6), 390–396. doi:10.1097/00000441-198912000-00006

Bond, M. (2020). *Experiences of mindfulness for clients with OCD: An IPA study* (Doctorate in Counseling). University of the West of England, Bristol.

Bottaro, G. (Ed.) (2018). *The mindful Catholic: Finding God one moment at a time.* Midvale, UT: Wellspring.

Bowen, S., Bergman, A. L., & Witkiewitz, K. (2015). Engagement in Buddhist meditation practices among non-Buddhists: Associations with religious identity and practice. *Mindfulness, 6*(6), 1456–1461.

Brendel, D. (2015). Altruistic World Online Library. *Harvard Business Review.*

Brinkmann, S. (2017). *A Catholic guide to mindfulness.* Birmingham, UK: CreateSpace Independent Publishing Platform.

Brodar, K. E., Crosskey, L. B., & Thompson, R. J. (2015). The relationship of self-compassion with perfectionistic self-presentation, perceived forgiveness, and perceived social support in an undergraduate Christian community. *Journal of Psychology and Theology, 43*(4), 231–242. doi:10.1177/009164711504300401

Chien, W. T., Tse, M.-K., Chan, H. Y. L., Cheng, H. Y., & Chen, L. (2022). Is mindfulness-based intervention an effective treatment for people with obsessive-compulsive disorder? A systematic review and meta-analysis. *Journal of Obsessive-Compulsive and Related Disorders, 32*, 100712. doi:10.1016/j.jocrd.2022.100712

Cludius, B., Hottenrott, B., Heike, A., Ulrike, P., Schröder, J., & Moritz, S. (2015). Mindfulness for OCD? No evidence for a direct effect of a self-help treatment approach. *Journal of Obsessive-Compulsive and Related Disorders, 6*, 59–65. doi:10.1016/j.jocrd.2015.05.003

Crowe, K., & McKay, D. (2016). Mindfulness, obsessive–compulsive symptoms, and executive dysfunction. *Cognitive Therapy and Research, 40*(5), 627–644.

de Koning, P. P., Figee, M., Endert, E., Storosum, J. G., Fliers, E., & Denys, D. (2013). Deep brain stimulation for obsessive–compulsive disorder is associated with cortisol changes. *Psychoneuroendocrinology, 38*(8), 1455–1459.

Dfarhud, D., Malmir, M., & Khanahmadi, M. (2014). Happiness & Health: The biological factors- systematic review article. *Iranian Journal of Public Health*, 43(11), 1468–1477. Retrieved from https://www.ncbi.nlm.nih.gov/pubmed/26060713

Didonna, F. (2009). Mindfulness and obsessive-compulsive disorder: Developing a way to trust and validate one's internal experience. In F. Didonna (Ed.), *Clinical Handbook of Mindfulness* (pp. 189–219). New York, NY: Springer Science + Business Media.

Enright, R. D. (1996). Counseling within the forgiveness triad: On forgiving, receiving forgiveness, and self-forgiveness. *Counseling and Values, 40*(2), 107–126.

Fairfax, H. (2008). The use of mindfulness in obsessive compulsive disorder: Suggestions for its application and integration in existing treatment. *Clinical Psychology & Psychotherapy, 15*, 53–59. doi:10.1002/cpp.557

Fisak, B., Rodriguez, H., & Kissell, K. (2019). The relevance of mindfulness and thought suppression to scrupulosity. *Journal of Cognitive Psychotherapy, 33*(2), 106–115.

Hall, J., & Fincham, F. (2005). Self-forgiveness: The stepchild of forgiveness research. *Journal of Social and Clinical Psychology, 24*(5), 621–637.

Hayes, S. C. (2004). Acceptance and commitment therapy, relational frame theory, and the third wave of behavioral and cognitive therapies. *Behavior Therapy, 35*(4), 639–665. doi:10.1016/S0005-7894(04)80013-3

Hayes, S. C., & Wilson, K. G. (2003). Mindfulness: Method and process. *Clinical Psychology: Science and Practice, 10*(2), 161.

Hertenstein, E., Rose, N., Voderholzer, U., Heidenreich, T., Nissen, C., Thiel, N., . . . Kulz, A. K. (2012). Mindfulness-based cognitive therapy in obsessive-compulsive disorder—A qualitative study on patients' experiences. *BMC Psychiatry, 12*, 185. doi:10.1186/1471-244X-12-185

Kämpf, M. S., Kanske, P., Kleiman, A., Haberkamp, A., Glombiewski, J., & Exner, C. (2021). Empathy, compassion, and theory of mind in obsessive-compulsive disorder. *Psychology and Psychotherapy*. Retrieved from https://pubmed.ncbi.nlm.nih.gov/34331362/

Key, B. L., Rowa, K., Bieling, P., McCabe, R., & Pawluk, E. J. (2017). Mindfulness-based cognitive therapy as an augmentation treatment for obsessive-compulsive disorder. *Clinical Psychology & Psychotherapy, 24*(5), 1109–1120. doi:10.1002/cpp.2076

Külz, A. K., Landmann, S., Cludius, B., Rose, N., Heidenreich, T., Jelinek, L., . . . Moritz, S. (2019). Mindfulness-based cognitive therapy (MBCT) in patients with obsessive-compulsive disorder (OCD) and residual symptoms after cognitive behavioral therapy (CBT): A randomized controlled trial. *European Archives of Psychiatry and Clinical Neuroscience, 269*(2), 223–233. doi:10.1007/s00406-018-0957-4

Lee, D. A., & James, S. (2013). *The compassionate-mind guide to recovering from trauma and PTSD: Using compassion-focused therapy to overcome flashbacks, shame, guilt, and fear.* Oakland, CA: New Harbinger Publications.

Moroń, M., Biolik-Moroń, M., & Matuszewski, K. (2022). Scrupulosity in the network of obsessive-compulsive symptoms, religious struggles, and self-compassion: A study in a non-clinical sample. *Religions, 13*(10), 879.

Moss, D., & O'Niell, B. (2003). *Just another technique? Possibilities and paradoxes in working with mindfulness.* 29–33. Retrieved from https://www.researchgate.net/publication/293571313_Just_another_technique_Possibilities_and_paradoxes_in_working_with_mindfulness

Neff, K. (2001). *Self-compassion: The proven power of being kind to yourself.* New York, NY: HarperCollins.

Neff, K. (2011). *Self-compassion: Stop beating yourself up and leave insecurity behind.* New York, NY: William Morrow.

Petrocchi, N., Cosentino, T., Pellegrini, V., Femia, G., D'Innocenzo, A., & Mancini, F. (2021). Compassion-focused group therapy for treatment-resistant OCD: Initial evaluation using a multiple baseline design. *Frontiers in Psychology, 11*, 594277. doi:10.3389/fpsyg.2020.594277

Ranabir, S., & Reetu, K. (2011). Stress and hormones. *Indian Journal of Endocrinology and Metabolism, 15*(1), 18–22. doi:10.4103/2230-8210.77573

Schanche, E., Vøllestad, J., Binder, P.-E., Hjeltnes, A., Dundas, I., & Nielsen, G. H. (2020). Participant experiences of change in mindfulness-based stress reduction for anxiety disorders. *International Journal of Qualitative Studies on Health and Well-Being, 15*(1), 1776094. doi:10.1080/17482631.2020.1776094

Shafran, R., Thoradson, D. S., & Rachman, S. (1996). Thought-action fusion in obsessive compulsive disorder. *Journal of Anxiety Disorders, 10*(5), 379–391. doi:10.1016/0887-6185(96)00018-7

Shapiro, L. J., & Stewart, S. E. (2011). Pathological guilt: A persistent yet overlooked treatment factor in obsessive-compulsive disorder. *Ann Clin Psychiatry, 23*, 63–70.

Strauss, C., Rosten, C., Hayward, M., Lea, L., Forrester, E., & Jones, A.-M. (2015). Mindfulness-based exposure and response prevention for obsessive compulsive disorder: study protocol for a pilot randomised controlled trial. *Trials, 16*(1), 167.

Tala, Á. (2019). Thanks for everything: a review on gratitude from neurobiology to clinic. *Revista Médica de Chile, 147*(6), 755–761. doi:10.4067/s0034-98872019000600755

Taren, A. A., Gianaros, P. J., Greco, C. M., Lindsay, E. K., Fairgrieve, A., Brown, K. W., . . . Creswell, J. D. (2017). Mindfulness meditation training and executive control network resting state functional connectivity: A randomized controlled trial. *Psychosomatic Medicine, 79*(6), 674–683. doi:10.1097/psy.0000000000000466

Tolin, D. F., Abramowitz, J. S., Kozak, M. J., & Foa, E. B. (2001). Fixity of belief, perceptual aberration, and magical ideation in obsessive–compulsive disorder. *Journal of Anxiety Disorders, 15*(6), 501–510. doi:10.1016/s0887-6185(01)00078-0

Toro, J., Cervera, M., Osejo, E., & Salamero, M. (1992). Obsessive-compulsive disorder in childhood and adolescence: A clinical study. *Journal of Child Psychology and Psychiatry, 33*(6), 1025–1037. doi:10.1111/j.1469-7610.1992.tb00923.x

Wegner, D. M., Schneider, D. J., Carter, S. R., & White, T. L. (1987). Paradoxical effects of thought suppression. *Journal of Personality and Social Psychology, 53*(1), 5.

Werner, K. H., Jazaieri, H., Goldin, P. R., Ziv, M., Heimberg, R. G., & Gross, J. J. (2012). Self-compassion and social anxiety disorder. *Anxiety, Stress & Coping, 25*(5), 543–558.

Wetterneck, C. T., Lee, E. B., Smith, A. H., & Hart, J. M. (2013). Courage, self-compassion, and values in obsessive-compulsive disorder. *Journal of Contextual Behavioral Science, 2*, 68–73.

Yim, J. (2016). Therapeutic benefits of laughter in mental health: A theoretical review. *Tohoku Journal of Experimental Medicine, 239*(3), 243–249. doi:10.1620/tjem.239.243

Appendix

These statements are provided by Anabelle Finger to demonstrate her courage to stand up to her OCD:

- I am an atheist. Despite believing that there is a larger possibility that God or gods do not exist, there will never be definitive evidence for either side; absolute knowledge is impossible.
- I do not believe in God/gods, nor do I subscribe to any organized religion.
- I think that believing in God or gods is akin to children believing in Santa Claus.
- I don't believe that praying accomplishes any goal. I believe that what happens as "a result" of praying is a coincidence or gap in human knowledge.
- I believe that the multiverse was created through multiple interacting forces rather than one all-knowing force.
- I do not believe that it is harmful for oneself or others to believe in a God or gods insofar as harmful actions are not taken to justify such beliefs.
- If God does exist, I think that it would be more probable for him to act as a changing force rather than as a dictator.
- I do not believe that there is one correct religion or doctrine.
- I do not believe that if there was a God, that he would be as stringent as organized religions make him out to be.
- I don't think that God would punish people for looking at sexual images/hearing sexual words and phrases (including watching suggestive scenes in movies and TV shows), because sex is one of humanity's basic needs.
- I don't believe that sex is a negative action, whether it is done for pleasure or procreation, outside or inside of marriage, as long as such act or acts are consensual.

- I do not think that masturbation is a negative action insofar as it doesn't interfere with a person's daily functioning, relationships, or hurt their physical health/mental health.
- I do not think that there is anything inherently wrong with being bisexual, homosexual, or transgender.
- I think that subscribing to a certain religion and/or believing in God or multiple gods can provide people with a false sense of control over their lives.
- Lack of belief in God or gods is not immoral. Instead, it is immoral to deprive humans of the ability to determine their own choices and values.
- I do not believe that atheism or agnosticism is a means to hedonism. People who don't believe in God or multiple gods can be as morally astute and have as much self-control as people who do.
- Beliefs or lack thereof (in any category) do not determine accomplishments or failures.
- Beliefs or lack thereof in God or multiple gods do not increase or decrease the threshold of what it means to be a good person or bad person, respectively.
- I do not believe that a person or persons have to believe in God or multiple gods and/or subscribe to mass beliefs in order to be a good person and have a fulfilling life.
- I do not believe that there is an afterlife, whether that be any variation of heaven, hell, or purgatory. Instead, when we die, both our physical body and consciousness cease to exist. However, a person's impacts, accomplishments, and failures, big and small, exist posthumously.
- I do not believe in the devil or demons. I believe that cases of possession are just cases of undiagnosed complex mental illness.
- I do not believe that God or multiple gods are the arbiter/arbiters of objective truth.
- I don't believe that religious texts are the word of God or multiple gods but rather people's interpretations of phenomena and how they view the world at a specific time. Although religious texts can provide relevant and important moral lessons, such lessons are not unique to religious texts.
- Good and bad actions get praised and punished as much on earth as they do in hell.
- I think that being detached from any sort of religion or God/gods is freeing.
- I think that when people rely on religion or their belief in God/gods too much, they become too rigid to think for themselves.
- I think that people who believe in God/gods/religion solely out of fear is not the same as believing in God/gods/religion out of fear and love.
- I do not believe that atheism is akin to satanism.

Resources

Finding Help

International Obsessive Compulsive Foundation: iocdf.org

Websites

Beyond OCD: https://beyondocd.org/

Catholic/Christian

OCD & Christianity Ian Osborne: https://ocdandchristianity.com/?page_id=26

Rules for the Scrupulous Person: https://www.phatmass.com/phorum/topic/128141-rules-for-the-scrupulous-person/

Latter-Day Saints

Understanding Scrupulosity (Religious OCD) Debra Theobald McClendon, PhD: https://www.churchofjesuschrist.org/study/ensign/2019/09/young-adults/understanding-scrupulosity-religious-ocd?lang=eng

Jewish

OCD Mikvah Checklist: Mikvah.org, Mivtza Taharas Hamishpacha

Books

Catholic/Christian

Ciarrocchi, J. (1995). *The doubting disease: Help for scrupulosity and religious compulsions*. New York, NY: Paulist Press.

O'Flaherty, V. M. (1973). *Therapy for scrupulosity.* In R. M. Jurjevich (Ed.), *Direct psychotherapy: Twenty-eight American originals.* Miami, FL: University of Miami Press.

Osborne, I. (2008). *Can Christianity cure obsessive-compulsive disorder? A psychiatrist explores the role of faith in treatment.* Grand Rapids, MI: Brazos Press

Santa, T. M. (2007). *Understanding scrupulosity: Questions, helps, and encouragement* (Rev. ed.). Liguori, MO.: Liguori/Triumph.

Jewish

Boncheck, A. (2000). *Religious compulsions and fears: A guide to treatment.* New York, NY: Feldheim.

General

Shapiro, L. (2015). *Understanding OCD: Skills to control the conscience and outsmart obsessive compulsive disorder.* Santa Barbara, CA: Praeger.

Summers, J. S., & Sinnott-Armstrong, W. (2019). *Clean hands: Philosophical lessons from scrupulosity.* New York, NY: Oxford University Press.

Summers, J. S., & Sinnott-Armstrong, W. (2019). Scrupulosity as a form of OCD. In J. S. Summers & W. Sinnott-Armstrong (Eds.), *Clean hands: Philosophical lessons from scrupulosity* (pp. 40–56). New York, NY: Oxford University Press.

Index

About the Author

Leslie J. Shapiro, LICSW, has been treating OCD and related disorders since 1989. In 1997, she was hired as one of the initial behavior therapists at the OCD Institute (OCDI) at McLean Hospital, the premiere residential treatment program for treatment-resistant OCD.

In 2009, Ms. Shapiro was awarded the first interdisciplinary career development research grant at McLean Hospital. The grant supported her pilot project on conscience related factors in OCD. She continues this research at the Office of Clinical Assessment and Research at the OCD Institute.

She is the author of two books on OCD: *Understanding OCD: Skills to Control the Conscience and Outsmart Obsessive Compulsive Disorder* and *Obsessive Compulsive Disorder: Elements, History, Treatments, and Research.* She has also written online OCD continuing education courses and has presented on OCD and related disorders in professional, academic, and community settings. Her other roles have included committee membership for Partners for Research Advancement in Nursing and Social Work at McLean Hospital, adjunct professor at the Boston University School of Social Work, and teaching, supervising, and training students and staff at the OCD Institute.

www.ingramcontent.com/pod-product-compliance
Ingram Content Group UK Ltd.
Pitfield, Milton Keynes, MK11 3LW, UK
UKHW021908150926
475560UK00003B/251